Critical Essays on Thomas Wolfe

Critical Essays on Thomas Wolfe

John S. Phillipson

G. K. Hall & Co. • Boston, Massachusetts

Library of Congress Cataloging in Publication Data

Phillipson, John S.
Critical essays on Thomas Wolfe.

(Critical essays on American literature)
Includes index.
1. Wolfe, Thomas, 1900–1938—Criticism and interpretation—Addresses, essays, lectures. I. Title.
II. Series.
PS3545.0337Z825 1985 813′.52 84–25141
ISBN O–8161–8692–8

This publication is printed on permanent/durable acid-free paper
MANUFACTURED IN THE UNITED STATES OF AMERICA

CRITICAL ESSAYS ON AMERICAN LITERATURE

This series seeks to anthologize the most important criticism on a wide variety of topics and writers in American literature. Our readers will find in various volumes not only a generous selection of reprinted articles and reviews but original essays, bibliographies, manuscript sections, and other materials brought to public attention for the first time. A welcome addition to our list, this volume contains sections on *Look Homeward, Angel*, *Of Time and the River*, the posthumous novels, the plays, the short fiction, and a concluding group of general studies. Among the reprinted essays are pieces by the leading Wolfe scholars, including Richard Walser, John Hagan, Richard S. Kennedy, Leslie Field, John L. Idol, Jr., and James D. Boyer. The original essays include John S. Phillipson's bibliographical survey of Wolfe scholarship in his introduction, a study of *Look Homeward, Angel* by Darlene H. Unrue, and a discussion of Wolfe's short stories by Webb Salmon. We are confident that this volume will make a permanent and significant contribution to American literary study.

JAMES NAGEL, GENERAL EDITOR

Northeastern University

For Aldo P. Magi

CONTENTS

INTRODUCTION

Psychologically, Thomas Wolfe affords an interesting case study. More than most people, he seems to have been adversely conditioned in some important ways by his childhood years. Born in Asheville, N. C., October 3, 1900, he was the last child of Julia A. Westall Wolfe and William Oliver Wolfe, and as such was babied beyond his years. Not weaned until three-and-one-half, he shared his mother's bed until the age of eight and was forced to keep his hair long until nine, when infestation with lice compelled its cutting. Some believe that this prolonged infantilism made impossible his later relating sexually to women his own age and helps to explain his love affair with a woman twenty years his senior. Because he made his fiction largely from his own life, the merits and demerits of Eugene Gant and George Webber are those of Thomas Wolfe. Their weaknesses and strengths are his, sprung from his own background and conditioning.

In 1906 Mrs. Wolfe opened a boarding house (now the Thomas Wolfe Memorial, a State Historic Site) at 48 Spruce Street in Asheville, just around the corner from 92 Woodfin Street, the house that W. O. Wolfe had built in 1881 for his second wife, and took Tom with her. Here he was to experience the lack of a sense of home that he was later to describe in *Look Homeward, Angel* when he had to yield his room to the boarders. He later got a morning newspaper route (his brother Ben was an assistant manager at a local newspaper) and in adulthood wrote of rising in "lilac darkness" to deliver his papers in "Niggertown." He also sold the *Saturday Evening Post* (his brother Fred had the local agency) and in time he was to write of his shame at making himself a nuisance to sell copies of the magazine. Fred (Luke in *Look Homeward, Angel*) was an outgoing, gregarious type; Tom, far more introspective, hated the world of hearty good fellowship that Fred represented. Ben, however, was a kind of idol for him, and readers of *Look Homeward, Angel* will long remember his odd combination of affection for his young brother and hand uplifted as for a blow. Ben's death in 1918, movingly described in this book, was one of the great shocks of Wolfe's life. (Later he was to dedicate *From Death to Morning* to Ben's memory.) His father's death in 1922, related with equal power in *Of Time and the River*, joins Ben's as being among the most powerful death scenes in world literature.

Upon completing prep school at sixteen, Wolfe wanted to attend the University of Virginia, but his father, foreseeing a career in politics for him, insisted upon the University of North Carolina. So it was that in the fall of 1916 Tom went off to Chapel Hill, where he became a popular and active undergraduate, a member of the Di-Phi Society of debaters, a fraternity man, and the editor of the school newspaper. In 1919 he won the Worth Prize, awarded annually by the Department of Philosophy for the best essay submitted. His contribution, titled *The Crisis in Industry*, had nothing to do with philosophy; Horace H. Williams, Wolfe's philosophy professor, recognized the essay as an innovation for a prize in philosophy but thought that "If Philosophy shall be able to throw any light upon the problem of Industry, . . . the effort justifies itself."[1]

Professor Williams was joined as an important influence upon Wolfe by William Stanly "Bully" Bernard, who taught Greek; by Edwin Greenlaw, English; and by Frederick Henry Koch, who founded the Carolina Playmakers. In 1919 Wolfe played the lead in his own one-act play, *The Return of Buck Gavin.*[2] Koch had studied with George Pierce Baker at Harvard, and it was his influence that induced Wolfe in 1920 to begin studies for a Master's Degree at Harvard, intending a career as a playwright. At Chapel Hill Wolfe wrote several folkplays, and at Harvard he was to see produced, in 1923, his full-length play *Welcome to Our City*. Despite its length and numerous scene changes (it ran from 8 p.m. to around midnight), some thought it the most original and innovative play that Harvard had done.[3]

Baker tried earnestly but unsuccessfully to win a commercial production of this play by the New York Theatre Guild, which was interested in it only if Wolfe would cut it. This he was unable to do; characteristically he lengthened it. In January 1924, he began teaching at New York University's Washington Square campus, where he was to remain for six years in what he called "odious bondage" while continuing to hope, at least for the first few years, for a career as a dramatist. But a second play, *Mannerhouse*, was also declined by the Theatre Guild, the Provincetown Theatre, and the Neighborhood Playhouse, the three groups that also had rejected his earlier play.[4]

In September 1925, returning from Europe on the *Olympia*, Wolfe met Aline Bernstein, noted stage designer and a director of the Neighborhood Playhouse who by coincidence was carrying a copy of *Welcome to Our City*, which the Playhouse had asked her to read. He was 24; she, 44. And so began the six-year affair that has become part of American literary history. The letters between them make for painful reading.[5] Mrs. Bernstein comes through as overly possessive, complaining bitterly if Wolfe, in Europe, did not write often enough; and on one occasion she cabled her intention of taking ship and tracking him down. Wolfe's letters to her about his European travels, however, make delightful reading.

It was Mrs. Bernstein who, by generous gifts of money, made possible several of Wolfe's trips abroad, where in 1926, in England, he began the novel that became *Look Homeward, Angel* after several changes of title, *O Lost* and *The Building of a Wall* being earlier titles considered for it. Published October 18, 1929, the book drew generally favorable responses, even in North Carolina, although in Asheville it caused a furore that took several years to die down. Even when reviewers found some fault with it, they tended to admire its powerful characterizations and effective descriptions

Among early reviewers Basil Davenport saw Wolfe as possessing with Rabelais "the same fundamental and most unusual quality, a robust sensitiveness," and found in his manner a hint of Joyce.[6] Geoffrey T. Hellman called it "an extraordinarily fine novel, not to be mentioned with all the forgotten blue-ribbon winners of the past few years."[7] Margaret Wallace accurately predicted that the final decision on his book rested, probably, "with another generation than ours."[8]

Nearly six years would elapse before Wolfe's second novel, *Of Time and the River*, appeared, and that it appeared then was due to Maxwell Perkins's taking the manuscript from Wolfe and declaring it finished. (One of the essays in the present collection treats of Perkins's editing of this novel.) Whereas *Look Homeward, Angel* covers about seventeen years and ends with Eugene about to leave Altamont for the great world outside the encircling mountains, *Of Time and the River* covers some six or seven, beginning with Eugene leaving for graduate work at Harvard, continuing with his teaching in New York City after failing to get a play produced commercially, visiting England and France, and ending with his seeing a woman named Esther at a ship departure. As Wolfe puts it, "At that moment of their meeting she got into his life by some dark magic, and before he knew it, he had her beating in the pulses of his blood. . . ."[9] This love affair with "Esther Jack" was to occupy large portions of *The Web and the Rock* and *You Can't Go Home Again*, published posthumously.

Reviewers and general readers alike, wondering whether *Look Homeward, Angel* was a one-time success by this new novelist, eagerly awaited his second book. On the whole they were not disappointed. *Of Time and the River* was published March 8, 1935, and Lewis Gannett commented that its pages "tumble, pour, roar, sing with . . . savage joy and fury."[10] Herschel Brickell called the book "the event of the publishing season."[11] Burton Rascoe found the novels of Wolfe "thrilling to contemplate and read."[12] Reviewers tended to mention the absence of formal structure but praised the book's huge vitality.

During the five-and-one-half years between publication of Wolfe's first two novels, his name was kept before the public by the appearance of two novelettes, "A Portrait of Bascom Hawke"[13] and "The Web of Earth."[14] There followed eight short stories and two poetical sketches, "The Names of the Nation"[15] and "For Professional Appearance."[16] Other short stories and sketches ensued, and the *Saturday Review of Literature* published "The Story of a Novel,"[17] recounting the production of *Of Time and the River.*

The year 1935 also saw publication of fourteen short stories and sketches (deciding which is which not always easy!), collected from magazines, under the title *From Death to Morning.* These are of variable quality: probably the best are "Only the Dead Know Brooklyn," "Circus at Dawn," "In the Park," and "The Web of Earth." Wolfe was to continue publication of short stories while he continued work on a projected series of novels that would begin in the late eighteenth century and end in the twentieth—books with titles like *Pacific End, The Hills Beyond Pentland,* and *The October Fair.* Because of Scribner's announcement of the series, it was widely believed that they were all written and awaiting publication. Wolfe also planned a novel about nighttime America, to be called *The Hound of Darkness,* and one about the Pullman car numbered K–19 that ran between New York and Asheville.[18]

In May 1937, Wolfe returned to Asheville for the first time since 1929 and found himself a celebrity, a circumstance described in a sketch or short story called "The Return of the Prodigal."[19] Renting a cabin in nearby Oteen, he tried to work but found his privacy being disturbed too much for significant accomplishment. At this time he was also seriously contemplating leaving Scribner's, largely because of a review of *The Story of a Novel* by Bernard DeVoto that charged Wolfe with being unable to produce publishable work without the expert help of Maxwell Perkins, Wolfe's editor at Scribner's.[20] Wolfe's account of Perkins's help in *The Story of a Novel* strengthened DeVoto's belief that Wolfe was helpless without his editor. These twin concerns, really one, in that both concerned his writing, drove him back to New York in early September 1937.

The following May he spoke at Purdue University,[21] continuing on to the West Coast for a vacation. Before leaving New York, he had delivered to his new editor, Edward C. Aswell of Harper & Brothers, his huge mass of manuscript, which he regarded as the first draft of a new novel entitled *The Web and the Rock.* On the West Coast he joined Edward C. Miller, a Portland newspaperman, and Ray Conway of the Oregon State Motor Association, at Miller's invitation, on a two-week tour of the eleven Western national parks to prove that all eleven could be visited in the space of the average workingman's vacation. By driving between 400 and 500 miles a day they did it, leaving Portland, Ore., June 20, 1938, and returning to Olympia, Wash., July 2, having "traveled 4,632 miles in thirteen days."[22]

Wolfe then went to Seattle, took a trip to Victoria and Vancouver, B. C., and became ill. The original diagnosis was pneumonia. He did not respond to treatment, however, and early in September was put on a train for Johns Hopkins Hospital in Baltimore. A nurse, Annie Laurie Crawford, from Asheville, accompanied him. At Johns Hopkins, his brain was found to be covered with tubercule bacilli; nothing could be done. On September 15 he died.

Up in New York, young editor Aswell faced some problems. He had advanced Wolfe $10,000 on the new novel, and Harper's had given Wolfe a contract stipulating that no changes were to be made in the text without Wolfe's approval. But Wolfe was now no longer available to give or withhold permission. (In 1962 Richard S. Kennedy, the most knowledgeable scholar in America on this matter, discussed Aswell's work on the posthumous novels, *The Web and the Rock* and *You Can't Go Home Again*, defending it as "creative editing" in an appendix to *The Window of Memory*. In editing Wolfe's huge manuscript, Aswell was guided by an outline prepared by Wolfe; by Wolfe's agent, Elizabeth Nowell, who knew many of Wolfe's intentions concerning the manuscript; and by Maxwell Perkins, Wolfe's literary executor. Two of the articles in the present collection discuss this editing.)

Published June 22, 1939, as *The Web and the Rock*, the first of the two posthumous novels had a new protagonist, George "Monk" Webber, but it was evident that Webber was merely Eugene Gant in disguise. (Scholars and critics generally agree that Wolfe should have kept Gant as his protagonist.) This book, like its successor, was still autobiographical, telling of a young man who comes to New York City from the South, wanting to become a writer; he sees Depression America, begins a love affair with Esther Jack, an older woman, and visits Germany. (The affair builds, of course, upon the final scene of *Of Time and the River*.)

Of this book, one reviewer, Ray Warwick, said that in it Wolfe has given us "the feel, taste, smell, the very heartbeat of American life as no other modern writer has done."[23] Louis Kronenberger, however, deplored the book's autobiography (despite an "Author's Note" claiming that this work was "a turning away from the books I have written in the past" and "the most objective novel that I have written.") He pictured Wolfe as a kind of "egocentric adolescent" whose books, though "marvelous" in parts, betray "the amateur and the adolescent." Wolfe never had values worth considering, he thought.[24]

You Can't Go Home Again, published September 18, 1940, received similarly mixed reviews. Claude Simpson called it a sequel to *The Web and the Rock*, heavily autobiographical, carrying on the story of George Webber, taking him again to Germany and ending the affair with Esther Jack. Simpson recognized the special merit of the chapter titled "I Have a Thing to Tell You," revised slightly from its earlier appearance in magazine form.[25] (The chapter and article tell of disillusionment with Nazi

Germany.)[26] Fanny Butcher found this final novel "the easiest to read, the simplest, the most certain of popularity, as it is the most brilliant."[27] Actually, each of Wolfe's four major novels has been praised by scholars or critics as his best. That none of his fictional works has ever been out of print is a tribute to his enduring popularity, though one admits that Wolfe is today not read as widely as he was fifty years ago.

In 1961 the late C. Hugh Holman edited *The Short Novels of Thomas Wolfe*,[28] these being "A Portrait of Bascom Hawke" (an expanded version of the portrait of Bascom Pentland in *Of Time and the River*), "The Web of Earth," "No Door" (an expanded version of a section in *You Can't Go Home Again* and *From Death to Morning*), " 'I Have a Thing to Tell You' " (the shorter version, from *The New Republic*), and "The Party at Jack's" (a shortened version of Book II of *You Can't Go Home Again*).

In his introduction to this book, Holman expounded an idea that has since found wide acceptance among Wolfe scholars: that Wolfe did his best work in relatively short pieces and that Perkins erred in insisting that the lengthy *Look Homeward, Angel* be followed by another long work. Wolfe himself wanted, first, *K–19* and, later, *No Door* to follow his first novel. Had his wish been followed, and had he remained consistent in it, Holman argued, his literary reputation both then and now might have been and might be higher. Characteristically, Wolfe had trouble giving adequate form to long works. These five writings demonstrate what he could do with the novelette.

The posthumous editing of Wolfe also yielded a second book of short stories and sketches, *The Hills Beyond*,[29] and ten chapters about George Webber's ancestors that had been cut from *The Web and the Rock*. In this collection the best stories are undoubtedly "The Lost Boy" and "Chickamauga." The rest is inferior.

II

Leslie Field, of Purdue University, has defended Wolfe against the charge, often made and still repeated today, that Wolfe can be read with pleasure only by the young.[30] "When one grows older and more mature, one puts away childish things," the saying goes. Of course young readers tend to like Wolfe; they read him, however, differently than does the adult experienced in literary matters and differently than does the literary scholar. Says Field:

> Serious and sensitive critics of Wolfe have focussed on a number of "mature" critical concerns as they examined *Look Homeward, Angel* over the years. They have been concerned with his Whitmanesque "discovery" of America; his concepts of time, faith, loneliness, and death; his gusto, his vitality, his Faustian qualities; his struggles stemming from ambivalent views of the city versus the country, the North versus the South; his use of

autobiography, folklore, myth, rhetoric, language, and symbolism; his humor and his comic spirit; his dramatic quality; his resemblance to and affinity for other writers; his search for a spiritual father, his romantic quest, and his use of the *Bildungsroman*.[31]

In the half-century years since his death, Thomas Wolfe has been the subject of many and varied studies. The first compilation of Wolfe bibliography, George R. Preston Jr.'s *Thomas Wolfe: A Bibliography*,[32] concentrated on describing primary source material, with citation of some reviews. Paschal Reeves's *Checklist of Thomas Wolfe*,[33] a 43-page booklet, was supplanted soon afterward by Elmer D. Johnson's *Thomas Wolfe: A Checklist*,[34] a much more substantial work citing both primary and secondary source material but not always accurately. John S. Phillipson's *Thomas Wolfe: A Reference Guide*,[35] an abstract-bibliography, was later supplemented by his "Thomas Wolfe: A Reference Guide Updated," covering Wolfe bibliography through the spring of 1981.[36]

Each issue of the semiannual *Thomas Wolfe Review* (from Spring, 1977 through Fall, 1980 the *Thomas Wolfe Newsletter*) carries an abstract-bibliography of primary and secondary Wolfe material. Published at the University of Akron, this journal is cited in the MLA and MHRA annual bibliographies, is abstracted in *Abstracts of English Studies*, and is listed in the *American Humanities Index*, issued by the Whitston Publishing Co. of Troy, N. Y., and the *Arts and Humanities Citation Index* of the Institute for Scientific Information in Philadelphia.

In 1974 the late Paschal Reeves edited *Thomas Wolfe: The Critical Reception*,[37] a collection of reviews of Wolfe's fiction, of obituaries, of his letters, and of his notebooks. The reviews, printed for the most part in full, are supplemented by checklists of additional reviews. Robert Raynolds's review of *Look Homeward, Angel* in *Scribner's Magazine* for December, 1929, that brought the two men together (they toured Vermont together in 1933), merely cited in the supplemental checklist, was finally reprinted in the *Thomas Wolfe Newsletter*, 3, No. 2 (Fall 1979), the issue commemorating the fiftieth anniversary of Wolfe's first novel.

Collections of critical essays about Wolfe include Richard Walser's *The Enigma of Thomas Wolfe: Biographical and Critical Selections*;[38] Leslie A. Field's *Thomas Wolfe: Three Decades of Criticism*;[39] Paschal Reeves's *Studies in Look Homeward, Angel*;[40] Louis D. Rubin, Jr., *Thomas Wolfe: A Collection of Critical Essays*;[41] and Richard S. Kennedy's *Thomas Wolfe: A Harvard Perspective*.[42] This last contains the papers read at the meeting of the Thomas Wolfe Society at Harvard University in May 1982, plus a talk on administering the Wolfe estate by the Administrator C.T.A., and, by Professor Kennedy, an original paper not read at the meeting, on the editing of the posthumous books based on an exhibition at the Houghton Library of Wolfe's manuscripts for these works.

Kennedy's paper can be connected with a controversy begun a few years ago with publication of an article by John Halberstadt attacking the editing of Wolfe's posthumous books.[43] This article charged that although Wolfe's contract with Harper's specified that changes in the book's title or text were to be made only with the author's written approval, examination of the manuscript that Wolfe had left with Edward C. Aswell revealed that Aswell's editing was far more drastic than had been thought. Sections were shifted about, collages of text were produced, and even two new characters were created.

Halberstadt later restated the argument of his *Yale Review* piece.[44] Kennedy then pointed out[45] that he had commented extensively on Aswell's "creative editing" of the posthumous books twenty years before in *The Window of Memory*.[46] Halberstadt's charges, he contended, sensationalized in a letter to the *New York Review of Books* and in an interview in the *Village Voice*, constituted "harmful mischief" that was damaging the reputations of both Aswell and Wolfe.

Kennedy denied "that Edward Aswell mishandled Wolfe's manuscripts by means of the editorial process, to the extent that Aswell is really the author of Wolfe's last novels; and . . . that he is blameable for concealing his editorial procedure." The first of these charges Kennedy found "false" and the second "grossly exaggerated." A detailed account and defense of Aswell's editing followed.

Halberstadt's accusation of fraud against Aswell produced letters to the editor in publications around the country.[47] Louis D. Rubin, a well known Wolfe scholar at the University of North Carolina, Chapel Hill, called the matter "a tempest in a teapot," and a man in England who claimed to have examined the manuscript thought that "a complete critical edition" of it was needed—"for Wolfe's sake." Kennedy, however, says that "anyone who has any knowledge of the matter regards it as unpublishable in that state." So the matter stands today.

The 1982 display at Harvard's Houghton Library of manuscripts and rare books included Wolfe's typed outline for *The Web and the Rock*, marked by Aswell for retention or discarding, plus examples of his editing. There was a need, in Aswell's judgment, to change names and points of view in places and, occasionally, to move material. Character traits had to conform to those presented elsewhere, and some changes were needed to lessen risk of a lawsuit. According to explanatory material accompanying the exhibit, Aswell contributed but one paragraph of his own, ending Chapter 11 of *You Can't Go Home Again.*

The Autumn 1965, number of *Modern Fiction Studies*, 11, No. 3, was a special issue devoted to Thomas Wolfe, containing nine essays and a selected checklist of Wolfe criticism compiled by Maurice Beebe and Leslie A. Field.

In biography, Agatha Boyd Adams's *Thomas Wolfe: Carolina Student*[48] has been superseded by Richard Walser's *Thomas Wolfe Under-*

graduate.[49] A second limited-focus biography, *Thomas Wolfe at Washington Square*,[50] by Thomas Clark Pollock and Oscar Cargill, looks at Wolfe's years of teaching at New York University. Two full-length biographies have appeared: Elizabeth Nowell's *Thomas Wolfe: A Biography*[51] and Andrew Turnbull's *Thomas Wolfe: A Biography*.[52] As this introduction is being written, in the spring of 1984, David Herbert Donald of Harvard University, an historian, is writing what will probably become the definitive biography of Wolfe, scheduled for publication probably in 1986. And in 1985 Louisiana State University Press will be publishing a collection of interviews by Wolfe, edited by Richard Walser and Aldo P. Magi.

Richard S. Kennedy's *The Window of Memory: The Literary Career of Thomas Wolfe*[53] concentrates upon Wolfe's career as a writer, using his "manuscripts, notebooks, diaries, . . . letters and . . . interviews with relatives, friends, and literary associates of Wolfe himself." An appendix discusses Wolfe's rough outline for what became *The Web and the Rock* and *You Can't Go Home Again*.

The Notebooks of Thomas Wolfe, edited in two volumes by Richard S. Kennedy and Paschal Reeves,[54] provides valuable primary source material about Wolfe.

Wolfe's correspondence has been well mined. *Thomas Wolfe's Letters to His Mother*,[55] edited with an introduction by John Skally Terry of New York University, was re-edited from the original manuscripts by the late C. Hugh Holman and Sue Fields Ross in 1968[56] with an introduction by the editors. This scholarly edition is the one to be relied upon for serious study of Wolfe. Oscar Cargill and Thomas Clark Pollock edited the rather slight correspondence between Wolfe and the chairman of the English Department at New York University when Wolfe taught there, 1924–31, under the title *The Correspondence of Thomas Wolfe and Homer Andrew Watt*.[57] This also includes letters between Wolfe and Harry Woodburn Chase. Elizabeth Nowell, Wolfe's first major biographer, also edited *The Letters of Thomas Wolfe*.[58]

The correspondence between Wolfe and Aline Bernstein has already been noted. In 1983 Richard S. Kennedy edited *Beyond Love and Loyalty: The Letters of Thomas Wolfe and Elizabeth Nowell*,[59] with an introduction by the editor. This book also contains a short story by Wolfe, never before published, titled "No More Rivers," and an account of the story's history. *American Literary Manuscripts* reveals the existence of a considerable number of additional unpublished letters by Wolfe in collections around the country.

Several other works of special interest deserve mention. Floyd C. Watkins's *Thomas Wolfe's Characters*[60] remains a work not since supplanted, and Mabel Wolfe Wheaton and Le Gette Blythe's *Thomas Wolfe and His Family*[61] concentrates on the family relationship as seen by one of his sisters. Also noteworthy are Carole Klein's *Aline*,[62] a biography of Mrs. Bernstein, and A. Scott Berg's *Max Perkins: Editor of Genius*.[63] Both contain much material about Wolfe. The survey and appraisal of Wolfe scholarship previously prepared for *Sixteen Modern American Authors*,[64] by the late C. Hugh Holman, has been updated for 1972–83 by Richard S. Kennedy for the revised edition of this work, to be published in 1985.

From the roster of major Wolfe scholars the names of Paschal Reeves (University of Georgia) and C. Hugh Holman (University of North Carolina) have had to be dropped during the past decade because of their deaths. Richard S. Kennedy of Temple University, John L. Idol, Jr., (Clemson University), Richard Walser (North Carolina State University emeritus), and Louis D. Rubin (University of North Carolina) continue to be productive; Walser as the most prolific writer on Wolfe in America. His investigations into Wolfe biography have given us *The Wolfe Family in Raleigh*[65] and *Thomas Wolfe's Pennsylvania*.[66] More recently he has been investigating the maternal side of Wolfe's family, the Westalls, with articles on this in the spring and fall issues of the *Thomas Wolfe Review* for 1984.

In 1983 Louis D. Rubin won the first Zelda Gitlin Literary Award for the best article on Thomas Wolfe published during the preceding calendar year. This was "In Search of the Country of Art: Thomas Wolfe's *Of Time and the River*."[67] This award, established by Paul Gitlin, Administrator C.T.A. of the Estate of Thomas Wolfe, in memory of his late wife, was first presented in May of 1983 at the meeting of the Thomas Wolfe Society in New York City. Leslie Field continues to be active in Wolfe scholarship at Purdue University.

Relative newcomers to the field of Wolfe scholarship include John Hagan (SUNY, Binghamton), whose paper "*Of Time and the River:* The Flight from Death" (printed in Richard S. Kennedy, ed., *Thomas Wolfe: A Harvard Perspective*[68] as "Thomas Wolfe's *Of Time and the River:* The Quest for Transcendence") won the Zelda Gitlin Award for 1984, announced at the Wolfe Society's meeting in Raleigh in May of this year (1984). Elizabeth Evans (Georgia Institute of Technology), author of the critical monograph *Thomas Wolfe*,[69] is also productive in Wolfe scholarship. James Boyer (Pennsylvania State University, Berks Campus), in "The Development of Form in Thomas Wolfe's Short Fiction," read at the Wolfe Society's 1982 meeting, focused on a matter of increasing scholarly attention: structure in Wolfe's works. Suzanne Stutman of Pennsylvania State University's Ogontz Campus is a more recent scholar of considerable potential, and a paper by Michael S. Mills, a graduate student at Temple University, at the 1983 meeting of the Wolfe Society in New York City, on the transformation of *O Lost* into *Look Homeward, Angel*, points to a new talent worth watching.

III

The principal concern of this book is with scholarship on Wolfe for, approximately, the past decade. Of the essays in this collection, the oldest dates from 1970. Six date from the 1970s, and the rest from the 1980s, including two printed here for the first time. Only one, Leslie Field's "*You Can't Go Home Again:* Wolfe's Germany and Social Consciousness," has appeared before in a collection.

Reflecting the generally greater interest in Wolfe's first novel than in any of his other works, the first five essays in this collection concern *Look Homeward, Angel.* Of these, two deal with the book's critical reception, one in his native state and the other in the nation, the two complementing each other. Professor Walser finds that no North Carolina reviewer condemned the book unreservedly, and Professor Bassett shows that Southern reviewers on the whole were no more hostile toward it than were Northern ones.

Jack D. Wages examines how Wolfe in *Look Homeward, Angel* uses names of real places and people, devises names for comic effect, and draws up catalogs of names in epic style, while John Hagan shows how in that novel Wolfe integrates themes, symbols, and images into a complex and satisfying whole. Darlene Unrue finds that Wolfe's first novel shares with books by Faulkner, McCullers, O'Connor, and others the quality called "gothic."

Examining the editing of Wolfe's second novel, Francis E. Skipp finds that Maxwell Perkins cut over seven hundred lines of lyrical prose from *Of Time and the River* and eliminated plain bad writing that Wolfe should never have written or should have had the good sense to delete.

Examination of the outline for Wolfe's intended final book (which actually became two) convinces Patrick Miehe that Edward C. Aswell, Wolfe's second editor, prepared this plan, not Wolfe. Richard S. Kennedy, however, believes that Wolfe planned the outline and that, in fact, Aswell could not have composed it. Richard H. Cracroft finds unity and structure in *You Can't Go Home Again,* a work that many have found formless, and Leslie Field sees this novel as Wolfe's "most politically minded work," in which Wolfe sought a social consciousness and maturity whose complete fulfilment was thwarted by his death. John L. Idol, Jr., considers how two of Wolfe's athletes, a football and a baseball player, reveal in *The Web and the Rock* and *You Can't Go Home Again* something about American life and "the emptiness of fame."

Phyllis L. Huffman examines Wolfe's satire on boosterism and civic greed in the South of the 1920s as expressed in his *Welcome to Our City* (staged at Harvard in 1923), and Jerry L. Rice finds *Mannerhouse* (staged at Yale in 1949) "an indifferent final attempt in the drama" for which Wolfe himself maintained but a sporadic interest while writing it.

Seven scholars examine Wolfe's short fiction. Guy Owen demonstrates that "An Angel on the Porch," published three months before *Look Homeward, Angel*, represents a conscious reshaping of a chapter from that novel to make it an effective short story. John S. Phillipson compares the facts of the military career of the Civil War veteran who told Wolfe the story that became "Chickamauga" with the story as Wolfe wrote it. Wolfe changed many details to make a more effective literary work. Gloria Guzi examines the weaving metaphor that unifies "The Web of Earth," and Timothy Dow Adams finds a pattern of movement in "The Lost Boy" that represents Wolfe's sense of change as a constant in human life.

William Domnarski finds "A Portrait of Bascom Hawke" worth reading and remembering, unlike the longer, more famous novels in being tightly constructed. Webb Salmon, in a previously unpublished essay, finds that "Only the Dead Know Brooklyn" is important in helping us understand Wolfe's theme of loneliness, basic in much of Wolfe's writing, and his search for release from the resultant grief. And, concluding the section on the short fiction, James D. Boyer traces Wolfe's change from an early distaste for city people (in New York) to a sympathy for and identification with them.

In the concluding section, dealing with various aspects of Wolfe, Larry Rubin shows how Wolfe's concept of the unity of time helps to explain his interest in history and emphasizes the contrast between permanence and change in human life. And John Boone Trotti presents the most detailed study yet on the Presbyterian element in Wolfe's life and work, while Kenneth Seib suggests that "Wolfe's narrative method is most often that of the miniaturist" rather than that of a magnifier of human actions.

John S. Phillipson

Notes

1. Thomas Wolfe, *The Crisis in Industry* (Chapel Hill, N.C., 1919), Introduction, unpaginated. Reprinted in facsimile 1978 by the Palaemon Press, Charlotte, N.C.

2. Later printed in Frederick H. Koch, ed., *Carolina Folkplays*, 2nd ser. (Chapel Hill, N.C., 1924), pp. 31–44.

3. An expanded version, abridged by Edward C. Aswell, was published in *Esquire* for Oct. 1957, pp. 58–84. The 1923 working script, edited by Richard S. Kennedy, was published in 1983 by the Louisiana State Univ. Press.

4. Thomas Wolfe, *Mannerhouse: A Play in a Prologue and Three Acts* (New York: Harper & Bros., 1948). This play is being re-edited by John L. Idol., Jr., of Clemson Univ. for publication in 1985.

5. Suzanne Stutman, ed., *My Other Loneliness: Letters of Thomas Wolfe and Aline Bernstein* (Chapel Hill: Univ. of N.C. Press, 1983).

6. *Saturday Review of Literature*, 21 Dec. 1929, p. 584.

7. Geoffrey T. Hellman, *New Republic*, 18 Dec. 1929, p. 122.

8. *New York Times Book Review*, 27 Oct. 1929, p. 7.

9. Thomas Wolfe, *Of Time and the River* (New York: Charles Scribner's Sons, 1935), p. 911.

10. *New York Herald Tribune*, 8 Mar. 1935, p. 17.

11. *New York Post*, 8 Mar. 1935, p. 7.

12. *New York Herald Tribune Books*, 10 Mar. 1935, pp. 1–2.

13. In *Scribner's* for Apr. 1932, pp. 193–98; 239–56.

14. Scribner's for July 1932, pp. 1–5; 43–64, where it is called "a complete short novel."

15. In *Modern Monthly* for Dec. 1934, pp. 521–25.

16. In *Modern Monthly* for Jan. 1935, pp. 660–66.

17. In the issues of Dec. 14, 21, 28, 1935, published by Scribner's in expanded, book form 21 Apr. 1936. For the dates of Wolfe's publications I am indebted to Aldo P. Magi's "Thomas Wolfe: A Publishing Chronology," in *Thomas Wolfe Review*, 7, No. 2 (Fall 1983), 14–20.

18. In *Scribner's* for Spring 1932, *K–19* was announced as Wolfe's second novel, and a dummy was prepared of it, complete with dust jacket, title page (showing 1932 as the year of publication), and prologue. A fascimile of this, published as *K–19: Salvaged Pieces*, edited by John L. Idol, Jr., was the 1983 special publication of the Thomas Wolfe Society.

19. Published in *The Hills Beyond* (New York: Harper & Bros, 1941), pp. 108–41.

20. "Genius Is Not Enough," *Saturday Review of Literature* 25 Apr. 1936, pp. 3–4; 14–15.

21. Edited by Leslie Field in *The Autobiography of an American Novelist: Thomas Wolfe* (Cambridge: Harvard Univ. Press, 1983), sharing space with *The Story of a Novel*, which had originally been a talk given by Wolfe at a Writers' Conference at the Univ. of Colorado in 1935.

22. According to Brian F. Berger, whose *Thomas Wolfe: The Final Journey* (West Linn, Oreg.: Willamette River Press, 1984 [P.O. Box 317, Zip 97068]) retells the story and prints a substantial number of new photographs showing Wolfe on that trip. Wolfe's own account of it was published by the Univ. of Pittsburgh Press in 1951 as *A Western Journal.*

23. In the magazine section of the *Atlanta Journal* for 25 June 1939, p. 10.

24. In the *Nation* for 15 July 1939, pp. 75–76.

25. In the *New Republic* for Mar. 10, 17, 24, 1937, pp. 132–36; 159–64; 202–07.

26. In the *Southwest Review* 26 (Autumn 1940), 132–35.

27. In the *Chicago Tribune* for 18 Sept. 1940, p. 12.

28. Published by Charles Scribner's Sons.

29. Published 15 Oct. 1941, by Harper & Bros.

30. See "*Look Homeward, Angel* and the Passage of Time," *Thomas Wolfe Newsletter*, 3, No. 2 (Fall 1979), 33–40.

31. "*Look Homeward, Angel* and the Passage of Time," p. 35.

32. C. S. Boesen, 1943, reprinted 1979 by the Greenwood Press of Westport, Conn.

33. Columbus, Ohio: Charles E. Merrill, 1969.

34. Kent, Ohio: Kent State Univ. Press, 1970.

35. Boston: G. K. Hall & Co.

36. In *Resources for American Literary Study*, 11, No. 1 (Sept. 1981), 37–80.

37. New York: David Lewis.

38. Cambridge: Harvard Univ. Press, 1953.

39. New York: New York Univ. Press, 1968.

40. Columbus, Ohio: Charles E. Merrill, 1970.

41. Englewood Cliffs, N.J.: Prentice-Hall, 1973.

42. Athens, Ohio: Croissant & Co. [P.O. Box 282, Zip 45701], 1983.

43. "The Making of Thomas Wolfe's Posthumous Novels," *Yale Review*, 70, No. 1 (Oct. 1980), 79–94.

44. In a letter to the editor of the *New York Review of Books* for 19 Mar. 1981, pp. 51–52, headed "Who Wrote Thomas Wolfe's Last Novels?"

45. "The 'Wolfegate' Affair," *Harvard Magazine*, 84, No. 1 (Sept.-Oct. 1981), 48–53; 62.

46. Chapel Hill: Univ. of N.C. Press, 1962.

47. These include the *Harvard Magazine*, the *New York Review of Books*, the *Chronicle of Higher Education*, the *Boston Globe*, and the *Washington Post* among others.

48. Chapel Hill: Univ. of N.C. Press, 1950.

49. Durham, N.C.: Duke Univ. Press, 1977.

50. New York: New York Univ. Press, 1954.

51. Garden City, N.Y.: Doubleday, 1960.

52. New York: Charles Scribner's Sons, 1967.

53. Chapel Hill: Univ. of N.C. Press, 1962.

54. Chapel Hill: Univ. of N.C. Press, 1970.

55. New York: Charles Scribner's Sons, 1943.

56. Chapel Hill: Univ. of N.C. Press, 1968.

57. New York: Oxford Univ. Press, 1954.

58. New York: Charles Scribner's Sons, 1956.

59. Chapel Hill: Univ. of N.C. Press.

60. Norman: Univ. of Okla. Press, 1957.

61. Garden City, N.Y.: Doubleday, 1961.

62. New York: Harper & Row, 1979.

63. New York: Dutton, 1978.

64. Durham, N.C.: Duke Univ. Press, 1974.

65. Raleigh, N.C.: Wolf's Head Press, 1976.

66. Athens, Ohio: Croissant & Co., 1978.

67. Published in *A Gallery of Southerners* (Baton Rouge, La.: Louisiana State Univ. Press, 1982) pp. 85–106.

68. Athens, Ohio: Croissant & Co., 1983.

69. New York: Ungar, 1984.

Look Homeward, Angel

The Angel in North Carolina

Richard Walser*

Every Wolfe buff worth his salt knows what happened in Asheville when *Look Homeward, Angel* appeared in the bookstores there. On Sunday, October 20, 1929, two days after its official publication date, the *Asheville Citizen* ran a review by Lola M. Love which was, we have recently come to learn, written with the unacknowledged but persuasive assistance of her fiancé George W. McCoy, friend of Wolfe and state news editor at the *Citizen*. With predetermined oneness of mind, they eschewed temptation and treated the novel as if its setting and characters had nothing at all to do with Asheville. "The book," they wrote, "is a genius' combination of reality, which will not shrink from even the most sordid details of everyday life, and of a child-like expression of the most delightful fantasy . . . clothed in a vibrant language . . . with living people."

On the same day in the *Asheville Times*, managing editor Walter S. Adams also praised the book as "an outstanding novel possessed of unquestioned literary merit. The portraiture is vivid, the style is incisive, the narrative flows with a freedom that sweeps along the most resisting reader." But Adams went a step further. He believed that "any resident of Asheville who knew this city and its people during the period 1900 to 1920 will not have the slightest trouble in filling in the names of the real persons whom Wolfe made characters in his book." These real persons, wrote Adams, are made to "wear their most unpleasant guises. If there attaches to them any scandal which has enjoyed only a subterranean circulation, it is dragged forth into the light. If they have any weaknesses which more tolerant friends are considerate enough to overlook, these defects are faithfully described. . . . The novel will be acclaimed by literary critics as a work of real distinction. But the suspicion is strong that Asheville people will read it not because of its literary worth but rather in spite of any artistic merit which it may possess. They will

*Reprinted from the *Thomas Wolfe Newsletter*, 3, No. 2 (Fall 1979), pp. 19–25, by permission of the University of Akron.

read it because it is the story, told with bitterness and without compassion, of many Asheville people."

And that is exactly what happened. In no time flat, the bookstores sold out all copies in stock. In the margins excited readers began annotating the names of local denizens whom Wolfe had written about. All hell broke loose in Asheville.

Elsewhere in North Carolina reviews of the book followed the Asheville pattern, though of course its reception by readers down state had none of that excessive local resentment displayed in Asheville and none of the pandemonium resulting from those marginal notes. It often depended on how knowledgeable the reviewer was with Wolfe's materials. If the reviewer had no intimate acquaintance with Asheville or Chapel Hill, with Durham or Raleigh, his comments were prone to be relatively objective. But if he was familiar with those towns, Wolfe usually received a reprimand for his apostasy and indelicacies. Either way, the novel was generally praised, though reviewers always felt compelled to point out whatever weaknesses they detected.

On publication day (October 18), Jonathan Daniels, who had known Wolfe during their student days at the University of North Carolina, wrote in his column "Looking Both Ways" in the Raleigh *News and Observer*: "Despite a thin veil of disguise the book is about North Carolina and even about definite North Carolina people." Daniels then got into the identifications game, matching several characters with their originals, and predicted that the novel might "become in North Carolina not a novel but the prize puzzle book of the year." He thought it "safe to add that no extra copies of it will be ordered by the Asheville chamber of commerce." On Sunday two days later, Daniels wrote an extensive review, concluding his first paragraph with this oft-quoted sentence: "In 'Look Homeward, Angel,' North Carolina and the South are spat upon." The state and her people, he reported, were viewed through the eyes of the Gants, and "Seeing any section through the Gant family would be like looking upon that section through the barred windows of a madhouse. In such a case the hysteria of the madhouse is apt to color the whole country outside. So it is here." Daniels had almost no words of praise for the novel, which, he opined, was "a book written in a poetic realism, the poetry of dissolution and decay. . . . The book is sensuous rather than cerebral. It pictures a life without dignity—cruel and ugly and touched only by a half-mad beauty. . . . There is beauty in it but it is not a beautiful book."

The Love, Adams, and Daniels reviews reached Wolfe in New York posthaste. On Monday, October 21, Wolfe made this entry in his ledger: "Read first reviews of my book today. All from North Carolina. *Asheville Citizen* generous and sympathetic. *Asheville Times* bitter and grossly personal and unfair. Raleigh *News and Observer*—Headline [Wolfe's First Is Novel Of Revolt—Former Asheville Writer Turns In Fury Upon

N. C. And The South] says I turn in fury upon North Carolina and the South and 'spit upon them.'" He then admonished himself: "Live and learn, Wolfe" (*Notebooks* 1:377).

Richard L. Young, like Jonathan Daniels, had been a student at Chapel Hill with Wolfe. He and Wolfe belonged to the same social fraternity. His review in the *Charlotte News* of December 15 was not so harsh as Daniels's. "North Carolinians should be proud of Thomas Wolfe," Young began, "for soon the nation will doubtless hail him as one of our greatest contemporary writers." The reviewer noted that the "dark, dry lust" and "the mean and the ugly" were treated in "fine literary style" on an equal basis with "the beautiful, the appealing and the gentle." Then, after pointing out a few analogues, Young offered the information that during their college years he had been "in daily intimate contact" with Wolfe and therefore was able to declare that "in some elements" the hero Eugene was "none other than Wolfe himself. The author will doubtless deny this," Young warned the reader. "Yet the restless, moving, idealistic Gant appears a counterpart of Wolfe, the young student, fresh from the mountains. The groping for the beautiful, the soulful, the big and great of life was Wolfe's as well as Gant's."

An undated, unidentified newspaper review headlined "Thomas Wolfe Tells Startling Story of North Carolina Life" is deposited among the Wolfe papers at the University library at Chapel Hill. The reviewer, who signed himself P.D.M., took the dirty-book-great-book approach. "All the joys, all the beauty, all the sorrows, all the filth and ugliness of life leap from the pages and strike the reader with terrific force," ranted P.D.M. "At times one will want to cast the book aside and go bathe, feeling that one has been crawling through a sewer for the past two or three chapters. Then, suddenly the story will soar to the heavens and cleanse itself in the light of bright stars and a mellow southern moon." There is more of this sort of thing. No doubt about it, P.D.M. has got himself into a rhapsody and one feels that at any moment he just may swirl off into the poetic mists. But instead of swirling off, P.D.M. unbosomed himself with the avowal that he had "lived many years in the cities that bear the brunt of this story [and knew] full well that families like the Gants . . . do exist." Wolfe, he declared, had not exaggerated the Gants, nor the "harlots," nor the "vice dens" and "bawdy houses," nor "the slime that flows daily along the gutters" in Raleigh, Durham, and Asheville. Though *Look Homeward, Angel* could not be called "a good book," it was nevertheless "a true story" about conditions so disgraceful that their disclosure by Wolfe "should awaken North Carolinians" to improve them. The novel, he predicted, would "be denounced by many, praised by few, but it is a story that will not die. . . . Generations yet unborn will know its fascinations." True, true, and its fascinations for P.D.M. seem to have been those vice dens and slimy gutters.

During the 1920's, Chapel Hill professors frequently wrote book columns for various North Carolina dailies. At least two of them—Howard Mumford Jones and Archibald Henderson—made brief comments on *Look Homeward, Angel.*

Jones's arrival at the University in 1924 was too late for him to have known Wolfe on campus. For his column "The Literary Lantern" in the *Greensboro Daily News* of Sunday, November 24, Jones, signing himself "The Book-Keeper," first provided an overlong discussion of *The New American Caravan,* textbook for college English classes, then gave *Look Homeward, Angel,* which he called a "prodigious novel," a mere one paragraph. The book, Jones thought, suggested that its author was interested "in the development of new techniques in fiction. I understand," he hastily went on, "that the published book is the result of a considerable blue penciling of the original manuscript; I hope I will not be thought ungracious if I say that the book was not blue-penciled enough. Mr. Wolfe has energy enough for two or three writers, and it is constantly leading him astray. But he has written a book of Rabelaisian gusto, extraordinary vigor, and baffling weaknesses—especially when it is a question of bringing his wide-ranging curiosity to focus on a single artistic aim." Professor Jones thought that "Ben, who is not supposed to be the 'hero,' is the real center of the story, for it is in his life rather than in Eugene's that we see the tragic fatuity of a renaissance egotism in the modern world." In spite of its defects, Jones concluded, the novel had "a power, a creative splendor, a drive and tension that lift it out of the class of ordinary fiction, and discover in its author a talent of unusual interest."

Professor Archibald Henderson, mathematician and biographer of Shaw, was unlike Jones in that he had known Wolfe at Chapel Hill, but not in the classroom. Both Henderson and Wolfe had been popular as banquet speakers and belonged to some of the same campus clubs and societies. There is evidence that the patrician Henderson was occasionally displeased with the antics of undergraduate Wolfe. His remarks on *Look Homeward, Angel* in the *News and Observer* of December 15 are sandwiched in between comments on a new North Carolina play and some half dozen paragraphs about Ward Greene's novel *Cora Potts.* Though not unkind, Professor Henderson's sentences seem to me to have a patronizing undertone, as if he, incredulous that the novel was as good as it was, were patting tall clodhopper Wolfe gently but reluctantly on the back. Prefacing his triple review, Henderson acknowledged his acquaintance with Wolfe, then made this statement: "Wolfe's novel was originally projected as a play, if I am correct in identifying this novel as embodying the story of which he wrote me more than once." (Henderson was wrong about that. On October 7, 1924, Wolfe had written him about a play he was then working on whose theme was to be "the rise and fall of a powerful Southern family, and of the decay of a great social system." This play was, of course, *Mannerhouse.*)

Here is his critical paragraph entire: "Mr. Wolfe's story has a large, epic sweep about it. The family which he unsparingly exposes in the course of its degeneration is a microcosm. But so focally is his attention concentrated upon this social group, to the exclusion of the rest of the world, that the story assumes macrocosmic proportions. There is a but half-concealed savagery in the denotement [sic] of the characters. Mr. Wolfe has slowly matured his powers in a long period of incubating this extended story; and it embodies a philosophic commentary upon life, notable in a first novel." Clearly this is an "elegant" Henderson putdown. Perhaps the professor was annoyed that he had been omitted from Wolfe's cast of characters.

If there were other reviews of *Look Homeward, Angel* in North Carolina newspapers in late 1929 or early 1930, I have not come upon them. (Not cited here are press notices announcing publication of the novel but expressing no opinion of it.) After the first of the year, however, two university literary journals ran belated reviews of Wolfe's book.

At Chapel Hill, in the *Carolina Magazine* of February 2, 1930, editor John Mebane launched immediately into effusive praise: "*Look Homeward, Angel* is a brilliant piece of work. All the artistic talents of a man are combined in a harmonious blending to produce a novel as nearly perfect as has been written in this country in many years. Mr. Wolfe is the true artist; he sees, he hears. . . . The book . . . is vibrant with colours [sic], with passion, with originality." It "is to be read slowly–slowly the poetry, slowly the masterful dialogue." Wolfe was, in Mebane's opinion, "a powerful and a beautiful writer."

Twelve miles away in Durham at Duke University, Thomas J. Shaw, Jr., wrote in the *Archive* of March, 1930, that the novel, "far too long," was "a poetic and ruthless but damning picture of frustrated revolt from the poverty and materialism of the world." Wolfe's style was "at places poetically beautiful, as in the description of the death of Ben; at other times it is a mere confusion of words. Professional teachers of English would delight in using their blue pencil without mercy. They might, and probably would, end by crushing the heart out of the book." Shaw thought he ought to point out that Wolfe's "none too flattering thumbnail sketches of Raleigh, Durham, Chapel Hill, and his native town (all thinly veiled under substitute names) can hardly contribute to the local vanity of the inhabitants thereof," but, taking one thing with another, he did not doubt that the novel, "undigested" though it was, yet carried "with it the power of truth, and even if [Thomas Wolfe's] future writing be but half as good he need feel no cause for shame."

By the spring of 1930 the period for writing reviews of a book published the previous autumn was over. Not a single one of the North Carolina reviewers had condemned the book outright. Many of them admired the richly drawn characters, the powerful dialogue, the poetic prose. Many commented on the North Carolina settings and personalities. Few of the reviewers had much of a notion about the theme of the book, and not a one of them found any significance in such obvious symbols as the angel and the ghost. Several called attention to the "repulsive" low-life passages, but they were for the most part eager to concede that such passages had relevance to current social issues. For some, the book was too long and should have been cut. In short, *Look Homeward, Angel* was accepted by North Carolina reviewers in just about the same way it was accepted all over America. Added ingredients were the identifications game and the local pride that Tar Heels might feel in their native son. Outside Asheville, the novel caused no great stir in North Carolina.

Great stir or not, book-minded North Carolinians down state were not unaware of the Asheville uproar. In a feature story headlined "Asheville People Smart Under Lash of Genius" (*Charlotte Observer*, March 30, 1930), May Johnston Avery wrote of how the town "awoke one morning to find herself the mother of a literary genius," of how "Asheville tip-toed around with the book in its hand," or how "Every one somehow hoped—and feared—they would find themselves within the pages," and of how Asheville businessmen would greet each other by saying, " 'Well, have you read it? Did you recognize so and so?' and some would laugh, while others whispered, 'Isn't it awful! I don't see how he could do it!' " As for the rest of North Carolina, she declared, "The book was accepted 50 miles away from Asheville in the same spirit as it was 10,000 miles away and . . . the genius of the man, and the agony of the flesh that was poured into it, was not missed."

Four months after publication of the book, wrote Avery, "Asheville had another reaction. They read the book again." On this "second look" the town began to see that the "individuality" of those portrayed in *Look Homeward, Angel* was "only a common trait of human nature." Avery then told how, as Asheville began to realize that Wolfe was merely "saying from first to last that men are strangers, that they are lonely and forsaken, that they live and die alone," the "wretched bitterness" which had earlier been so rampant "softened." The town finally seemed to understand that "all great achievement is bought with a price, and," noted Avery, "Asheville now looks proudly at Tom Wolfe, writer, not from his lost land but from his home land."

Soon thereafter Asheville's benediction was felt throughout the state, but not always was it accepted everywhere right away.

To wind up these paragraphs on how Wolfe's angel fared during her first months in North Carolina, perhaps I may be permitted to relate a personal experience and tell how I came upon *Look Homeward, Angel.*

My last full student year at Chapel Hill was 1929–30. At that time, I heard of the Wolfe novel but was too busy with Milton and Keats to read it. Back in my hometown of Lexington in central North Carolina during the summer of 1930, I was stopped one day by a boyhood friend of mine who knew of my literary bent. "Have you seen that terrible Asheville book?" asked Jimmy. He told me that his father, a former Asheville man, had purchased the novel but was so ashamed of it that it was now hidden on the library shelf behind the *Encyclopaedia Britannica.* Jimmy's father was superintendent of the Methodist Sunday School. "It's a dirty book," said Jimmy. Well, I'd had enough *Samson Agonistes* and *Endymion* for a spell, and on that particular day a "dirty book" was more what I needed than Book III of *The Faerie Queene.* "Get it for me, Jimmy." I promised him that nobody would ever know. The next day he brought it over. "I've got to have it back by Friday," said Jimmy. He was afraid his father would go looking behind the *Britannica.* I had three days.

I read it in two. At this late date I can't recall if I was titillated by those pages narrating what went on in Exeter's red-light district or by that scene when "Miss Brown" took all of Eugene's medals. I probably was. But most definitely indeed do I still recall the effect upon me of Wolfe's vocabulary—glorious adjectives like *phthisic* and *frore* and *nacreous* and *synchronic*—and sentences like "The bell rang under the sea." I knew that the Gants and Pulpit Hill, and Eugene's suffering were mine. At age twenty-one, I too felt myself to be lost, lost, lost.

No, *Look Homeward, Angel* was not such a book as Jimmy had described. It was one of the great books, alongside *Moby Dick* and *Middlemarch.* From that day to this my opinion has not changed, and as far as I'm concerned, the angel who came to North Carolina in October, 1929, has never for a moment left the state.

The Critical Reception of *Look Homeward, Angel*

John Earl Bassett*

Richard Walser's recent article "The Angel in North Carolina" puts into much needed perspective the response of Thomas Wolfe's home state to *Look Homeward, Angel.*[1] Wolfe scholars for many years have assumed that despite superlative reviews elsewhere in America the South reacted in a generally negative way. Elizabeth Nowell writes of the "outraged protest" in Southern newspapers and the "most personal sense of betrayal" in the review by Jonathan Daniels.[2] Paschal Reeves emphasizes the "heated reviews it provoked in his native state of North Carolina," the anger and furor the book evoked in Asheville.[3] Wolfe

*Reprinted from the *Thomas Wolfe Review,* 6, No. 1 (Spring 1982), pp. 45–49, by permission of the University of Akron. © 1982 by the University of Akron, Akron, Ohio.

himself, of course, invested much in the belief that upon "the book's publication, I became an exile from my native town."[4] In speeches and such books as *Notes on a Novel* and *You Can't Go Home Again* he played self-indulgently upon the alienation forced on the honest artist in his own region. A reconsideration of the known reviews and of nine previously unlisted reviews—six from the South—however, suggests that Southern reviews of Wolfe's first novel were generally as favorable as those from the North.[5]

Four favorable articles in important New York newspapers were instrumental to the success that *Look Homeward, Angel* did have. In late October and early November 1929, Harry Hansen (*World*), though he poked fun at Wolfe's stylistic excesses, Margaret Wallace (*Times*), and Margery Latimer (*Herald-Tribune*), and Kenneth Fearing (*Post*) praised the novel's originality, drive and vigor, rich emotion, ambition, and vital, full characterizations. In a previously unlisted review, however, Dorothy Dayton (*Sun*), while admitting the book's vital energy, ridiculed it for a total lack of intellectual control and rigorous thought. That was apparently one of only two negative reviews in Northern newspapers; in the other William E. Harris (*Boston Evening Transcript*) said Wolfe "simply turned on the spigot" and poured forth a torrent of undisciplined, ununified sentimental prose.

Northern magazines in the late fall and early winter praised Wolfe as one of the most important voices in American fiction. Except for an attack by the priggish Edwin Fairley in the *Christian Register*, a second Bostonian, who claimed such foul smelling trash should be burned, the only unfavorable review was a short unsigned item in *Nation*; and that was a matter of emphasis. Like the sympathetic reviews, but in different proportions, it praised vitality but regretted incoherence, formlessness, overwriting, and undercutting. Established reviewers like Basil Davenport, Burton Rascoe, Geoffrey Hellman, John Chamberlain, Frances Robbins, Robert Raynolds, Carl Van Doren, and Agnes W. Smith lauded the young writer's Rabelaisian vitality, largeness of vision, truthful passion, and robust characterizations.[6]

These critics were, of course, more distanced personally than those in the South; but the criteria in both regions were precisely the same: praise for characters, passions, sensuous vividness, reservations for unevenness and formlessness. A few in the South commented on the painful realism of the portraits, but only in one or two cases negatively. Asheville newspapers printed no conventional reviews, but rather news articles with some discussion of reactions to the book. The article usually cited as reflecting initial local hostility is one by Walter S. Adams in the *Times*.[7] Actually this was written before the novel was even in local bookstores. Adams *predicted* that some residents might "be shocked into chills," and others "annoyed" but that many others would "snicker and laugh." Although Adams implicitly indicted Wolfe for laying bare his characters "with bitterness and without compassion," he fully praised the novel's vivid portraiture, incisive style, and forceful narrative. The ambivalence in the article was Adams's self-confessed inability to distance himself from such a local and personal work. The other significant local article, by Lola M. Love, was not even so mixed. She breezily recorded an interview with Julia Wolfe, talked of the author's childhood, physical traits, and reception by "New York publishers," and praised the book for its combination of "sordid details," "delightful fantasy," and excellent characterizations. She did not predict hostility or anger in Asheville. We know that such did ensue. Five months later, when May Johnston Avery reevaluated the local response, she wrote that many had been indignant at Wolfe's "disloyalty" and afraid of being identified, although others were upset they had not been included. By spring the atmosphere had altered, as the first reaction had worn itself out: Asheville was calling *Look Homeward, Angel* a great work and "now looks proudly at Tom Wolfe." One kinsman said, "Well, I don't care what Tom said about me. I'm proud he is in my family."

Also identified with North Carolina's bitterness is Jonathan Daniels' review in the Raleigh *News and Observer*. Daniels had been at Chapel Hill with Wolfe before returning to his family's newspaper. He did write that Wolfe seemed greatly hurt inside "by something that he loved" and that in reaction to that and in rejection of the "Victorian morality and the Bourbon aristocracy of the South" he had turned on North Carolina to spit in its face. It is hard, however, to find in Daniels' review the sense of personal betrayal that Reeves does—even as one might find it in Adams's article. As Daniels himself said many years later, the evaluative part of the review was "generally favorable," but some people confused his evaluation with his speculation about the novel's genesis.[8]

Elsewhere in Carolina Richard L. Young, another fellow alumnus, praised Wolfe and his novel unreservedly; Archibald Henderson, on the faculty at Chapel Hill, wrote about the book condescendingly but favorably; and Howard Mumford Jones, a Northerner then teaching at the University of North Carolina, remarked in a syndicated review that the novel's Rabelaisian gusto, vigor, power, and splendor marked Wolfe as a most important new talent. Similar adjectives were used not only by columnists for university magazines at Duke and Chapel Hill but also by the Richmond reviewer "Zoilus," who argued that in its Elizabethan vigor the novel expanded vivid local particulars into universal dimensions. Stringfellow Barr, editor of the *Virginia Quarterly Review*, was equally laudatory. More significantly, just a few months before his conflict with the Nashville Agrarians, he identified Wolfe, in contrast with the backward-looking Stark Young, as "the first novelist of the new dispensation in the Southern States," the first of a generation which could analyze a new and more incisively a South which must rid itself of false regional myths and its obsession with the War Between the States and Reconstruction. Only a few weeks earlier, Donald Davidson, the most unreconstructed Agrarian, granted *Look Homeward, Angel* rather grudging praise. He could not quarrel with Wolfe's "superb performance," his powers of observation and insight into character; but he could say that the novel "has a sickness in its marrow, a sickness of divided aims" that reflects the mind of a confused author who believes that a writer's art and artistry can be separated from his life, his personal and political and social values. Fully involved with the Agrarian cause, Davidson, not unlike Marxist critics of the day, implied that modern Northern capitalist industrialism fostered an alienation of the writer's self from his work that had infected even a serious young Southern author like Wolfe.

Elsewhere in the article, however, Davidson calls Wolfe's novel "brilliant," "powerful," and "magnificent." The only decidedly negative review in the South, outside of an unsigned article in the Louisville *Courier Journal*, was one by Julia K. Wetherill Baker, a high-toned critic for the New Orleans *Times-Picayune*, who penned several sympathetic reviews of Faulkner's early novels. Even Baker, after lamenting that Wolfe does not satirize but only makes faces, and creates bad smells, disgusting sights, and vulgarities, admitted "there is fine material in this chaotic book," and good characterizations. More representative reviews were those in the Baltimore *Sun* and Savannah *News*. Constance Brendon compared Wolfe favorably with Dreiser in pathos and profound understanding of humanity; Adah Young praised his ability to create beauty out of a panorama of life's painful experiences.

In conclusion it appears that Southern reviewers were quicker to express reservations toward *Look Homeward, Angel* in 1929, but on balance were no more negative than reviewers in the North. Of seventeen known reviews in the North, four were predominantly negative; of fifteen in the South no more than three were. In any case Wolfe had become a recognized new talent, one who would soon be praised also by Sinclair Lewis, Hugh Walpole, Richard Aldington, and William Faulkner, and whose second novel in 1935 would attract a much broader set of reviews. Faulkner critics might be interested but not surprised to know that in December 1929, when the Chicago *Tribune* listed the forty most interesting novels of the year, *Look Homeward, Angel* was included; *The Sound and the Fury* was not.[9]

A CHECKLIST OF AMERICAN REVIEWS OF *LOOK HOMEWARD, ANGEL*[10]

A[dams], F[ranklin] P. New York *World*, Feb. 6, 1930, p. 6.
Adams, Walter S. Asheville *Times*, Oct. 20, 1929, pp. 1–2.
Anon. *Chapel Hill Weekly*, Oct. 18, 1929, p. 2. News article.
Anon. *Tar Heel*, Oct. 24, 1929, p. 1. News article.

Anon. *University of North Carolina Alumni Review*, Nov. 1929, p. 45. News article.

Anon. Louisville *Courier Journal*, Nov. 24, 1929, Sec. 4, p. 3.*

Anon. *Atlanta Journal*, Dec. 1, 1929, magazine, p. 22.*

Anon. *Nation*, 130 (Feb. 19, 1930), 225.

Anon. *Booklist*, 26 (May 1930), 315.

Avery, May Johnston. Charlotte *Observer*, March 30, 1930, Sec. 3, p. 6.

B[aker], J[ulia] K. W. New Orleans *Times-Picayune*, Feb. 23, 1930, p. 25.*

Barr, Stringfellow. *Virginia Quarterly Review*, 6 (Spring 1930), 310–313.

Brendon, Constance. Baltimore *Evening Sun*, Nov. 30, 1929, p. 6.*

Chamberlain, John. *Bookman*, 70 (Dec. 1929), 449–450.

Coon, Horace. *Ms.: A Magazine for Students of Creative Writing*, Dec. 1929, p. 6.

Daniels, Jonathan. Raleigh *News and Observer*, Oct. 20, 1929, p. 2–M.

Davenport, Basil. *Saturday Review of Literature*, 6 (Dec. 21, 1929), 584.

Davidson, Donald. Nashville *Tennessean*, Feb. 16, 1930, Automotive Sec., p. 7.

Dayton, Dorothy. New York *Sun*, Nov. 16, 1929, p. 8.*

Fairley, Edwin. *Christian Register*, Jan. 9, 1930, p. 31.

Fearing, Kenneth. New York *Evening Post*, Nov. 16, 1929, p. 12m.

Hansen, Harry. New York *World*, Oct. 26, 1929, p. 15.

Harris, Cora Annette. Charlotte *Observer*, Oct. 20, 1929, Sec. 3, p. 7, News article.

H[arris], W[illiam] E. *Boston Evening Transcript*, Nov. 9, 1929, Book Sec., p. 2.

Hellman, Geoffrey T. *New Republic*, 61 (Dec. 18, 1929), 122.

Henderson, Archibald. Raleigh *News and Observer*, Dec. 15, 1929.

Jones, Howard Mumford. Charlotte *Observer*, Nov. 24, 1929, Sec. 3, p. 6. Syndicated review.

Latimer, Margery. New York *Herald Tribune Books*, Nov. 3, 1929, p. 20.

Love, Lola M. Asheville *Citizen*, Oct. 20, 1929, p. 8–C.

Mebane, John. *Carolina Magazine*, Feb. 2, 1930, p. 8.

Rascoe, Burton, *Arts and Decorations*, Feb. 1930, p. 106.

R[aynolds], R[obert]. *Scribner's Magazine*, Dec. 1929, pp. 36, 38 (adv.).

Robbins, Frances L. *Outlook and Independent*, 153 (Dec. 25, 1929), 669.

Shaw, Thomas J., Jr. *The Archive* (Duke U.), Mar. 1930, pp. 23–24.

S[mith], A[gnes] W. *New Yorker*, Nov. 16, 1929, pp. 111–112.*

Van Doren, Carl. *Wings* (Literary Guild), Feb. 1930, p. 17.

Wallace, Margaret. *New York Times Book Review*, Oct. 27, 1929, p. 7.

Williams, Sidney. Philadelphia *Inquirer*, Nov. 16, 1929, p. 12.*

Young, Adah. Savannah *Morning News*, Jan. 5, 1930, Sec. 3, p. 5.*

Young, Richard L. Charlotte *News*, Dec. 15, 1929, p. 5–B

Zoilus. Richmond *Times-Dispatch*, Nov. 10, 1929, Part 2, p. 3.*

Notes

1. *Thomas Wolfe Newsletter*, Fall 1979, pp. 19–25.
2. *Thomas Wolfe: A Biography* (Garden City, 1960), p. 150.
3. *Thomas Wolfe: The Critical Reception* (New York, 1974), p. xix.
4. This comment, from the famous Purdue speech, is quoted by Reeves, p. xx.
5. The essential checklists for reviews of the novel are the Reeves volume; John S. Phillipson, *Thomas Wolfe: A Reference Guide* (Boston, 1977); Elmer D. Johnson, *Thomas Wolfe: A Checklist* (Kent, Ohio, 1970); and those earlier checklists mentioned by C. Hugh Holman, "Thomas Wolfe," in *Fifteen Modern American Authors*, ed. J. R. Bryer (Durham, 1969). As a basis for additional research I used the newspaper collection at the Library of Congress; I checked each American newspaper from 1929 there and searched through February 1930 those that carried book reviews regularly.
6. Carl Van Doren's review was in the promotional circular of the Literary Guild, so perhaps should be granted less weight.
7. The Asheville *Times* on Oct. 20 (p. 5–A) carried an advertisement by the Arcade Book Shoppe for *Look Homeward, Angel,* which was called "a work of permanent value over and above the supreme interest it holds for local people."
8. *Thomas Wolfe* (Columbia, S.C., 1961), p. 13.
9. Dec. 14, 1929, p. 18.
10. Items marked * are, I believe, neither listed in one of the checklists nor mentioned in an article, such as Walser's elsewhere. The Smith review seems to be one Andrew Turnbull refers to in his biography as being in *The New Yorker.* I have not mentioned British responses, a subject needing detailed study. Only reviews by Richard Aldington, Gerald Gould, Frank Swinnerton, and one in *TLS* seem to be known, plus Canadian reviews by Felix Walter and Morley Callaghan.

Names in *Look Homeward, Angel*

Jack D. Wages*

Names are important in the novels of Thomas Wolfe, especially in his first and best novel, *Look Homeward, Angel* (1929), in which well over three-hundred characters and places are mentioned by name or described. My purpose in this paper is to discuss briefly only a few of

*Reprinted from the *Thomas Wolfe Newsletter*, 1, No. 2 (Fall 1977), pp. 29–34, by permission of the University of Akron.

numerous functions of naming in his first book: his use of the names, sometimes modified, of real persons and actual places, his use of names for comic effect, and his use of epic-like catalogues of names.

That Wolfe is sensitive to names of characters is obvious from that early passage when Eugene is about to be born. When the baby finally arrives, in spite of W. O.'s rantings and posturings, the attending physician speaks:

> "Well, what are you going to call it?" inquired Dr. Cardiac, referring thus, with shocking and medical coarseness, to this most royal imp. Eliza was better turned to cosmic vibrations. With a full, if inexact, sense of what portended, she gave to Luck's Lad the title of Eugene, a name which beautifully, means "well born," but which, as any one will be able to testify, does not mean, has never meant, "well-bred."[1]

With characteristic rhetorical flourish, tinged with a measure of the comic, Wolfe notifies the alert reader that names will, indeed, be of significance as he makes a distinction that one finds made by numerous writers of the Southern Renaissance from Ellen Glasgow to Eudora Welty.

Wolfe's uses of the charactonym and of the place name are varied and interesting. One reason for the violent reception of the novel in Asheville is Wolfe's practice of using real names or modifying them only slightly. His thinly disguised place names include: Pulpit Hill for Chapel Hill. Sydney for Raleigh, Old Stockade for Old Fort, Spring Street, the address of Dixieland, for Spruce Street, the address of Old Kentucky Home, and so on.

Some names, such as those of his twin brothers who died young, Grover Cleveland and Benjamin Harrison, he does not alter; other names he changes to create charactonyms. For example Wolfe's sister, Mabel, becomes in the novel *Helen*, and she is in a number of ways the "light of the family." Our charactonyms are ironic. *Eliza*, a shortened form of *Elizabeth*, functions very well as an ironic charactonym, as do *Luke* (a character based on Wolfe's brother, Fred) and Lily, a prostitute.

One student of Wolfe's writing has divided the charactonyms of the first novel into a number of categories, including those which were actual names, those with the same number of syllables as the actual names, those in which only one name was changed, those in which nationality of names was preserved, those indicative of irony, etc.[2] Whereas these aspects of Wolfe's naming techniques have received some attention, two functions of naming mentioned above—as humor and as epic catalogues—have received hardly any scrutiny, despite the fact that both areas of Wolfe's writing have been noted and occasionally commented upon.[3]

Often, Wolfe creates humor by manipulating names. Early in *Look Homeward, Angel*, one is confronted with the essentially comic scene of W. O. Gant going to meet his prospective father-in-law, Eliza's father,

Major Will Pentland. To make the situation even less comfortable for Gant, the room is filled with other assorted relatives of Eliza who prove to function as the audience—really Swiftian clackers—for Major Pentland. Eliza's father turns to Gant and says:

"It's W. O. Gant, isn't it?" he asked in a drawling unctuous voice.

"Yes," said W. O., "that's right."

"From what Eliza's been telling me about you," said the Major, giving the signal to his audience, "I was going to say it ought to be L. E. Gant."

The room sounded with the fat, pleased laughter of the Pentlands (p. 12). Major Pentland's dubious ability to pun on names is clearly appreciated by his ready-made audience of relatives, if not by his future son-in-law. One additional example, perhaps, will more than suffice. As the major is introducing W. O. to the family, arranged around the room, Uncle Bacchus is reached.

> "They call him Back-us everywhere else," said Will, including them all in a brisk wink, "but here in the family we call him Behind-us." (p. 13)

Major Pentland's attempts at humor, his inveterate punning, and W. O.'s silent suffering, not only aid in characterization, but they also serve as a kind of foreshadowing of the not altogether amiable relationships between these two men later in the novel.

At approximately the same level of sophistication are examples of humor drawn from Eugene's undergraduate days at Pulpit Hill. Overheard during a dormitory study session is the following:

> "Gene!" yelled Harold Gay, hurling a thick volume from him. . . . "What do you know about history? Who signed the Magna Charta?" "It wasn't signed," said Eugene. "The King didn't know how to write, so they mimeographed it." "Correct!" roared Harold Gay. "Who was Aethelred the Unready?" "He was the son of Cynewulf the Silly and Undine the Unwashed," said Eugene. "On his Uncle Jasper's side," said Elk Duncan, "he was related to Paul the Poxy and Genevieve the Ungenerous." (pp. 404–405)

Still another example of undergraduate "humor," or what passed for undergraduate humor in Wolfe's day, is the series of pranks, involving names, about which Eugene is able to reminisce with considerable pleasure:

> He would go to Exeter or Sydney; sometimes he would go to little towns he had never before visited. He would register at hotels as "Robert Herrick," "John Donne," "George Peele," "William Blake," and "John Milton." Sometimes, at hotels of ill-repute, he would register, with a dark buried glee, as "Robert Browning," "Alfred Tenny-

son," and "William Wordsworth." Once he registered as "Henry W. Longfellow." "You can't fool me," said the clerk, with a hard grin of disbelief. That's the name of a writer." (pp. 497–498)

Wolfe has often been charged with overwriting the "lyrical" passages of *Look Homeward, Angel*; however, a passage in Chapter 14, at the beginning of Part Two of the book, well demonstrates the varied, and I believe, well-integrated style of Wolfe. That is, it shows Wolfe's ability to write at least violet, if not purple, passages of prose, which are redeemed by the appropriate measure of humor and irony, humor created through devices of naming. He begins:

> Nacreous pearl light swam faintly about the hem of the lilac darkness; the edges of light and darkness were stitched upon the hills. Morning moved like a pearl-gray tide across the fields and up the hill-flanks, flowing rapidly down into the soluble dark. (p. 144)

There follows a comic interchange between the habituées of the local, all-night diner and "laughter howls out into the tender dawn" (p. 145). As usual, in a book by Wolfe, the passage is a long one, several pages long; but, one section deserves mentioning here as a humorous use of names. The passage is a parody of what may well become the society column of the newspaper to appear later that morning.. Harry Tugman declaims:

> "Members of the Younger Set were charmingly entertained last night at a dinner dance given at Snotwood, the beautiful residence of Mr. and Mrs. Clarence Firkins, in honor of their youngest daughter, Gladys, who made her debutt this season. . . . Miss Catherine Hipkiss, affectionately known to members of the local younger set as Roaring Kate, supervised the checking of overcoats, evening wraps, jock-straps, and jewelry. Attending were the Misses Aline Titsworth, Lena Ginster, Ophelia Legg, Beatrice Slutsky, Helen Shockett, Lofta Barnes, and the Messrs. I. C. Bottom, O. I. Lovett, J. Broad Stern, etc. (pp. 149–150)

The following section of the chapter begins: "Virginal sunlight crept into the street in young moteless shafts. At this moment Gant awoke" (p. 150).

Look Homeward, Angel traces the growing awareness of the boy, Eugene, as he grows, matures, and searches for his identity. One path he takes is reading. At one stage of his development, a number of the books that he has been reading are named, including:

> . . . the *Iliad* and the *Odyssey* read at the same time as *Diamond Dick*, *Buffalo Bill*, and the *Algers*, and for the same reason; then, as the first years waned and the erotic gropings become more intelligible, he turned passionately to all romantic legendry, looking for women in whom blood ran hotly, whose breath was honey, and whose soft touch a spurting train of fire. (p. 85)

He often imaginatively recreates some of these stories as his own day-dreams, and he chooses, for his imaginary name in this heroic world of his day-dreams, Bruce-Eugene Glendenning.

At one point in the narrative, after Bruce-Eugene has lived through a particularly harrowing dream-adventure in which he slays his dragon and wins his pure maiden, the narrator states:

> Ah, me! Ah, me! Eugene's heart was filled with joy and sadness—with sorrow because his adventure was done. He pulled his clotted handkerchief from his pocket and blew the contents of his loaded heart into it in one mighty, triumphant and ecstatic blast of glory and sentiment. Ah, me! Good old Bruce-Eugene. (p. 89)

This imaginary, secret name becomes, then, a kind of signal—a form of communication between narrator and reader—signifying poignant feeling, perhaps eliciting a smile if not a chuckle, a nostalgic fondness for the time in all our lives when such daydreams are possible.

This name, Bruce-Eugene, is invoked several times later in the novel. For example, we see Eugene on his college campus, still able to summon the name from his past. In a rather sophomoric state of depression resulting from being ostracized temporarily by his friends, Eugene muses:

> I think I'm hell, thought Eugene, and they say I stink because I have not had a bath. Me! Bruce-Eugene, the Scourge of the Greasers, and the greatest fullback Yale ever had! Marshal Gant, the savior of his Country! Ace Gant, the hawk of the sky, the man who brought Richthofen down! Senator Gant, Governor Gant, President Gant, the restorer and uniter of a broken nation, retiring quietly to private life in spite of the weeping protest of one hundred million people, until, like Arthur of Barbarossa, he shall hear again the drums of need and peril.
>
> Jesus-of-Nazareth Gant, mocked, reviled, spat upon, and imprisoned for the sins of others, but nobly silent, preferring death rather than cause pain to the woman he loves. Gant, the Unknown Soldier, the Martyred President, the slain God of Harvest, the Bringer of Good Crops. Duke Gant of Westmoreland, Viscount Pondicherry, twelfth Lord Runnymede, who hunts for true love, incognito, in Devon and ripe grain, and finds the calico white legs embedded in sweet hay. Yes, George-Gordon-Noel-Byron Gant, Chatterton Gant, and François-Villon Gant . . . and Proteus Gant . . . and Mumbo-Jumbo Gant. (pp. 493–494)

This humorous string of imagined pseudonyms is, of course, an example of the manner in which Wolfe often includes epic-like catalogues in a book which has been called—with some justification—an attempt at American epic in prose. Of numerous such "epic" catalogues throughout the book, many of which exhibit various forms of Wolfeian humor and comic exaggeration, the following example exhibits still another use of the technique of allusion in the novel.[4] After both the birth and the name of Eugene have been announced, the narrator "refreshes our historical memory" in order to place the event of Eugene's birth in a larger context. A small portion of the "epic" catalogue celebrating Eugene's birth reads as follows:

> By 1900, Oscar Wilde and James A. McNeill Whistler had almost finished saying things they were reported as saying, and that Eugene was destined to hear, twenty years later; most of the Great Victorians had died before the bombardment began; William McKinley was up for a second term, the crew of the Spanish navy had returned home in a tugboat.
>
> Meanwhile . . . Pope Sixtus the Fifth had come and gone; Belisarius had been blinded by Justinian; Henry James Pye, Poet Laureate of England, was with his fathers; Simonides, Menander, Strabo, Moschus, and Pindar had closed their earthly accounts. . . . Finally, only thirty or forty million years before, our earliest ancestors had crawled out of the primeval slime; and then, no doubt, finding the change unpleasant, crawled back in again. (pp. 29–30)

Among other purposes, such a catalogue of names serves to reinforce Wolfe's tripartite view of time in the novel.[5]

Of Wolfe's writing, one scholar has stated that his "work stands vast, flawed, imperfect, and in its own way magnificent; and it flings down a challenge to the serious critic that has largely been ignored."[6] As these few naming techniques in *Look Homeward, Angel*, which are noted above, indicate, an onomastic approach to each of Wolfe's major works would surely be a rewarding method of taking up this challenge.

Notes

1. Thomas Wolfe, *Look Homeward, Angel* (New York: Charles Scribner's Sons, 1929), pp. 28–29. Subsequent references to the novel, made parenthetically in the text of this study, are to this edition.

2. Randall Vance Brock, "A Study of Charactonyms in Selected Works by Thomas Wolfe," M.A. Thesis, East Texas State University, 1974. Also, see Floyd C. Watkins, *Thomas Wolfe's Characters: Portraits from Life* (Norman: University of Oklahoma Press, 1957), pp. 4–37.

3. For discussions of the epic nature of Wolfe's writing, see C. Hugh Holman, " 'The Dark, Ruined Helen of His Blood': Thomas Wolfe and the South," in *South: Modern Southern Literature in its Cultural Setting*, ed. Louis D. Rubin, Jr., and Robert Jacobs (New York: Doubleday & Co., Inc. 1961), pp. 177–197, rpt. in *Thomas Wolfe, Three Decades of Criticism*, ed. Leslie A. Field (New York: New York University Press, 1968), pp. 17–36, and Richard S. Kennedy, "Thomas Wolfe's Fiction: The Question of Genre," in *Thomas Wolfe and the Glass of Time*, ed. Paschal Reeves (Athens: University of Georgia Press, 1971), pp. 1–44. Discussions of humor include Paschal Reeves, "The Humor of Thomas Wolfe," *Southern Folklore Quarterly*, 24 (Dec., 1960), 109–120, and Bruce R. McElderry, Jr., "The Durable Humor of *Look Homeward, Angel*," *Arizona Quarterly*, 11 (Summer, 1955), 123–128, and *Thomas Wolfe* (New York: Twayne, 1964), pp. 64–66, 164.

4. An interesting form of allusion is discussed by Mark D. Hawthorne, "Thomas Wolfe's Use of the Poetic Fragment," *Modern Fiction Studies*, 11 (Autumn, 1965), 234–244.

5. One of the best treatments of time in Wolfe's fiction remains the often reprinted essay by Margaret Church, "Thomas Wolfe: Dark Time," PMLA, 64 (September, 1949), 629–638.

6. C. Hugh Holman, "Thomas Wolfe," in *Sixteen Modern American Authors, A Survey of Research and Criticism*, ed. Jackson R. Bryer (New York: W. W. Norton & Company, Inc., 1973), p. 618.

Structure, Theme, and Metaphor in Thomas Wolfe's *Look Homeward, Angel*

John Hagan*

The taste-makers have long since passed it by, and the fiftieth anniversary of its publication in October 1929 went almost without remark, except in the South. One of the main reasons for this comparative neglect, I believe, is the still prevailing notion that Wolfe's first novel, though undeniably powerful in some respects, is mere "formless autobiography," the product of a *naïf* who had no "ideas" and only a rudimentary technique. To be sure, Wolfe was hardly a flawless writer, and the pattern of his book is not of the tightest; its structure could never be called rigorously Jamesian. But organic unity, formal cohesion, and thematic control of a larger and looser kind—of a sort to be found, for instance, in *Moby-Dick*, *Bleak House*, and *War and Peace*—are demonstrably present. Accordingly, in this paper I should like to show how the novel's various themes, images, and symbols are integrated in a rich, complex, many-layered whole, and reach their appropriate culmination in the brilliant and extremely moving last chapter.

I

Drawing upon late nineteenth- and early twentieth-century concepts earlier embodied in fiction by writers like Zola, Hardy, and Dreiser, the narrator of *Look Homeward, Angel* boldly sketches in the famous opening three paragraphs an uncompromisingly deterministic picture of the human condition which becomes a leitmotif throughout.[1] Wolfe's protagonist, Eugene Gant himself, shares these ideas. Lacking any firm, traditional religious beliefs, he becomes early in life a "fanatical zealot in the religion of Chance," the secular faith of the philosophical mechanist (pp. 160. Cf. 434). Moreover, though there is, after all, good

*Reprinted from *American Literature*, 53, No. 2 (May 1981), 266–85.

fortune as well as bad, the novel's conception of determinism, like that of the Naturalists in general, tends to be bleakly pessimistic. At the time of the death by typhoid fever of his eldest son, Grover, at the St. Louis Fair in 1904, W. O. Gant feels the dreadful power of "the inexorable tides of Necessity" (p. 49). Later, a conspicuous and embarrassing skin irritation which Eugene has inherited from his mother's family convinces the young man that "there was no escape" from his biological heritage (p. 479); he was "touched with the terrible destiny of his blood, caught in the trap of himself and the Pentlands, with the little flower of sin and darkness on his neck. . ." (p. 490).

Heredity and other deterministic forces—variously called "destiny," "chance," "necessity," and "accident"—thus constitute a "trap" within which Eugene feels himself confined. At the same time, one of the very traits he has inherited from his father makes it impossible for him to resign himself to such a condition. This trait is his enormous, "Rabelaisian" lust for life and boundless exuberance, his surging energy and huge, "Faustian" hunger, under the compulsion of which he is ready to hurl himself against whatever constrains him from devouring experience to the utmost. The whole thrust of his life, therefore, becomes a heroic struggle for freedom, for if heredity and other deterministic forces themselves cannot be overcome, he never loses his faith that there are many other thwarting circumstances, analogous to them, which can be. His very first bid for liberation takes place only a few months after his second birthday when he slips away from his negligent babysitter into the driveway of a wealthy neighbor and is almost trampled by a horse drawing a grocery wagon. "It was his first escape" (p. 35), the narrator points out, and he "carried the mark of the centaur [on his forehead] for many years" (p. 36). The image of the centaur as a symbol of liberation also appears in Chapter 29 in Eugene's "whinnying squeal—the centaur-cry of man or beast, trying to unburden its overladen heart in one blast of pain and joy and passion" (p. 348), and again in Chapter 39 in the description of him as "a centaur, moon-eyed and wild of mane, torn apart with hunger for the golden world" (p. 502). Still other metaphors of his desire for physical and spiritual escape are among the novel's most pervasive tropes—that of trains (on which he and others travel or whose haunting whistles, bells, and rumbling wheels he hears from a distance); that of the "door"; and that of "journeys," "quests," and, above all, "voyages," of which the comic antithesis is the intellectual incompetence of his eccentric school-teacher, John Dorsey Leonard, who "skirted Virgil because . . . [he] was a bad sailor—he was not at all sure of Virgilian navigation. He hated exploration. He distrusted voyages" (pp. 180–81).

From one point of view, of course, the quest for liberation marks Eugene as a late avatar of the archetypal Romantic rebel and outsider, individualist and man of feeling, metaphysical seeker and poet. Indeed, one of the paradoxical features of his consciousness is the way in which early nineteenth-century Romanticism and late nineteenth-century Pessimistic Determinism meet in it and clash. The coexistence in the same character of these different kinds of sensibility—the Romantic-poet and the Naturalistic-scientific—is one of the chief sources of the novel's dramatic tension. But it is not only the quest for liberation that links Eugene with the early Romantics and their typical heroes and plots. He is a Romantic in a more specific way, which we may loosely call "mystical," and which, as many recent critics have pointed out, is associated with the Platonic and Neoplatonic doctrine of "pre-existence" as developed by Wordsworth in his great ode, "Intimations of Immortality."[2] On one level at least, the "home" of the title toward which the angel is implored to look is the life before birth, where alone can be found the true home of the spirit. An even more obvious reference to this realm is the fourth paragraph of the famous lyrical prose-poem which serves as an epigraph to Part One of the novel and supplies a recurrent refrain: "Remembering speechlessly we seek the great forgotten language, the lost lane-end into heaven, a stone, a leaf, an unfound door" (pp. i. cf. 4, 465). The "door," which Wolfe often uses as a symbol of escape in general, here acquires the additional, fairy-tale-like meaning of an entrance specifically into the paradise of pre-existence—an entrance whose location is also marked by the "stone" and the "leaf." Finally, Eugene's recollections of this paradise—of which there are several scattered throughout the book—are defined by two other important images, those of sound (voices, bells, or music) and water: "somewhere within or without his consciousness he heard a great bell ringing faintly, as if it sounded undersea, and as he listened, the ghost of memory walked through his mind, and for a moment he felt that he had almost recovered what he had lost" (pp. 31. cf. 32, 166, 244–45, 435).

Now, the point to be made about these mystical experiences is that, far from being merely "poetic" embellishments or merely exotic indicators of Eugene's "sensitivity," they provide every phase of the central story of his quest for liberation with a crucial frame of reference. In opposition to the bleak, deterministic prison-house of "destiny," "chance," "necessity," and "accident" in general and various other constricting circumstances in particular, they feed Eugene's passionate and, at bottom, religious yearning for transcendence, for escape into beauty and order, permanence and perfection—his desire, in a word, for an Earthly Paradise. For although *Look Homeward, Angel* is in many ways a Naturalistic novel, its protagonist is an imaginative young man of torrential vitality and idealism for whom a Naturalistic view of life can never be enough. His gargantuan hunger for this-worldly experience in all its manifestations coexists with a profound need to believe that such experience can be fabulous and enchanted, and provide a genuine "home" for his heart's desire. The other-worldly realm of pre-existence and the ecstasy which recollection of it arouses become for him not only an image of paradise lost, but a model, an archetype, of the paradise which can be regained in the here and now. For no matter how often he is made aware of "the nightmare cruelty of life" (p. 379), Eugene remains to the end a "Myth-maker" (p. 325), a visionary, a romancer, an American Adam, who is always seeking to return to the paradise from which he feels he has been expelled.

Specifically, his efforts to preserve this poetic conception of experience in the face of circumstances that are always threatening to destroy it consist of various struggles—carried on more or less simultaneously in complex counterpoint—to achieve some measure of ideal existence by escaping from five major constraining conditions: loneliness, family, hometown, native region, and (taken together) time and death. The first four of these quests terminate in his decision at the end of the novel to go to Harvard, and the last in his discovery at the same point of his vocation as an artist, a discovery which resolves at the deepest level the other quests as well.

II

Eugene's sense of the lost paradise of pre-existence is one of the main sources of the intense feelings of loneliness which he begins to have even as an infant. But his loneliness is also due to more ordinary causes, typical of many other *Bildungsromane*. For both his temperament and his values effectively isolate him from everyone in his family (except his older brother, Ben) and from most of his fellows in school and college too. During his Freshman year at the state university, in particular, he is so "desperately lonely" that "he saw himself in his clown's trappings and thought of his former vision of success and honor with a lacerating self-contempt" (p. 329). The clown image, in fact, is one of the novel's chief symbols of his loneliness in general, just as that of the centaur is of his quest for liberation. Terrified by the seemingly huge size of the family members bending over his crib, "he saw himself an inarticulate stranger, an amusing little clown, to be dandled and nursed by these enormous and remote figures" (p. 31). And many years later, when participating in a ludicrous Shakespeare Tercentenary pageant, he is dressed by the Leonards in "a full baggy clown's suit, of green linen" (p. 308) that prostrates the spectators in "wild, earthshaking, thundercuffing" laughter (p. 312).

His quests to escape from this loneliness take three main directions: for the knowledge and stimulus to his imagination which can be gained from books; for "life" itself, which is to be found only outside of books; and for self-acceptance and independence. In each of these kinds of experience he seeks a "door" that will admit him to that fabulous and ideal "home"—that paradise of pre-existence regained on earth—for which he so painfully yearns, and in the possibility of which he never loses his faith.

One of his earliest desires is for the knowledge which can be acquired from speech and reading, for while he is still in his crib he realizes precociously that "his first escape must come through language" (p. 30). Books, he soon learns, can liberate him from his loneliness because they introduce his vivid imagination to a "vast, enchanting, but unperplexing world" outside the confines of his narrow, immediate surroundings (p. 70). Great teachers partake of the same glow for him. His years at the Leonards' private school "bloomed like golden apples" (p. 180), because "the school had become the centre of his heart and life—Margaret Leonard his spiritual mother" (p. 192). To her "he turned his face up . . . as a prisoner who recovers light" (p. 178), convinced that "the way through the passage to India, that he had never been able to find, would now be charted for him" (p. 179).

Ever since childhood, Eugene's voracious reading in cheap fiction has also been providing him with another mode of escape from loneliness in self-flattering daydreams. Several of these fantasies are of high adventure or of grandiose achievements which win him acclaim or power. He rivals his mother's epic acquisitiveness in visions of princely wealth (pp. 85, 164, 229), and compensates for his clumsiness on the playing-field by imagining himself performing "heroic game-saving" feats of athletic prowess (p. 169). Especially comic are his fantasies of glory at the time of America's entrance into the First World War, in which he is debarred from participating because of his youth: "he longed for that subtle distinction, that air of having lived and suffered that could only be attained by a wooden leg, a rebuilt nose, or the seared scar of a bullet across his temple" (p. 445. cf. 427). Even after the war is over, delusions of grandeur of still other kinds afford him an escape from his loneliness—now become almost paranoid—when he revels in thoughts of himself as "Senator Gant, Governor Gant, President Gant . . . Jesus-of-Nazareth Gant," and the like (p. 493).

Eugene's daydreams are also often highly erotic. For sex too can be an escape from loneliness into a kind of glory, provided, of course, that it is sanctified by "love" and the woman, however passionate, is "pure." Although Eugene's lust is strong, his romantic, idealistic temperament makes it impossible for him to be satisfied with "pagan love" alone (p. 90). Building elaborate structures of wishful thinking on the basis of popular society novels and the silent movies, he imagines preposterously elegant men and women making love "in kid gloves, to the accompaniment of subtle repartee . . . beyond all the laws of nature . . . exquisitely and incorruptibly" (p. 132), and himself as "Bruce-Eugene" or "The Dixie-Ghost," the noble, unblemished hero who never fails to enjoy the delights of passion with the most beautiful and ardent yet virtuous women (pp. 85–90, 225–27).

More importantly, his quest for liberation from loneliness eventually takes him from books into "life" itself, when he comes to believe that the marvelous can be found in "real" (as distinct from merely imaginary) experience too—that the Ideal and the Actual, Romance and Reality, are one. "Facts" which fail to conform to this belief simply cease to be "facts" at all for him. Even when he learns certain unpleasant truths about Mrs. Leonard and her relatives, for example, he flatly refuses to believe them: "all the facts that leveled Margaret down to life . . . were as unreal and horrible as a nightmare . . . Eugene believed in the glory and the gold" (p. 187). In the same way, after he has lost faith in the bookish teachings of Vergil Weldon, his professor of philosophy at Pulpit Hill, he is sustained by his conviction that "the world was full of pleasant places, enchanted places, if he could only go and find them. . . . He always felt sure things would be better elsewhere" (p. 491. cf. 128, 132, 160, 325, 424–25). Thus, "he was devoured by a vast strange hunger for life" (p. 498); "the world lay before him for his picking"—not, as for Adam and Eve, a world radically different from Eden, but an Eden itself, "full of opulent cities, golden vintages, glorious triumphs, lovely women, full of a thousand unmet and magnificent possibilities. Nothing was dull or tarnished. The strange enchanted coasts were unvisited. He was young and he could never die" (p. 502). By the end of the novel, to be sure, he has not given up his quest for formal learning, for he is about to leave for graduate study at Harvard. But Harvard has come to mean much more to him than books; it too is a part of fabulous, liberating "life": "it was not the name of a university—it was rich magic, wealth, elegance, joy. . . . And he felt somehow that it gave a reason, a goal of profit, to his wild ecstasy" (p. 502).

Meanwhile, during the summer following his first year at Pulpit Hill, his quest for a paradise in "real life" has also resulted in a romance with one of his mother's boarders, named Laura James. No less than his earlier erotic fantasies that were fed by books, the two main parts into which Chapter 30, which records their brief love affair, is divided are dominated by imagery of enchantment. In the first (pp. 357–69), he and Laura declare their love for one another in what might be the preternatural, mythical realm of one of his favorite poets—that "chief prince of the moon and magic" (p. 351)—Coleridge. "The moonlight fell upon the earth like a magic unearthly dawn. It wiped away all rawness, it hid all sores. It gave all common and familiar things . . . a uniform bloom of wonder" (p. 368). As the pair embrace, Eugene's "limbs" are "numbed" by a "passion . . . governed by a religious ecstasy"; and, after they have parted for the night, he falls asleep to the sound of a cock's "distant elfin minstrelsy" (p. 369). Equally idyllic, though taking place in daylight, is the scene in the second part of the chapter (pp. 369–80), in which Eugene and Laura picnic on the following afternoon in a cove in the hills. The comparison of her body to a "Maenad's" which might "grow into the tree again" (p. 380) unmistakably links her to "the flitting wood-girls growing into bark" who have appeared earlier in one of Eugene's recollections of pre-existence (p. 245). The setting too is a counterpart of the pre-natal realm—a landscape which combines features of pagan pastoral, the Biblical Paradise, and fairy tale (pp. 376–78, 380). Here, forgetting the passage of time and the "pain and conflict" of the town, which "lay in another unthinkable world" (p. 377), the lovers "clung together in that bright moment of wonder . . . believing all they said" (p. 380).

Laura, of course, ultimately puts Eugene's trust to a severe test: in their Eden there is a "snake," both literal and figurative (pp. 376–77). The young girl betrays "the apple tree, the singing, and the gold" (p. 380), because she has been secretly engaged to someone else, and only a few days after leaving Altamont marries him. Eugene is crushed; having sought escape from loneliness in a "real life" paradise of love, he appears to have been left more lonely than before. Nevertheless, he soon recovers: his very loss of Laura, together with other experiences, teaches him that there is yet another way in which loneliness can be escaped—a way already suggested by his juvenile fantasies of demonic "isolation and dominance over sea and land . . . victorious dark all-seeing isolation" (pp. 74–75) and of "opulent solitude" (reminiscent again of pre-existence) in "kingdoms under the sea, on windy crags, and . . . [in] the deep elf kingdoms of the earth's core" (p. 229). For if there are many times when he finds his loneliness and the self-contempt it can breed an intolerable bondage, there are others when he eagerly embraces the proud self-acceptance which can be fostered by loneliness itself, and rejoices in his solitary state as a field for the development and display of heroic independence (pp. 427, 431, 436, 440).

During his last year at the state university his hope of finding a "vast Utopia of . . . loneliness" (p. 440) reaches its climax. Although he is troubled at first by a repetition of the students' mockery, and driven almost mad with shame by the Pentland rash, which has appeared on his neck and made him absurdly conscious of all his other physical blemishes, he eventually begins "to take a terrible joy in his taint" (p. 489), because he has come to believe that the truly great men of the world have also been "tainted"—"wasted and devoured by the beautiful disease of thought and passion" (p. 490). By thus persuading himself of his kinship with such "lords of the earth," "Eugene escaped forever from the good and the pretty into a dark land that is forbidden to the sterilized" (p. 490), wherein "he felt that . . . there was in him a health that was greater than they could ever know" (p. 491). In more appealingly modest and comically self-ironic moods, he even achieves enough objectivity to live comfortably with the heretofore intolerable idea that he may not be the genius he has always liked to think himself after all; "over that final hedge [of self-knowledge], he thought, not death, as I once believed—but new life—and new lands" (p. 494). The magic of one such "new land," Harvard, consists precisely in his faith that there he will be able to cultivate his "proud loneliness" to the fullest (p. 502).

III

In various ways, then, Eugene seeks to escape into some kind of Earthly Paradise from the prisons of loneliness constituted by his exile from the realm of pre-existence, by his family, by school and college, and by Laura's rejection. At the same time, his family, hometown, and native region spur his quest for liberation because they are the sources of additional discontents.

Eugene's attitude toward his family is by no means always simple. The words that the narrator uses to describe the boy's feelings at the time of Ben's death suggest his ambivalent reactions to them generally: "there was no moment of hate that was not touched by a dozen shafts of pity: impotently, he wanted to seize them, cuff them, shake them, as one might a trying brat, and at the same time to caress them, love them, comfort them" (p. 458). For this very reason, his relations with them are more painful than they would have been otherwise, and his frustrations all the greater. The characteristic image of home for him becomes that of entrapment (pp. 66, 112, 117, 180, 404, 412, 422, 440, 457, 458, 482). Prominent also is water imagery, which, as I have remarked, can symbolize the very different "home" of pre-existence: the boarding house is "a smothering Sargasso" (p. 244), in which his mother, Eliza, is " 'going to strangle and drown us all' " (p. 365), and a "deep pit" of "death and darkness" in which Eugene's "soul plunged downward, drowning . . . : he felt that he could never again escape from this smothering flood of pain and ugliness" (p. 458). The sense of liberation he feels after delivering his newspapers—a job which his parents have forced upon him—is like that felt by "a sailor drowned within the hold, who gropes to life and morning through a hatch" and by "a diver twined desperately in octopal feelers, who cuts himself from death and mounts slowly from the sea-floor into light" (p. 248). The phrase, "octopal feelers," in turn echoes an earlier reference to Eliza's extraordinary memory as "a great octopus" (p. 64). Moreover, Ben's "messy" death reminds Eugene of his childhood "hatred of the semi-private bathroom, his messy discomfort while he sat at stool and stared at the tub filled with dirty wash, sloppily puffed and ballooned by cold gray soapy water" (p. 458); and Ben himself, succumbing to pneumonia, is, in the words of the doctor, " 'Drowning! Drowning!' " (p. 461)

But if there is no hope for Ben, Eugene refuses to give up hope for himself. Even as Ben lies dying, the key symbol of the door reappears when Eugene "paced restlessly up and down the hall or prowled through the house a-search for some entrance he had never found" (p. 457).

Although his sister Helen's erratic oscillation between love and hatred in her treatment of him has always been extremely painful because it has plunged him "unexpectedly from Elfland into hell" (p. 117), he never loses his faith that "each time . . . you die, you will be born again" (p. 482). And if Helen is transformed on such occasions from a "bountiful angel" into "a snake-haired fury" (p. 117), he can always turn to another angel: "come lower, angel," he implores; "whisper in our ears. We are passing away in smoke and there is nothing today but weariness to pay us for yesterday's toil. How may we save ourselves?" (p. 244). This angel who can point the way to liberation is, on one level at least, the angel of the novel's title too, and the "home" in the direction of which it is exhorted to look is not only the other-worldly realm of preexistence, but the literal home of Eugene and his family.

Nor is it indifferent to his prayers: the way to his fullest escape from the family is opened at last with Ben's death and Eliza's sale of the original house on Woodson Street, for with these two events "the great wild pattern of the family had been broken forever" (p. 504) and its "final disintegration" assured (p. 505). When the family berated Eugene earlier for getting drunk for the first time, he bitterly declared his seventeen-year " 'apprenticeship' " with them over (p. 420); at the end of the novel he translates this into his adamant demand to be allowed to go to Harvard. Just as the glamorous university has symbolized for him liberation into knowledge, "life," and proud independence, it now symbolizes liberation from his crumbling family into " 'beauty' " and " 'order' " (p. 422), and "he waited for departure as a prisoner for release" (p. 422).

Of course, the university can arouse this euphoria in Eugene not only because it will free him from loneliness and his family. It is important because it is one of several experiences which also release him from the prison of Altamont. At the beginning of the novel, he is quite satisfied with the community (p. 89); as he matures, however, he comes increasingly to see the mountains as an entrapment (pp. 352, 407), the town itself as small, cramped, and ugly, and himself as a Gulliver among the Lilliputians (pp. 343, 375). Nor is it only the physical ugliness of Altamont that offends and oppresses him. There is an intellectual and moral ugliness in the place too, which is epitomized by the small-town mentality of his slow-witted, insensitive teacher, John Dorsey Leonard (pp. 193–96). Although cowardice induces Eugene to participate in the "ugly and revolting" persecution which Leonard conducts against a harmless, effeminate young Jew (p. 193), he does so not without a "piercing shame" that grows even more acute with the passing years (pp. 195–96).

The process which eventually leads to his final rupture with Altamont and its values consists of a series of journeys into various parts of the South, each of which, in one degree or another, convinces him that the "land of timeless and never-ending faery" (p. 132) lies only just beyond his native hills. These journeys fall into two phases, the first consisting of those which he makes between the ages of four and twelve with one or another of his parents, and the second, and more decisive, those which he makes at the age of fifteen and afterwards by himself. The climax of the latter journeys is his trip to Virginia during the last summer of the First World War—a trip which not only helps him develop his independence, but becomes an "initiation to the voyage" of the rest of his life and "a prelude to exile" (p. 431). In fact, it is on this occasion, for the first time since his love affair with Laura, that that ideality of the actual, that romantic quality of "real life," in which Eugene so passionately believes, fully manifests itself again. Travelling by train across a landscape symbolically bathed in the same Coleridgean enchantment as the lovers' nocturnal meeting, he stares "bewitched upon the great romantic country clumped with dreaming woodlands and white as a weird dawn beneath the blazing moonlight" (p. 425). Richmond, too, after this "lonely and magnificent approach through the night," thrills him "by its very casualness. All the little ticking sounds of a city beginning its day, the strange familiarity of voices in an alien place, heard curiously after the thunder of the wheels, seemed magical and unreal" (p. 425).

Eugene's adventures in Virginia, furthermore, are related to the important pattern of water symbolism which, as I have already noted, is frequently associated by Wolfe with both the other-worldly paradise of pre-existence and entrapment by the family. Beginning with his earliest travels with his mother, the image is also used to symbolize escape from Altamont, for certain of the faraway places in the South which Eugene visits are intimately connected with water and thus stimulate his hunger for "great ships and cities" alike (p. 197). The sound of the sea at Charleston, South Carolina, for example, fills his mind with exotic images of "strange dusky faces, palm frondage, and . . . the little tinkling sounds of Asia" (p. 304). While cruising out into the Roads at Newport News, in particular, he experiences for the first time "a music and a glory in his heart" that he feels he will be able to sustain forever (p. 426). And soon after, in a great romantic cry, he both identifies with the sea, and appeals to it as the Eternal Mother who "will bring me to the happy land . . . wash me to glory in bright ships" (p. 436).

As a result, then, of all these journeys to Virginia and elsewhere, Eugene is ready at the end of the novel to leave Altamont permanently. But in doing so, as the sea imagery implies, he will also be going away for the first time from the South as a whole. Indeed, he has come to believe more and more that, like his father, who is an "exiled" Northerner, he is "'a stranger in a strange land'" (p. 10). Building on this feeling, Margaret Leonard evokes in him a fantasy of "faery London" (p. 290), and arouses his desire for the "Paradise" of Oxford (p. 321).

By the end of the book, though he has set very definite sights on a very definite place (Harvard), the rest of the world he hungers to explore has dissolved into a vast, romantic blur. As we have seen in discussing his quest for "life" as an escape from loneliness, myth and the reality of the lands beyond the South become indistinguishable, fusing into a seamless whole; reality, it seems to him, *is* mythic (pp. 161, 491, 504).

Physical liberation from the South thus becomes one of the main objects of Eugene's quests. At the same time—and as in the case of Altamont—the South threatens him with intellectual and moral imprisonment too. If he is fully to escape his region, the myth which he constructs of the world beyond the South must eventually replace another, more insidious kind of myth—the sentimental one of ante-bellum Southern glory—constructed by the slave-owning aristocracy. During the time covered by the action of the novel, indeed, the latter myth, with its picture of "the romantic life of plantation and canefields . . . moonlight . . . dancing darkies on the levee," and so forth (p. 129. cf. 127, 302–03), makes Eugene very much its prisoner. Unlike the other trammels in the novel, it is one from which he neither escapes nor from which he sees any need to escape until "years later" (p. 127). Yet that he does finally emancipate himself from it the narrator makes emphatic, the process (like that of the journeys from Altamont) occurring in two phases. First, after having lived for awhile in the North, Eugene reaches a time "when he could no longer think of the barren spiritual wilderness, the hostile and murderous intrenchment against all new life—when their [the Southerners'] cheap mythology, their legend of the charm of their manner, the aristocratic culture of their lives, the quaint sweetness of their drawl, made him writhe—when he could think of no return to their life and its swarming superstition without weariness and horror" (p. 127). At this stage, nevertheless, "so great was his fear of the legend, his fear of their antagonism, that he still pretended the most fanatic devotion to them, excusing his Northern residence on grounds of necessity rather than desire" (p. 127). The second phase is reached when he finally realizes that "these people had given him nothing, that neither their love nor their hatred could injure him, that he owed them nothing, and he determined that he would say so, and repay their insolence with a curse. And he did" (p. 128).

IV

The most inclusive trap from which Eugene's quest for an Earthly Paradise compels him to seek escape, of course, is that of time and death, the ultimate expression of those blind, remorseless laws of "destiny," "change," "accident," and "necessity" that govern the godless, naturalistic universe as a whole. Personal encounters with the agonizingly protracted dying of his father and the deaths of his brother Grover, his college roommate (Bob Sterling), Laura James, and especially his beloved Ben assure that a dread of mutability and mortality is never far from his mind. Indeed, his sensitivity to the brevity of human life, to the "lostness" and dreamlike strangeness of the past, and to the dizzying rush of himself and the world he has known to extinction and oblivion is shown in many ways throughout the novel to be extremely acute. It is a vital element in his insatiable energy and partakes of the same intensity, for life and joy are precious to him, as they were for Keats, precisely because he knows they are so fleeting. His loneliness, insofar as it springs from a sense of expulsion from the timeless paradise of pre-existence into the temporal world, is directly related to the same awareness, and the latter encompasses and exacerbates his sense of entrapment by family, hometown, and native region as well. Furthermore, as I shall show, a complete resolution of his quests to escape from these other traps can come only when he is able to meet the supreme test of conquering time and death themselves.

This conquest is achieved when he discovers his vocation as an artist in the novel's last chapter—a discovery toward which numerous signs (e.g., his precocious interest in language, his ravenous love of reading, his maturing critical powers and taste, his rich fantasy life, and his actual writings) have been steadily pointing the way. Before looking at the chapter in detail, however, we must consider for a moment how an earlier one prepares for it. This is the famous Chapter 36 which describes Eugene and his brother Luke's visit to Horse Hines's mortuary, where they view Ben's corpse and make arrangements for his funeral, and which reaches its grotesque climax when the undertaker, regarding with great complacency the job of embalming he has done, decides that he needs to apply only one last touch to make his work of "art" perfect:

> "Just a moment!" said Horse Hines quickly, lifting a finger. Briskly he took a stick of rouge from his pocket, stepped forward, and deftly, swiftly, sketched upon the dead gray cheeks a ghastly rose-hued mockery of life and health.
>
> "There!" he said, with deep satisfaction; and, rouge-stick in hand, head critically cocked, like a painter before his canvas, he stepped back into the terrible staring prison of their horror.
>
> "There are artists, boys, in every profession. . . . Did you ever see anything more natural in your life? . . . That's art, boys!" (p. 477)

At this point Eugene, unable to contain himself any longer, falls to the floor, almost strangling with laughter, and screams, "'A-r-t! Yes! Yes! That's it!'" (p. 477). Needless to say, the episode is a masterpiece of macabre comedy—and an especially bold one at that, since it follows almost immediately the magnificent, extremely moving account of Ben's death. But it also makes a serious point, which can easily be missed, in relation to Eugene's discovery of his vocation. For when Hines attempts to give the appearance of "life and health" to Ben's corpse, he is only trying to perform, in however bizarre and parodic a way, that very function of triumphing over time and death which belongs to genuine art itself, and Eugene, in crying out hysterically as he does, seems to recognize this fact. The moment thus becomes for the young man an epiphany, completing his earlier recognitions of the power of Gant's stonecutting and of Homer's poetry to transcend flux (pp. 83, 334–35), and leading directly to the resolution of his own quest for transcendence in Chapter 40.[3]

The action of this last chapter falls into four main parts, the first three recapitulating matters which the novel has considered earlier. Thus, the opening passage (pp. 514–17 [paragraph 17]) reminds us of Eugene's unusually powerful imagination by showing how, after arriving at his father's shop on the eve of his departure for Harvard, he conjures up Ben's "ghost" and imparts life and animation to Gant's stone angels. The second part of the chapter (pp. 517 [paragraph 18]–19 [paragraph 5]) then dramatizes once more the power of Eugene's phenomenal memory, which calls forth into the Square "the thousand forms of himself and Ben" as they were in childhood, and for an instant holds in radiant stasis "all the minutes of lost time" (p. 519). Eugene also hints to the "ghost" of Ben how he has experienced faint memories of the even farther past of pre-existence (p. 518), and recalls having had such recollections as a child (p. 519). In turn, this awareness of time, loss, and death leads immediately into the third part of the chapter (p. 519 [paragraphs 6–8]) where, in a "vision" of history which echoes Shelley's "Ozymandias," Eugene perceives again the tragic ephemerality of mankind in general in contrast to the permanence of the earth itself.

Finally, the fourth—and most difficult—part of the last chapter (pp. 519 [paragraph 9]–22 [paragraph 2] consists almost entirely of a still more "terrible vision" (p. 519) of Eugene's own personal future—a vision in which he sees that all of his quests for the Earthly Paradise have ended only in frustration and defeat (p. 519). He also sees himself as turning at this time to Ben for an answer: where are " 'an end to hunger, and the happy land?' " " 'Where is the world' " he is seeking? (p. 520). Ben's elliptical reply is that " 'There is no happy land. There is no end to hunger. . . . *You* are your world' " (p. 520). That is, to find what he is searching for his brother must explore himself, for this is the only reality which is accessible and knowable to him. Apparently misunderstanding this advice, Eugene resolves in despair to give up his quest entirely and simply wait for the final, inevitable voyage into the " 'one land unvisited,' " death itself (p. 520). But now Ben reiterates what he has just said, and Eugene, at last grasping the point, is marvelously revived. " 'Fool,' said Ben, '*this* is life. You have been nowhere!' " (p. 521). Besides death, " 'there is one voyage, the first, the last, the only one' " still left (p. 521)—the voyage into himself—and Eugene immediately and exultantly vows to embark on it. How this journey will end he doesn't know, for when he asks Ben the vision suddenly fades away (p. 521). But no matter; Eugene has been strengthened by his brother's counsel, and, as dawn comes and the ghost of Ben disappears and the angels are once more frozen in their places, he turns with bold, new confidence to his departure for Harvard and the beginning of his great voyage of self-discovery.

The question to be asked, of course, is what this whole episode means in relation to the quest pattern of the novel in general and the quest for transcendence of time and death in particular. Most obviously, the chapter is an allegory of education and hence a microcosm of the *Bildungsroman* pattern which governs the book as a whole. Eugene is the pupil and the "ghost" of Ben is the teacher; whereas previously the former has learned from experience, here he learns from his brother. But what he learns now is that he must give his quests a vital new direction. Heretofore, looking "homeward" has meant seeking for the Earthly Paradise in the world outside himself: as an escape from loneliness he has sought it in books, "life," and physical isolation; as an escape from his family, Altamont, and the South, he has sought it in far and exotic places; and as an escape from time and death he has sought it in consoling thoughts of Ben's liberation from suffering (pp. 467, 470), of his resurrection in the form of the flowers which grow above his grave (pp. 486–87), and in scenes, like those glimpsed from the windows of speeding trains, which create an illusion of timelessness (pp. 133–34, 159). Now, however, under Ben's tutelage, he understands that he must seek the Earthly Paradise—look for his spiritual "home"—somewhere else as well. For if death is in Arcadia (the traditional meaning of the Latin motto, "*Et ego in Arcadia,*" which crosses his mind at one point in his conversation with Ben's "ghost" [p. 520]), in another sense Arcadia is a deathless place within himself, and there he must go to find it.

But what exactly does discovering himself mean? What is the nature of the self which we may presume Eugene will eventually find? The language which both he and the narrator use to describe "the lost land of himself" is practically identical with that which is used elsewhere in the novel to describe the paradisaical realm of pre-existence (p. 521). Any full recovery of pre-natal memories, however—not to mention a return to the pre-natal life itself—is of course impossible, for these memories are, by their very nature, fleeting and elusive, and, according to Wordsworth, become progressively more so as the child grows into youth and adulthood. Like all his other quests, therefore, Eugene's quest for his hidden self can only be for some metaphorical equivalent of the pre-natal paradise. What, then, is this something?

Although Wolfe does not explicitly tell us, the answer is clearly implied by the last chapter in its first three sections, which show how Eugene, who is painfully aware of the tragic ephemerality of man and his works, and longs to achieve the permanence, immutability, and timelessness symbolized by the enduring earth and the realm of preexistence, does actually triumph over time and death for a moment by the power of his imagination and memory, working together, to call back the past, raise the dead (Ben), and animate the lifeless angels. And what are imagination and memory for Wolfe if not the essential components of art itself, without which, indeed, the achievements of imagination and memory can only be fleeting? As memory immortalizes the past, so art must immortalize memory. Art, in fact, is doubly symbolized in the last chapter: first (and as elsewhere), by the angels themselves—those replicas of the angel which W. O. Gant, the artist *manqué*, saw as a boy in Baltimore and has futilely longed all his life to carve (p. 4)—and then by the fact that Eugene's imagination brings those angels to life, making them *his* creations, *his* works of art, just as, in bringing to life on the same occasion his earlier self through memory, he has created "his son, his boy" (p. 518). By thus symbolically dramatizing the power of art to triumph over the flux of life and render it timeless and beautiful, the first three sections of Chapter 40 implicitly provide the reader with the answer to the question which, in the last section, Eugene fails to get from Ben: what he will ultimately discover as he pursues his "ghost along the labyrinthine ways" (p. 521) will be the enormous creative resources of his imagination and memory—in short, nothing less than his vocation as an artist. It is in the direction of this discovery that he had been moving throughout his story.

With the forthcoming discovery of his artistic vocation, then, Eugene will have achieved, in the only way possible for him, his quest for liberation from time and death. But, by the same token, this discovery will permit a resolution of all his other quests too, and is thus ultimately the controlling theme of the entire novel. For Eugene will be able to escape from the traps of loneliness, family, town, and region, and pursue his quest for the Earthly Paradise, not only in the ways we have already seen, but by making them the very subject of his art—by transcending them through a supreme act of re-creation. Heretofore, he has failed to understand this. Early in the novel, for example, when he tried to avoid facing the unpleasant truths which he had come to learn about Margaret Leonard and her relatives, and which he feared might plunge her "in the defiling stream of life," he believed mistakenly that "it was not truth that men live for—the creative men—but for falsehood" (p. 186), and at the time of Ben's death he regretted that he and his brother had spent their lives in the "mean cramped huddle of brick and stone" that is Altamont, instead of in more glamorous and exotic places like "Gath or Ispahan . . . Corinth or Byzantium" (p. 450). During his conversation with Ben's "ghost" in Chapter 40 he makes this last point again, when he insists that stone angels should not walk in such an unremarkable place as Altamont's Square, but only " 'in Babylon! In

Thebes! In all the other places' " (p. 517). Beauty may be truth, and truth beauty, he is saying, but not here! Similarly, the name of Harvard appeals to him not only because the university it designates is far away, but because it is "enchanted" and sounds to him "like Cairo and Damascus" (p. 502). He has yet to learn what the narrator, paraphrasing Romantics like Wordsworth, Coleridge, and Carlyle, has known from the beginning—that "it is the union of the ordinary and the miraculous that makes wonder" (p. 397). When he does discover that it is art which can effect this union, he will have come to know at the same time that the "door" to the Earthly Paradise can be found anywhere—even in ugly, humdrum Altamont—through the exercise of his creative power itself. Whereas Ben, who is "lost" and can find no "door" because he has felt neglected by his family, acquired no satisfying vocation, and failed to discover any meaning in life as a whole, willingly embraces death as an escape from his frustrations and torments, Eugene will both find himself and affirm life by recapturing the past—including Ben himself—in timeless artistic form. As he once suspected on his trip to Charleston, Eugene now knows that "his gateway to the lost world" really lies behind him in the experiences he has already had and those waiting to be shaped by his hand (p. 297). Thus, although in the last paragraph of the novel, the town Square already seems "far and lost" to him, and he has become "like a man who . . . turns his eyes upon the distant soaring ranges" (p. 522), he and the angel of the title—which has now become his muse—will ultimately "look homeward" in the broadest sense of all, by immortalizing the family, the town, the region, and his own life there in art.

Notes

1. Thomas Wolfe, *Look Homeward, Angel* (New York: Charles Scribner's Sons, 1957), p. 3. Henceforth all references to the novel will be to this edition and will be given above in parentheses.

2. There have been several important discussions of this Platonic-Wordsworthian aspect of Wolfe's novel. Especially valuable are the following: Louis D. Rubin, Jr., *Thomas Wolfe: The Weather of His Youth* (Baton Rouge: Louisiana State University Press, 1955), Chap. 3; and Larry Rubin, "Thomas Wolfe and the Lost Paradise," *Modern Fiction Studies* 11 (1965), 250–58.

3. The best discussion of the last chapter I have found is Richard Walser, "The Angel and the Ghost," in *Thomas Wolfe and the Glass of Time*, ed. Paschal Reeves (Athens: Univ. of Georgia Press, 1971), pp. 63–65. As my remarks above will show, I agree completely with Walser's thesis that this chapter is "the poetic account of a young man's transformation into artist" (p. 64), but I examine the subject in closer detail and with some different emphases.

The Gothic Matrix of *Look Homeward, Angel*

Darlene H. Unrue*

Once the term Gothic referred to a style of medieval architecture and by extension to a group of eighteenth and nineteenth century novels that bore certain "medieval" traits; but since the advent of psychoanalytic theory, the term when applied to literature has come to refer loosely to particular elements within some modern literary works. Although modern critics have peered into the past and have pointed out that certain earlier works now stand revealed as Gothic in spirit, increased attention has been given to modern American Gothic, and especially to Southern American Gothic.

Notably missing from the list of twentieth century American Gothic writers is Thomas Wolfe. The list almost always includes William Faulkner, Carson McCullers, Tennessee Williams, and Flannery O'Connor and sometimes includes Truman Capote, Robert Penn Warren, Eudora Welty, and Ralph Ellison. And yet some of Wolfe's work shares with that of the above writers many of the same characteristics. This is particularly true of *Look Homeward, Angel,* and an examination of that work illustrates well the distinction between simply romantic elements and Gothic elements and again defines those parts of the Southern experience that are especially well expressed through the Gothic mode.

Look Homeward, Angel is admittedly an example of the twentieth century American romantic novel. Recent critics have treated the novel as representing a developmental stage in the American novel, at once lyrical and philosophical and devoted to answering the question of what it means to be a novelist writing in America. Critics like Louis D. Rubin, Jr., point out that many young aspiring American writers have been able to draw inspiration from Wolfe's novels, which seem to speak directly to them in ways that other American novels treating the same question, like some of Dos Passos' works, for example, cannot.[1]

Perhaps one of the reasons for the personal appeal of Wolfe, and of *Look Homeward, Angel* especially, is that Wolfe is more than simply a lyrical writer, and *Look Homeward, Angel* is more than merely a romantic novel. A closer look reveals that it abounds in archetypal Gothic images that appeal to readers subliminally; it shares with other Southern Gothic works the significant elements of both Southern and Gothic setting (bells, darkness, wind, a decaying mansion, labyrinths, an abyss, and eerie music), a quest, imprisonment, a ghost, and themes of isolation and fear of annihilation.

The matrix of prototypical Gothic novels is a journey that leads to knowledge. Usually the journey is made by a virtuous heroine or a

*This article is published here for the first time by permission of the author.

noble hero, or later is undertaken by a brooding villain-hero. The journey, often into strange lands, includes imprisonment along the way and confrontations with numerous dangers and evils, usually within the labyrinths and cellars of Gothic castles; but the more serious and horrifying the journey, the greater the victory if and when the sadder but wiser traveler returns home. Thus, the journey becomes an archetypal quest. The Gothic quest differs from the more general romantic quest primarily by the intensity of the extreme experiences completed against the backdrop of thunder and lightning, howling winds, wailing ghosts, and screeching demons, all of which are archetypes, some psychoanalysts believe, for the anxieties and fears of us all.

Look Homeward, Angel superficially is concerned with an actual world of people, buildings, and social problems; it is concerned more specifically with the quest, or initiation, of the novel's hero, Eugene Gant. Having been alienated from his mother and having lost his dear brother Ben, Eugene at the end of the novel finally understands that he must break irrevocably with his family and go out into the world on his own. But the process that has led to that awareness has been a long and agonizing spiritual journey. In order to evoke the intensity of the suffering, Wolfe has drawn heavily upon stock Gothic images, relying upon their psychological weight to carry much of the meaning of the story.

Just as many an imprisoned Gothic hero has contemplated his sad fate, an adolescent Eugene recalls infant impressions of being imprisoned, not within a gloomy castle, but first within a crib and second within a physical self:

> And left alone to sleep within a shuttered room, with the thick sunlight printed in bars upon the floor, unfathomable loneliness and sadness crept through him: he saw his life down the solemn vista of a forest aisle, and he knew he would always be the sad one: caged in that little round of skull, imprisoned in that beating and most secret heart, his life must always walk down lonely passages. Lost. His brain went black with terror. He saw himself an inarticulate stranger, an amusing little clown, to be dandled and nursed by these enormous and remote figures. He had been sent from one mystery into another: somewhere within or without his consciousness . . . he heard a great bell ringing faintly, as if it sounded undersea, and as he listened, the ghost of memory walked through his mind, and for a moment he felt that he had almost recovered what he had lost.[2]

That passage is permeated with a feeling of isolation and terror evoked by the images of prison bars, lonely, dark passages, a distant bell, and a ghost (even if only the ghost of memory). It is significant that the passage can be compared fruitfully with a passage from Maturin's classic Gothic work *Melmoth the Wanderer* (1820). In the early work John Melmoth has extracted from the Englishman Stanton's manuscript an account of the latter's discovery that he is imprisoned in a madhouse. Stanton sees that he is alone, hears bells, and discovers that the door to his room is locked. He calls aloud, and his voice is echoed by many others "in tones so wild and discordant" that he stops in "involuntary terror." As the day goes on and as his loneliness and fear increase, he tries the window, seeing for the first time that it is grated. As he looks out into the humanless courtyard, he sickens with "unspeakable horror" and sits down miserably in "complete darkness." When he shakes the door "with desperate strength" and utters "the most frightful cries, mixed with expostulations and commands," his cries are echoed by maniacs' malignant voices, which sound like "wild and infernal yells of joy.[3]

Both Wolfe's passage and Maturin's are imbued with what Denis de Rougemont has called "night mysticism" and with what Elizabeth Kerr has called the "dream side of the psyche, the essence of Gothicism which reveals the instinctual unconscious aspects of the psyche and abounds in literal and figurative dream-nightmare imagery effects."[4] Eugene's infant reveries also contain two of the three kinds of images Irving Malin deals with in *New American Gothic*, the "voyage into the forest" and also, as in Stanton's account, the enclosing place that represents retreat or imprisonment or both. As a variation of the second kind of image, Malin refers to the "other room" in the haunted castle which is the "final door through which the ghost-like forces march." It is a variation on the haunted castle itself, what Malin calls "the metaphor of confining narcissism, the private world." For literal examples of the metaphor, he refers to Faulkner's insane asylum at Jackson that shuts up Benjy Compson and Darl Bundren, the jail in Jefferson, and Miss Reba's brothel in Memphis.[5] Of course, Stanton is in a real madhouse, and Eugene is in a crib in the family home. Yet both Maturin and Wolfe, as well as Faulkner, have chosen the same motifs to translate those feelings of isolation, imprisonment, and terror into terms the reader can understand.

The dominant symbol and the focus of Gothic literature is the castle, or its equivalent, what G. R. Thompson terms "the most obvious single objective correlative" derived from *The Castle of Otranto* and indeed "suggested by the term 'Gothic' " itself.[6] The haunted castle is the other image that Malin considers, and he notes that in American Gothic "the 'castle' must be less ancient and magnificent and may be merely a ruined mansion like Faulkner's Old Frenchman's place or the Sutpen mansion."[7] The equivalent in *Look Homeward, Angel* is Dixieland (perhaps its very name suggests that like Emily Grierson's decayed mansion it, too, is a symbol of the Old South). Not precisely a mansion, it is the creaking old boarding house of which Eugene's mother, Eliza, is the proprietress. It is the edifice that contains Eugene's crib, and it is also that with which Eugene identifies his physical self in a brilliant illustration of a Jungian archetype. Eugene refers often to "the bleak horror" of Dixieland and thinks of it as the catalyst for his own infinite loneliness and the symbol of his spiritual imprisonment. The boarding house and his awareness of isolation blend in one passage which mirrors the terrors of his mind. Eugene has drunk himself into a stupor with a concoction of gin, rye, and bourbon:

> Then a divine paralysis crept through his flesh. His limbs were numb, his tongue thickened until he could not bend it to the cunning sounds of words. He spoke aloud, repeating difficult phrases over and over, filled with wild laughter and delight at his effort. Behind his drunken body his brain hung poised like a falcon, looking on him with scorn, with tenderness, looking on all laughter with grief and pity. There lay in him something that could not be seen and could not be touched, which was above and beyond him—an eye within an eye, a brain above a brain, the stranger that dwelt in him and regarded him and was him and that he did not know. But, thought he, I am alone now in this house; if I can come to know him, I will.
>
> He got up, and reeled out of the alien presences of light and warmth in the kitchen; he went out into the hall where a dim light burned and the high walls gave back their grave-damp chill. This, he thought, is the house.[8]

That passage exhibits clearly the way in which the fear of external dangers, common in some early Gothic fiction, has become exclusively the fear of internal, or psychological, dangers. And the physical Gothic castle has become here the physical, conscious self.

The old Gothic fiction was filled with extraordinary plights that evoked awesome fears. One common fear was that of annihilation, especially as a result of falling from great heights into black and bottomless pits. Often the castle, established high on an Alpine peak, provided the means of developing that kind of fear, and often a gaping chasm either within the edifice, as in Poe's "The Pit and the Pendulum," or in the mountain terrain, evoked the terror. One of the most dramatic scenes of all of Gothic fiction occurs at the end of Lewis's *The Monk* (1796) when the demon hurls Ambrosio into a mountain abyss:

> Darting his talons into the monk's shaven crown, he sprang with him from the rock. The caves and mountains rang with Ambrosio's shrieks. The demon continued to soar aloft, till reaching a dreadful height, he released the sufferer. Headlong fell the monk through the airy waste; the sharp point of a rock received him; and he rolled from precipice to precipice, till bruised and mangled, he rested on the river's banks.[9]

Wolfe also finds useful the image of the chasm or the pit inhabited by demons. Wolfe's pit, like that of the best of the older Gothic works, is a symbol for the fear of annihilation or the fear of the unknown side of the psyche. Eugene is especially susceptible to these horrifying fantasies when he is an impressionable boy, struggling to find meaning in his cruel existence. One passage is extraordinarily reminiscent of Lewis's passage:

> And when the bells broke through the drowning winds at night, his demon rushed into his heart, bursting all cords that held him to the earth, promising him isolation and dominance over sea and land, inhabitation of the dark: he looked down on the whirling disk of dark forest and field, sloped over singing pines upon a huddled town, and carried its grated guarded fires against its own roofs, swerving and pouncing with his haltered storm upon their doomed and flaming walls, howling with thin laughter above their stricken heads and, fiend-voiced, calling down the bullet wind.[10]

Another such passage occurs when Eugene and his sister Daisy attend a fair in St. Louis. Daisy in "furtive cat-cruelty" has taken Eugene with her into "the insane horrors of the scenic railway," and "they plunge bottomlessly from light into roaring blackness." When the blackness does yield, it is to "gloom peopled with huge painted grotesques, the red maws of fiendish heads, the cunning appearances of death, nightmare, and madness." As the car rolls "downward from one lighted cavern to another," he hears laughter like that in Stanton's madhouse and in which his sister joins. He is paralyzed by the belief that he has "surrendered all his hope" to "the lewd torture of demons masked in human flesh," and as he and Daisy emerge into the "warm and practical sunlight," he is "half-sensible" and "purple with gasping terror."[11] Eugene's fears can be recognized as irrational, based not upon the threat of external dangers but rather upon his internal fear of self-confrontation.

Many evocative passages in *Look Homeward, Angel* suggest the older Gothic works. For example, when the adolescent Eugene is sent to Niggertown to "capture" a new servant, he searches "fetid cellars" through "all the rank labyrinths." He suffers profoundly in isolation with his emerging psyche, and in one passage he thinks of himself as "holding in fief the storm and the dark and all the black powers of wizardry" as he crouches "against a lonely storm-swept house"; he feels a touch and looks "haunter-haunted, pursuer-pursued, into the green corrupted hell-face of malignant death."[12] Both those passages might be compared, for example, with one from Walpole's *The Castle of Otranto* (1764), in which Isabella flees into the depths of the castle from the villainous Manfred.[13] The castle's decay, darkness, and deep caverns symbolize Isabella's fear of the unknown just as the images in Wolfe's passage symbolize Eugene's fear of his unknown self.

Such Gothic passages occur regularly in *Look Homeward, Angel,* but perhaps the strongest Gothic link in the novel, and the inspiration for some of Wolfe's most poetic writing, is the presence of a ghost. In the older Gothic fiction the ghost followed an ancient literary tradition, having appeared in the Greek and French classical drama, in English drama, and in folklore. Like all facets of the ancient world, the ghost is admired by the Gothic writer, who uses the spectre primarily for any of three reasons: to create an atmosphere of fear, to reveal information, or to make a moral statement that could not be made without the help of a *deus ex machina.* A typical Gothic ghost is that which appears in Clara Reeve's *The Old English Baron* (1778); Sir Philip Harclay, returning to England after thirty years in French and Mohammedan wars, is visited by the ghost of his best friend and provided sufficient information to avenge the wrongs that have been brought upon his house in his absence.

The ghost in *Look Homeward, Angel* is the spirit of Eugene's brother Ben, whom Eugene frequently identifies as his other self. Darkness and wind attend Eugene's calling upon the ghost ("O lost, and by the wind grieved, ghost come back again!"). When the ghost comes, like many a Gothic ghost, it comes to instruct. The ghost of Ben tells Eugene that a physical journey in search of self-knowledge—in search of reality—is futile. In answer to Eugene's question "Where is the world?" the ghost of Ben replies, "Nowhere. You are your world."

Throughout the last pages of the novel Eugene confuses the ghost of Ben with his own spirit. And his seeking of that ghost/spirit is the psychological equivalent of the search for a "father," a source of strength. A final passage in this novel illustrates well one of the modern directions of the Gothic. These thoughts are Eugene's:

> O sudden and impalpable faun, lost in the thickets of myself. I will hunt you down until you cease to haunt my eyes with hunger. I heard your foot-falls in the desert, I saw your shadow in old buried cities, I heard your laughter running down a million streets, but I did not find you there. And no leaf hangs for me in the forest; I shall lift no stone upon the hills; I shall find no door in any city. But in the city of myself, upon the continent of my soul, I shall find the forgotten language, the lost world, a door where I may enter, and music strange as any ever sounded; I shall haunt you, ghost, along the labyrinthine ways until—until? O Ben, my ghost an answer?[14]

In this passage Thomas Wolfe has used the images of labyrinths without doors, ghosts, and strange music to dramatize his hero's search for self-knowledge and deliverance—a psychological search, but also a twentieth-century version of the old Gothic quest.

It remains to consider Wolfe in comparison with other Southern Gothic writers in order to determine what he shares with them and what he does not. Elizabeth Kerr concludes that the South provided William Faulkner and other Southern writers with "a reality which could be depicted with the strong contrasts of the Gothic genre to reveal social and psychological truths less accessible to purely objective and realistic treatment." She goes on to say that "with a foundation of realistic displacement which conceals Gothic structure beneath the representation of modern society, all the strategies of point of view, discontinuity, ironic inversion, exaggeration, and parody are employed to give new meaning to old formulas."[15]

There were elements in the South of the 1920s that made it ripe for Gothic fiction, and there were circumstances in Thomas Wolfe's experience that made him turn naturally in *Look Homeward, Angel* to Gothic motifs and symbols. Modern Southern Gothic writers, unlike their ancestor Poe, have not set their works in "the misty mid regions of Weir" or exclusively in the landscape of the soul. In this respect the family line runs more clearly from George Washington Cable than from Poe.[16] One of the characteristics of Southern Gothic writing is that it often concerns itself with time and place as well as with horror. In "A Rose for Emily," for example, Faulkner devotes his entire long second paragraph to establishing the exact setting. And Wolfe, like Cable, Faulkner, and other Southern Gothicists, provides in *Look Homeward, Angel* a strong sense of time and place. Like Miss Emily's decayed ancestral home, Dixieland is described in realistic detail as a big "frame house of eighteen or twenty drafty high-ceilinged rooms"; "rambling, unplanned, gabular" and "painted a dirty yellow," it later is referred to by Eugene as "the tomb."

Setting thus becomes crucial to the thematic development of much of Southern Gothic. Edward Stone believes that setting is crucial because the real setting, in the midst of social turmoil, is that against which Southern Gothic writers are reacting and which they embroider upon with Gothic images. The 1920s indeed were a period of rampant industrialism in the South and of a transformation of traditional social structures; the times would have been unduly troubling to a sensitive and poetic young person. In discussing the development of American Gothic fiction Stone also describes one of the common themes as the frightening burden of an isolated and alienated sensibility exploring its own emotions and one of the Gothic terrors as the vision of a landscape ravaged by modern industrialism.[17] The incessant theme of loneliness and alienation in *Look Homeward, Angel*, expressed by the pervasive repetition of the "O Lost!" motif, can be traced to both these sources.

Thus, the young and sensitive Thomas Wolfe, writing in the upper South in the 1920s, was trying to work out through art his search for himself and his revulsion for the change that was taking place in his society. A part of the repugnance of Dixieland, a repugnance so strong that it evokes nightmare terrors, is that it represents the opposite of what Eugene wants. He wants aesthetic nourishment, and Dixieland is an ugly symbol of twentieth-century American capitalism and of his mother's total absorption in the profit motive. He fears imprisonment in Dixieland in that he fears imprisonment in a materialistic society that does not allow the poetic soul to flower. It is understandable that he responds childishly to the train whistle that will take him out of it;

in his ignorance he fails to see that the train shares many of the characteristics of Dixieland. Ironically, it is the train, often a symbol of twentieth-century industrialism and progress, that obsesses him as the means of escape to knowledge, at least until the ghost of Ben tells him not to look outward for life's meaning but to look within.

The infant, child, and adolescent Eugene Gant, trying to find his way in the spiritual landscape of terrors and horrors, confronts his world's absurdities in grotesque characters and nightmares which will continue through the twentieth century into the theatre of the absurd and into the novels of black humorists like Pynchon, Barth, and Vonnegut. Thomas Wolfe and other writers who have sought to present in fiction man's searches and his internal terrors have turned frequently to the iconography of the Gothic. Because each human being's inner kingdom is private, there is no absolute description that will render it intelligible to the reader. The Gothic symbol, with its inherent wealth of emotion, has offered writers one means by which to give form to the abstract hope of fulfillment and the fear of annihilation, a hope and a fear that form the underlying conflict in such Southern American fiction. It is significant that after *Look Homeward, Angel,* when Wolfe was finished with his theme of initiation, when his autobiographical hero Eugene Gant had found his ghost within at the same time that he repudiated the materialism of his society, Wolfe turned naturally away from the Gothic; in subsequent novels he embraced a wider romantic mode as his hero confronted a larger social perspective than that of Altamont, a perspective that focused on a landscape more eternal than the dreamlit Gothic region of the soul.

Notes

1. See Louis D. Rubin, Jr., "Thomas Wolfe Once Again," *North Carolina Historical Review,* 1, No. 2 (Spring 1973), 169–89; and William Styron, "The Shade of Thomas Wolfe, *Harper's,* 236 (April 1968), 96–98.

2. *Look Homeward, Angel* (1929; rpt. New York: Charles Scribner & Sons, 1957), p. 31.

3. Charles Robert Maturin, *Melmoth the Wanderer* (1820; rpt. London: Oxford Univ. Press, 1968), p. 36.

4. See Denis de Rougemont, *Love Declared: Essays on the Myths of Love,* trans. Richard Howard (New York: Pantheon, 1963), p. 11; and Elizabeth Kerr, *William Faulkner's Gothic Domain* (Port Washington, N.Y.: Kennikat Press, 1979), p. 9.

5. Irving Malin, *New American Gothic* (Carbondale: Southern Illinois Univ. Press, 1962), pp. 11, 80.

6. G. R. Thompson, ed., introduction to *The Gothic Imagination: Essays in Dark Romanticism* (Pullman: Washington State Univ. Press, 1975), p. 6.

7. Malin, p. 11.

8. *Look Homeward, Angel,* p. 412.

9. Matthew Gregory ("Monk") Lewis, *The Monk* (1795; rpt. New York: Grove Press, 1959), pp. 419–20.

10. *Look Homeward, Angel*, p. 74.

11. *Look Homeward, Angel*, p. 46.

12. *Look Homeward, Angel*, pp. 111–12.

13. See *The Castle of Otranto* (1964; rpt. New York: Collier Books, 1963), p. 104.

14. *Look Homeward, Angel*, p. 521.

15. Kerr, p. 28.

16. See Edward Stone, "Usher, Poquelin, and Miss Emily: The Progress of Southern Gothic," *Georgia Review*, 14 (1960), 433–43; Stone traces the development of American Gothic by a comparison of Cable's "Jean-ah Pouqelin" with Faulkner's "A Rose for Emily."

17. Stone, p. 433.

Of Time and the River

Of Time and the River: The Final Editing

Francis E. Skipp*

Toward the end of December 1933 Thomas Wolfe and his editor at Charles Scribner's Sons, Maxwell Perkins, began to prepare for publication more than a million words of what Wolfe called "Of Time and the River." Although Wolfe went on writing to the extent of about 500,000 words during the months that followed, by the early fall of 1934 Perkins, cutting *en bloc*, produced a working typescript of about 415,000 words.[1]

The book was in galleys by October, but the typescript had gone to the printer bearing the marks of 142 additional cuts which shortened it by some 33,500 words. Lyrical prose that made the story line go slack came out. So did residual pockets of what Perkins apparently considered to be banal, irrelevant, redundant, or in bad taste. To analyze this cutting-in-detail, the evidence of which survives upon the typescript, is to enlarge our understanding of Perkins as an editor and Wolfe as an author.[2]

On leaves 437–40 Perkins placed characteristic brackets at the corners of a section eighty lines long and cut it all with a swift line running down the center of each page from top to bottom. This long passage, unmistakably lyrical in tone, is concerned with Eugene's penchant for accumulating all sorts of odds and ends, a characteristic he knows he inherited from the string-and-bottle-saving Eliza. It is a catalogue in rhythm, rich in the associations each item draws from the boy's memory. Toward the end of the passage occurs this paragraph:

> And for this reason, all these dreary and worthless accumulations of past time are pitiable mementos of this passion, the lifeless relics of man's bitter hug on life. Is it an old letter, a post-card scrawled with a few commonplace words, a note written years ago by someone met

*Reprinted from *Papers of the Bibliographical Society of America*, 64, No. 3 (1970), 313–22.

> one time and never seen again? Oh, keep it, keep it! Perhaps someday we will find a use for it, discover in it a rare and priceless value. Perhaps the person who wrote this will then have died, and all that we should have to make him live in memory—to hear him speak again, to see him as he was—will be the few scrawled words of this dull note. It is a jumble of scrawled words upon a thousand scraps of paper made out a thousand times at midnight in our room when we were twenty-one: keep it, keep it—perhaps there is a flash of fire here, a sinew of bright blood and agony, the priceless stuff of proud beginnings. Perhaps from this we shall preserve for other men the way the snow came at a certain time, and the way the sun was shining, the sound of gravel raked outside our window on a path, a boy's shout, or the hoof and wheel upon a morning street long long ago. [leaf 448]

This passage would seem to be as good as many which Wolfe published. Like Whitman, Wolfe here becomes more pronounced in his rhythm as his emotion rises. He reaches a peak of intensity in the pulse-beat of the spondee "bright blood" and thereafter descends to the lower key of melancholy recollection in a diminuendo of smooth iambs broken only by another spondee where the sound again conveys the sense in "boy's shout" and ends in the appropriately long vowels of "upon a morning street long long ago." And in addition to whatever poetic qualities the passage may have, it shows one reason why Wolfe wrote in the first place—to give an objective and more permanent existence to his memories.

Perkins cut the passage, however, regardless of its poetic qualities and the insight it provides into its author. He put it in the category he called "dithyramb" and disposed of it. There is an unmistakable odor of scorn about Perkins's choice of the word "dithyramb" to describe Wolfe's lyrical passages, and it is difficult not to conclude that he valued it less than he valued solid story and characterization. It is scarcely surprising, therefore, that when he was faced with an enormous typescript that obviously had to be cut, his hand fell heavily on the lyrical passages.

Wolfe was sometimes willing to retain tentative lines merely because they were "the priceless stuff of proud beginnings." On pages 664–65 of *Of Time and the River* (New York 1935) are Eugene's notebook jottings for one December day in Paris—descriptive metaphors and random musings. They give an interesting view of the mind of the literary artist before the shaping process begins, before he evaluates the images, inchoate thoughts, and verbal rhythms that float up into his consciousness. In the typescript there were about twice as many jottings as the book now contains. Before Perkins made his cut there appeared after the lines "The gull swerves seaward like a hope—September full of departing leaves and wings" these additional notebook entries:

A star I never saw before
The latticed hearts of whores
The windy bells across the snow
The loosened
Heard windy bells across the sheeting snow
The sunsets in the blinded eyes
How through my jaundiced heart the conspiratorial world
"Burn off my rust"
"Batter against my heart"
By the waters of Babylon
Painter of ghostly woods Olympian
B-long—B-long—B-long—B-long—Snap—Tap

Then after the published lines "He sat alone four thousand miles from home—the lonely death of seas at dawn," the lines cut from the typescript continue:

The debauched swine
His heart danced madly to the jazz
The island of my life
The sin's winter
How muttering life goes up and down
Purge
Our lives last inch
Bronchial horsecough
The sounding gong-notes of a drum
Green lily-depths
The sunken mouth of toothless age
The lake washed wings of dipping birds
Smooth bellied fish that glimmer in a pool
As one looks at a sleeping person and will not waken her
because—because. [leaves 1, 193–1, 194]

Perkins plainly saw what Wolfe was attempting here, for he made no effort to cut selectively, to choose the more striking lines and reject the obvious failures. His only basis for cutting was that of disproportionate development. From an artistic point of view Perkins probably was right, but the intrinsic interest of the lines themselves, transcribed virtually without modification from one of Wolfe's pocket notebooks, is such that his decision in this instance might be regretted. To Wolfe, "priceless stuff" was lost thereby, and, as was the case with all such detailed cutting, there could be no hope of preserving it in manuscript for later publication.[2a]

Where Perkins apparently recognized and cut the banal, the trite, the anticlimactic or the false he was on more defensible ground. If these numerous cuts irritated Wolfe it was probably because Wolfe quickly recognized their justice and was chagrined that he himself had written the material in the first place, or having written it, had not cut it on his own initiative. Here is a passage from the section Wolfe called "The River People," that portion of "Proteus: the City" that takes place on the Hudson River estate of Joel Pierce and his family. It is an analytical description of Joel's sister, Rosalind:

> Her beauty was wonderfully like that beauty which one sometimes sees in girls in England—a beauty that is at once Madonna-like in its noble purity, and warm and plain and living as earth, at once strong and robust as all natural life is, and equal to all life's natural shocks and burdens, and yet so fresh, fair and delicate that it haunts one like a dream. Nevertheless, no one could have mistaken her for an English girl: she was so unmistakably American that there were no words, no language, to tell the reason for it, yet she was so indubitably, as one saw the moment that he looked at her. It was the real America, the true America, the America we all have in our hearts, and live and hunger for, and always know that we shall find. It was not the accursed America of the illustration drawings, not the Harrison Fisher America of empty, brainless little faces, sweet rose-leaf lips and pure, sweet eyes and tooth-paste, moving-picture liveliness. It was not the America of the slender painted doll—the America of long, graceful legs, slender hips, pretty little nubs and buds and pippins of bright, infertile breasts, and slender little cups of shallow bellies and little sterile, tender, nervous grisettes of quick-coming———! It was not the little come-on, phony, flash-and-tease America, the horrible little flirt-and-twitch-it, get-your-man-by-baby-talk and roll-your-roguish-eyes America, it was not the horrible, cheap little empty doll with sawdust entrails that they have foisted off on America:—it was the real thing, the real America of the big hips and the melon-heavy breasts, the strong, wide hands with tender palms, the sweet warm mouth as fragrant as a flower, as rich and tender as the earth, and good for love and bold new adventuring and loyalty and courage and hard labor—the grand and sweet and casual America of the plains, the mountains, and the rivers, and it was deep as a well, and wider than a barn door, and as true and rich and fertile as the earth. [leaves 941–942]

There are a number of literary sins here, of course. Eugene's consciousness is at work, comparing Rosalind's beauty to girls in England, but Eugene's basis for such a comparison lies yet in his future. Perkins would pick out this inconsistency unfailingly. Eugene's frothing scorn for the slender painted doll occupies a disproportionate place in the passage in both length and intensity, competing for the central emphasis with Rosalind herself. The last three clauses are ludicrously, though unintentionally, suggestive. But dwarfing these peccadilloes is the cardinal sin of banality.

At the end of a letter to Ernest Hemingway written on 28 March 1934, Perkins had added, "Old Tom has been trying to change his book into a kind of Marxian argument (having written most of it some years before he ever heard of Marx), and I have been trying to express to him . . . that what convictions you hold on economic subjects will be in whatever you write, if they are really deep."[3] Perkins was right in principle, and he was right in cutting those passages where Wolfe violated it. Almost all instances where Wolfe steps before the curtain and comments upon the action are instances where he is trying to make his book speak a vaguely Marxian argument in technically improper passages tacked flimsily to the narrative. When old Gant is dying—actually dying at last—his friends and relatives come to the house and stand in small groups quietly talking, awaiting news of his condition. Among the visitors are both propertied men and laboring men. Helen, his devoted daughter, after trying to persuade herself that Gant had been the proprietor of his own "place" (her euphemism for "shop"), finds that her vision of Gant as a businessman is suddenly displaced by her recollection of his powerful workman's hands as they lay at his sides upon the deathbed. She realizes suddenly that his real friends were working men, and "having joined this group of working men . . . immediately felt an indefinable but powerful sense of comfort and physical well-being which the presence of such men as these always gave her. . . . She not only felt an enormous relief and joy to get back to these working people, it even seemed to her that everything they did . . . gave her a feeling of wonderful joy and happiness" (pp. 254–55). In the typescript at this juncture Wolfe steps in to ask rhetorically:

> Why is this? The reason is not hard to find. The true fellowship of working people is not one of mind and spirit but of blood, unless one comes from people who have worked with their [hands] their lives are jaded, feverish, impotent and sterile, their only dignity a feeble mocking of their own futility, a stale irony of hugging desolation to the bone and while enjoying lavish incomes, of crying "we are lost"—the child of the worker recoils from them with hatred and disgust, they smell bad to him and their whole lives stink, and thereafter his feeling toward them is tinged by the contempt and hatred of one who has known orchards, morning, and the smell of supper; has heard his father's great voice sounding from the darkness of the vineclad porch in summer, and hearing then the sound of great wheels pounding on the rail across the river, the tolling bell, the whistle's wail, has felt joy and glory stirring in his guts; and like a runner straining at the leash has had his vision of new lands, morning, and a shining city, the loves of glorious women, the fortunate and happy life of the enfabled rich! [leaves 467–68]

This passage was manifestly the worst sort of nonsense with a curious *nonsequitur* ending that nullified whatever validity its beginning possessed. In cutting it Perkins did Wolfe's reputation a great service.

On other occasions Perkins's reasons for cutting were more ambiguous. Kenneth Raisbeck (Francis Starwick in the novel) had been a close friend of Wolfe's at Harvard. When on 29 September 1931

Raisbeck came to a violent and mysterious death in a Westport, Connecticut, graveyard, Wolfe, according to Philip Barber, a friend of both men in "47 Workshop" days, was violently shocked. A few days later, dropping in at Yale, where Barber then was assisting George Pierce Baker, Wolfe told an excited story:

> He said that Raisbeck had borrowed a car to drive to New Haven [Barber reported] . . . and had picked up a young man for company. On the way, somewhere near Greenwich where Route One passes a cemetery, Raisbeck overcome by lust (this was Tom's word) had abruptly stopped the car, dragged the young man out of the car and into the cemetery in an attempt to assault him; the young man had fought back but was losing the fight when his hand found a stone with which he hit Raisbeck on the head, killing him. Leaving Raisbeck among the graves the young man had run away.[4]

An autopsy revealed subsequently that Raisbeck had died of acute meningitis, a disease distinguished by its sudden onset and violent termination. The examining physician thought that Raisbeck, in unbearable pain, had stopped his car, staggered into the graveyard, and died in a mortal spasm that produced upon him the marks suggesting violence at another's hands.[5]

Weighing the evidence more soberly as the days passed, however, Wolfe in October wrote to a friend unidentified by the editor of Wolfe's letters:

> Of one thing I feel reasonably convinced now—that Kenneth came to his death by natural causes, that he was not murdered. Of these other facts which you and——have told me, I don't know what to say or think—I have at times a sickening sense of horror and doubt, but I think that these things must now remain forever in mystery, buried in our memory or obliterated by our faith. My final sense about the matter is this: I remember him as he was when we were students together at Harvard, as my friend—as the remarkable, fine and brilliant person I believed and I believe him to have been.[6]

And yet Wolfe was unable to leave his sinister construction of the fate of Kenneth Raisbeck buried in his memory and obliterated by his faith. *Of Time and the River* now gives Wolfe's apostrophe to drunkenness in Chapter XXXV, a lyrical passage following upon a speakeasy bacchanal celebrated by Eugene and Francis Starwick. The second paragraph on page 281 ends with the lines "for they were drunken, young, and twenty—immortal confidence and immortal strength possessed them—and they knew that they could never die." The next paragraph commences with the invocation "Immortal drunkenness!" But in the typescript, standing between the two paragraphs, are these lines, cut by Perkins: "And in ten years time, one of them, destroyed by the corruption of his soul, would be found mangled, horribly mutilated, beaten to death by a maniac in a graveyard in New England." [leaf 524]

Perkins might have cut these lines because they were libelous or because they anticipated action not within the time-scope of the novel or because they showed in their author an immature want of charity. Possibly he eliminated them because they offended his taste, for elsewhere he cut sordid descriptions or passages of horror when they seemed to him excessive. The material Perkins cut from the now-famous scene of Gant on his deathbed shows the editor's sense of decorum opposed to Wolfe's lack of reticence even in matters where his affection and loyalty were strongly involved, his obsession with the need to put everything he remembered into every scene he wrote. Perkins had let stand the stark horror of Gant's moment of death, but when Helen embraced the body he suppressed the most harrowing touches Wolfe had given the scene. As Helen hurled herself upon the dead man, Wolfe had written: "'Oh, papa, papa'—she caught the body in her arms, and oblivious of the bloody froth and greenish matter that covered it, she hugged it to her, rocking back and forth, showering kisses on the cold, dead face and lips and moaning to it with demented broken phrases."

Perkins cut all but the three spoken words and then let stand six lines which became paragraph three, page 269, of the novel as far as the phrase "with a dead man in her arms." Between that phrase and the clause introducing the lines of dialogue which now end the paragraph, Perkins cut the lines "a corpse already cold and stiff with death, and not yet decently composed or straightened out, a corpse whose head shook stiffly, grotesquely, indecently, as she rocked with it and to which she was oblivious." [leaf 524]

Another cut, made primarily on grounds of taste, is of interest if only for the reason that Wolfe thought highly enough of it to rework it a little and use it in *The Web and the Rock.* While the train that is carrying Eugene toward Baltimore is still in the mountains of Old Catawba it toils slowly upward past a mountaineer's shack where a woman "stands in the doorway . . . holding a dirty little baby in her arms" (p. 26). Here the paragraph in the novel ends, but in the typescript the description as Wolfe originally intended it continues with these additional lines: ". . . her ever-pregnant belly, like some foul ripeness fructifying from the dregs of nature, coarsely prepared, bulged outward from her gaunt starved frame beneath the unconcealing hanging of a gingham gown. And around her lop-edged skirts are clustered three or four more little dirty tow-haired children, all gaunt, wide-eyed and staring with slow stunned wonder at the train." [leaf 49]

It is possible that this cut was made to prevent the overdevelopment of a passage which, after all, described a thing seen from a train, slowly moving though it was. When Wolfe reworked this description for the later novel the slattern was placed amidst the poor whites of Libya Hill, and the good phrase was inapplicable.

Finally there is this passage (leaf 747) with which Wolfe intended to complete the paragraph now ending on line two, page 422 of the novel, and thus to round out his impressions of a group of persons he had come to know in the city:

> Already he had seen from repeated and damning evidences how their envenomed souls fed on any rumor of corruption, how they shrank back in terror or shame before the proofs of life and richness: he saw with what a slimy thirst they lapped up every scandal of whoredom, cuckoldry, and treachery, baring their teeth in rat-like snickers at every sterile abomination of lesbic and pederastic loves, how even the barren and exhausted humor of their theaters was tricked out with the slimy garbage of a filthy and brutal innuendo, and how their souls shrank back resentfully, full of hate and shame if one spoke the words and gave the proof of love and faith and mercy.

Eugene's judgments here bear unmistakably the stamp of Wolfe's approval and show us something frightening and ugly in the author. We wonder how Perkins justified this cut to Wolfe, who only could have seen the editor's action as pusillanimous.

Maxwell Perkins had made his most drastic cuts in the typescript by eliminating more than seven hundred lines of Thomas Wolfe's lyrical prose. It was there that Wolfe had expressed his most deeply felt insights and certainties, and in giving up these passages, he lost what was closest to his heart. The most extensive cutting Perkins did after eliminating the lyrical passages was in disposing of banality, falseness, irrelevancy, digression, disproportional development, and related faults. These were cuts which Wolfe ought to have made for himself, for they represented plain bad writing or at the very least an inadequate sense of what was to the point and what was not.

Notes

1. The block cuts are to be found by comparing the published novel to the "Expanded Analytical Outline of *Of Time and the River*" which Wolfe prepared for Perkins early in 1934 (Thomas Wolfe Collection of William B. Wisdom, Houghton Library, Harvard, catalogue number *46AM–7 [24–L]). The outline describes a novel in fourteen sections. Perkins cut from Section One a long history of "Old Catawba" and much of Eugene's train journey east, thus disposing of 100,000 words. From Section Two, Eugene's encounter with evil in the person of "Dinwood Bland" was cut entirely. Wholly cut also was Section Three, "Young Man's Vision of the City" and "The Hudson River Joins the Harbor" (which Wolfe called "very long"). For its want of proportion, Perkins cut a minor scene in Section Five, a four-way conversation which had grown to 80,000 words. Most importantly, Perkins and Wolfe discovered that the manuscript described "two cycles" and decided to end *Of Time and the River* with Section Seven, the meeting between Eugene and Esther Jack. As a consequence, Sections Eight through Fourteen were

set aside to become the posthumously published *The Web and the Rock* (New York 1939).

2. The typescript of 1,633 leaves is in the Thomas Wolfe Collection of William B. Wisdom at the Houghton Library, Harvard. It is in three boxes with the catalogue designation *46AM-7(47) (1), (2), and (3). The extracts given herein are used by the kind permission of the Harvard College Library and of Mr. Pincus Berner, Administrator, C.T.A., Estate of Thomas Wolfe.

2a. This article was accepted for publication before the appearance of *The Notebooks of Thomas Wolfe*, ed. Richard S. Kennedy and Paschal Reeves, 2 vols., Chapel Hill, 1970. The notebook passages are given by Kennedy and Reeves in I,72–73.

3. John Hall Wheelock (ed.), *Editor to Author: The Letters of Maxwell E. Perkins* (New York 1950), p. 93.

4. Philip W. Barber, "Tom Wolfe Writes a Play," *Harper's Magazine* 216 (May 1958), 76.

5. Elizabeth Nowell, *Thomas Wolfe: A Biography* (Garden City 1960), p. 207.

6. Elizabeth Nowell (ed.), *The Letters of Thomas Wolfe* (New York 1956), p. 313.

The Posthumous Novels

The Outline of Thomas Wolfe's Last Book

Patrick Miehe*

At his death in 1938 Thomas Wolfe had completed and left in the hands of his editor, Edward Aswell, an immense draft for a novel concerning the life of a fictional character named George Webber. Aswell, finding this work unfit for publication, subsequently altered and rearranged the posthumous manuscript to such an extent that it emerged from his office as no more than a jumble of discrete segments. The original novel as conceived by Wolfe was lost, apparently irretrievably. Twenty-five years later, however, in the appendix to his critical study, *The Window of Memory: The Literary Career of Thomas Wolfe*, Richard S. Kennedy reprinted what he termed "Thomas Wolfe's rough outline of his last book,"[1] a document best described as being a veritable table of contents. Furthermore, Mr. Kennedy claimed that the outline "was left with Wolfe's final manuscript in the hands of Harper editor Edward Aswell. Each piece in the manuscript bundle was labeled according to its place. . . ."[2]

The outline,[3] if Mr. Kennedy's claims are authentic, at last provides a key to the structure and substance of the posthumous manuscript as it was before Edward Aswell extensively revised, cut, and reordered the work to form what are now three novels: *The Web and the Rock*, *You Can't Go Home Again*, and *The Hills Beyond*. With this key one could theoretically rebuild Thomas Wolfe's manuscript from the debris left by Edward Aswell's editing. This significance, however, hinges on Thomas Wolfe having indeed been the outline's author, and having indeed left it with a well-labeled draft—assertions Mr. Kennedy offers without substantiation. For the past ten years, Wolfe scholars have been willing to take his claims at face value. I believe it is time the pertinent manuscripts were examined.

There is, for example, Edward Aswell's description of the circum-

*Reprinted from the *Harvard Library Bulletin*, 21, No. 4 (1973), 400–01. © 1973 by the President and Fellows of Harvard College, Cambridge, Mass.

stances in which he obtained the manuscript, a description which fails to align with Mr. Kennedy's statements that Wolfe gave Aswell a carefully outlined and titled draft:

> On the evening he was to leave I went to his room in the old Chelsea Hotel on 23rd Street to get the manuscript. The writing was done, and when I arrived Tom was sorting and arranging the pages. He sat at a table in his shirt-sleeves with a pile of manuscripts a foot high in front of him. He had already sorted at least twice as much before. Rapidly he went through the remaining sections to make sure everything was in order. . . . Now and then he would decide that a chapter or section didn't belong in the book and he would discard it, throwing it on the floor. All around him the floor was littered with discards. . . . Tom did not know at the time, and I do not know now, whether it is to be published as one book or as several books. . . .[4]

Thereafter, whenever Aswell described the posthumous manuscript he repeatedly emphasized its chaos, *never* mentioning an outline or labels.

As for the outline itself, the following clearly establishes its true author:

(1) The outline never formed a part of the William B. Wisdom collection of Wolfe manuscripts but was given to Houghton Library by Edward Aswell himself with this preface, "These are notes I made to help bring order out of chaos while editing the posthumous MSs. of Thomas Wolfe."[5]

(2) The outline's typeface mirrors the typeface of manuscripts that are definitely the product of Edward Aswell's typewriter.

(3) The outline, as well as the labels to which Mr. Kennedy refers in the posthumous manuscript, occasionally contains as part of the typed title such parenthetical descriptions as "a variant" or "duplicate"—terminology Edward Aswell as editor would easily use but quite untypical of any titling by Thomas Wolfe.

There is no doubt that the outline reprinted in Mr. Kennedy's otherwise brilliant book is the work not of Thomas Wolfe but of Edward Aswell, and that the enticing attributions made by Mr. Kennedy are at best no better than wishes.

Notes

1. Richard S. Kennedy, *The Window of Memory: The Literary Career of Thomas Wolfe* (The University of North Carolina, 1962), p. 415. The outline itself is reprinted on pages 415–437.

2. *Window*, p. 415.

3. The outline in question is in the Houghton Library and has the call number bMS Am 1883 (1336).

4. Houghton Library, bMS Am 1883 (1337).

5. Houghton Library, bMS Am 1883 (1336).

Thomas Wolfe's Last Manuscript

Richard S. Kennedy*

I thought I had done with Thomas Wolfe but, alas, no. Patrick Miehe, the librarian who catalogued the Wisdom Collection of Wolfe papers in the Houghton Library, has published an article[1] which questions the authorship of the document which I had called "Thomas Wolfe's Rough Outline of his Last Book" and which I had published as an appendix to my book, *The Window of Memory: The Literary Career of Thomas Wolfe*.[2] He asserts that the outline was not composed by Wolfe at all and that the "true author" was Edward Aswell, Wolfe's editor at Harper and Brothers. Since the document is the principal piece of evidence which allows us to know Wolfe's intentions about the huge unfinished novel that he left in his editor's hands just before his fatal Western journey in 1938 and since Aswell published three volumes of fiction drawn from that manuscript but diverging considerably from the outline, it is a most important element in the assessment of Wolfe's later career and in the directions it was taking.

What I will do in this essay is to demonstrate beyond reasonable doubt that Wolfe planned the elaborate scheme for the novel which appears in the outline, that his secretary, Gwen Jassinoff, typed the title pages which were used to label each so-called "chapter" in the manuscript and typed (or supervised the typing of) the outline which Mr. Miehe questioned, and that it was impossible for Edward Aswell to have composed the outline. Also I feel that it is necessary that I place my argument within an extensive and detailed context so that there can be no quibbling about this in the future.

Early in 1938, Thomas Wolfe had been trying to pull together the first draft of a novel he had contracted to deliver to Harper and Brothers entitled "The Life and Adventures of the Bondsman Doaks," and he drew up a long tentative outline.[3] As the weeks went by, the project underwent several changes of plan and Wolfe drew more and more upon manuscript material that he had accumulated since 1935. Although early in the year his idea had been to have the work begin with his autobiographical hero, Joe Doaks, in his mid-twenties, by March Wolfe had decided to include the ancestry, childhood, and early youth of his hero, whom he renamed George Webber, and he gave the book a new title, "The Web and the Rock."[4] Two months later, while preparing to give a talk at Purdue University's Annual Literary Banquet, scheduled for 19 May, Wolfe decided on a way to conclude his ever-lengthening work: he planned to convert the Purdue speech into George Webber's justification for his literary life and for his decision to part from his friend and editor, Foxhall Edwards.[5]

*Reprinted from the *Harvard Library Bulletin*, 23, No. 2 (April 1975), pp. 203–11.

By 6 May Wolfe was nearing the end of his huge first draft and he told Aswell that he was "going to be pretty busy for several days next week assembling the manuscript and packing away the other manuscript I shall not use."[6] He asked Aswell if he could leave all his literary hoard in his care—not only the novel but three large wooden packing-cases full of the accumulated material of the past two decades.

He was apparently well along in assembling this material by 9 May, for that evening he gave large sections of it to his agent, Elizabeth Nowell, to look over. Although her approach to Wolfe and his work was usually tough and jocose, this time she broke down to express some unusual open-hearted praise for what he had accomplished:

> . . . ever since I was there Monday night I've been thinking how swell the first big hunk—and all the later hunks—of the book are . . . nobody else in the world would get the real flavor of those tough, salty, swell old guys like Bear and Zack and the way they talked and thought and lived so perfectly . . . and what's more nobody in the world but you could bring that to life . . . And come through to the swell and right-in-the-present-and-future stuff like the last parts of the book: The whole New York modern life, the literary racket, the German Nazi stuff, the ruined town and the Parson and the police, and . . . well, the whole analysis of the world right this minute.[7]

During the week Wolfe continued inserting additional pieces he had written in earlier years and for other projected fictional schemes. He wrote Miss Nowell on 12 May: "This is packing up day—I approach with considerable fear and trembling the job of assembling a good part of the manuscript I have done in the last three or four years. We are trying to arrange and audit it, so to speak, in some convenient form. Aswell is going to keep it for me until I get back, but I don't know whether it would be a good idea to let him read it now or not."[8] What Wolfe meant by "arrange and audit" becomes clear in a letter he wrote to Herbert Muller of Purdue on 16 May, the day before he left New York:

> For the past week my secretary and I have been engaged on the labor of assembling, putting in sequence, typing and binding the manuscript of my new book . . . Of course, the book is not finished yet . . . but for the first time since I began it, I begin to feel a sense of wholeness . . . All of this will be bound and minutely titled, section by section, and given to the editors at Harpers tomorrow to read and hold for me until I come back and go at it again . . .[9]

When Wolfe said "bound" he perhaps meant tied up in bundles, but I think it more likely he was referring to the fact that each "chapter" was held together by a paper clip. At any rate, almost all of the title pages he prepared for each chapter are still extant and they correspond exactly to the Parts, Books, and chapters in what I call the Rough Outline. For example, one of the early chapters has this title sheet:

Part I

The Hound of Darkness
(1793–1916)

Book III

The Web and the Hound
(1906–1916)

Chapter

Caliban
(Three O'clock)[10]

All of the title sheets, except one, were typed on Wolfe's typewriter, which produced well aligned 10-pitch elite copy and which can be identified by a capital H with a broken top at the left-hand corner. At least two of the title sheets have been revised in Wolfe's hand and several others show revisions in the hand of Miss Jassinoff.[11] Some title sheets do not have the name of the Part and Book if they are attached to chapters other than the first one in each Book. Other title pages which are not for the first chapter in each Book have the Part title and the Book title crossed out. All of this indicates, it seems to me, that the Rough Outline (which is really a kind of table of contents) was composed by merely making a typed copy of the title sheets in sequence.

At 5 p.m. on 17 May, Edward Aswell came to the Chelsea Hotel to pick up the manuscript and found Wolfe still not packed for the train journey and still going through his stack of manuscript, occasionally taking out a chunk and throwing it on the floor. These sheets were gathered up by Miss Jassinoff, and since the packing cases had gone off to the Harper warehouse, they were later placed in a "large reddish brown manila envelope."[12] Aswell left at 8:40 p.m. carrying two huge bundles of manuscript under his arms, and, as later testimony will show, he also had a copy of the Rough Outline with the manuscript. Wolfe then flew off to catch a 9 o'clock train.

Although Wolfe had suggested to Aswell that "it would perhaps be a good idea if you could familiarize yourself so far as possible with this first great batch of manuscript"[13] and although the editor wired Wolfe on 1 July, "Your new book is magnificent in scope and design,"[14] Aswell did not give the manuscript more than a superficial examination.

As everyone knows, Wolfe caught pneumonia on his Western trip and died from complications on 15 September 1938. His uncut, unpolished manuscript, with some gaps still to be filled in, was in the hands of young Edward Aswell, who had offered Wolfe an advance of $10,000 on a novel he had never seen and whose career now depended on his ability to edit the work successfully. The contract specified that the work could be cut by the publishers but could not be otherwise altered. The literary executor, Maxwell Perkins, insisted that these terms of the contract be adhered to.[15]

About two weeks after Wolfe's death, Elizabeth Nowell wrote to Aswell from her childhood home in New Bedford, Massachusetts, where she had been stranded as a result of the terrible hurricane of 21 September 1938:

> So I take it that you've agreed to go ahead and work on publication of the Web and The Rock, and I'm so glad that I don't know what to say . . . I brought up all his remaining manuscript that I had with me here—chiefly the story "No More Rivers" which the Yale Review was going to publish after he'd gone over it once more . . . But in with it I had a carbon copy of the list of material in the Web and the Rock, of which Miss Jassinoff[16] said you had the original with the script. Lots of those things itemized in the list I've read, and know where they come from, what Wolfe thought of them, etc. So I'm now going to mark up my copy with comment of what I know, and will mail it down to you today or tomorrow.[17]

This is a very clear description of the document now in the Houghton Library, the only surviving copy of what I called "The Rough Outline of Thomas Wolfe's Last Book."[18] It is a carbon copy, fourteen pages on white paper with no watermark, typed on an unidentified typewriter with a 12-pitch elite typeface.[19] Its margins are covered with fifty-seven of Miss Nowell's comments which range in length from a short phrase to a short paragraph. Edward Aswell gave it to the Harvard Library in 1949 along with a few other Wolfe manuscripts in his possession and a good many letters and memoranda of his own. Accompanying the document is a sheet of paper with a Harper and Brothers letterhead on which he has written: "These are notes I made to help bring order out of chaos while editing the posthumous Mss. of Thomas Wolfe." The notes he refers to are rather few and unsubstantial compared to Miss Nowell's annotations. For the most part, they consist of an "X" beside seventy-nine of the chapters; a Roman numeral beside forty-five chapters (the ones that he used for *You Can't Go Home Again*); and the word "Out" beside fifty-nine of the chapters. He has written "Dup" or "Duplicate" by five of the chapters; he has written out the titles of chapters fourteen times; he has made only three comments on the place or duplication of titles.

Besides the testimony of Miss Nowell's letter, there is one further indication that Miss Jassinoff was in charge of typing the Rough Outline: one of the entries of Part, Book, and Chapters is not typed at all; it is written out in Miss Jassinoff's hand [Plate IV] Miss Nowell identifies it for Aswell by an arrow and the statement "Miss Jassinoff wrote this." Since I did not include it when I published the Outline in the appendix of my book, I will give it now. It should appear on page 526 after "The Quality of Gus."

Part III

Love's Bitter Mystery
(1925–1930)

Book ——
Time is a Fable
Ambleside: The Toothless Tailor[20]

In February 1950, a few months after Aswell had deposited this manuscript in the Harvard Library, I interviewed him in New York in his office at the McGraw-Hill Book Company, of which he was then editor. I asked him about his editing of *The Web and the Rock* and *You Can't Go Home Again* and specifically whether he used only the material referred to in the "general outline" (as I called it then) or whether he had drawn upon other material in Wolfe's manuscript hoard.[21] My notes of his reply make clear that Wolfe and not he was the author of the outline and they also reveal his bewilderment about Wolfe's work at the time he undertook his editorial labors:

> When Wolfe died, Aswell didn't know where to start. Book written at various times, main character had several different names. He was at a loss, worked with the Papers, occasionally consulted Max Perkins, etc. finally worked out the 2 books. He followed Outline where he could, but many links were yet unwritten, e.g. about bank's failure in his home town, etc. Aswell supplied a few links, picked up what materials he thought would fit in, etc. finally the books published.

I do not wish to pursue the evidence further into a tedious overkill. It seems to me that the case for Wolfe's authorship and for Miss Jassinoff's activity in the typing has been substantiated. There are, of course, a number of unanswered questions. (1) If Aswell had the original copy of the Rough Outline, what happened to it? Did he send it to Perkins so that he could consult him about it and thus was left with only Miss Nowell's annotated copy for his own use? (2) Why was the Rough Outline typed on another typewriter rather than Wolfe's? Did Wolfe have to call in a public stenographer or one of Miss Nowell's secretaries for additional help in the rush of work during those last days? (3) When was the Outline typed up—before or after the last sifting through the manuscript stack? (4) What "chapters" were discarded at the last minute and placed in the "large reddish brown manila envelope"? Were they the stories previously published in *From Death to Morning*, such as "Death the Proud Brother," "One of the Girls of our Party," and "In the Park"? Or were they odd scraps left over from *Look Home-*

ward, Angel, such as "Gus: The Cafeteria" (originally a sketch of Luke Gant at the Norfolk Naval Base), or left over from *Of Time and the River,* such as "The Old Red Irish" (originally a part of the discourse on the Boston Irish)? Or were they just a few of the variant versions? There are no answers at this time.

I would like to conclude with two general comments. First, it is understandable that Mr. Miehe was misled by the evidence he examined. Given Aswell's ambiguous statement attached to the Rough Outline, given the resemblance between the two typefaces, and given the confusions of Wolfe's departure and his peculiar habits of composition, Mr. Miehe very well might question Wolfe's authorship. But anyone who knew very much about Wolfe and Aswell would certainly not attribute the authorship to Aswell. In the first place, the Outline is very characteristic of Wolfe. Several examples of his zest for compiling chapter titles and his tendency toward elaborate schematization are published in *The Notebooks of Thomas Wolfe*[22] and others are scattered throughout his unpublished papers. In the second place, it is highly improbable that Aswell could have known enough about Wolfe's work and his intentions to have developed the Outline. Aswell and Wolfe were total strangers until November 1937, and although Aswell saw Wolfe from time to time over the next six months, he, unlike Perkins and Nowell, knew very little about the work Wolfe was doing. Beyond all this, there are unpublished letters which prove that it was impossible for Aswell to have composed the Outline, for he had not even finished reading through Wolfe's manuscript by the time Miss Nowell sent him her carbon copy of the Outline.[23]

My second general comment has to do with the question, frequently raised, whether or not one could reconstitute and publish the text of Wolfe's manuscript as he left it in Aswell's hands. My answer is that I think it could be done, although we could never be certain about the discarded pieces in the manila envelope. But the result would hardly be worth the effort. After all, it was an unfinished work which Wolfe himself called an "enormous skeleton"[24] and likened to "the bones of some great prehistoric animal."[25] Many of the pieces that Wolfe listed in the Outline were kept only because he hoped to work a part of them in somewhere—for example, he placed "The Hospital" at the beginning of the last Book, "A Farewell to the Fox," even though he had already used a version of this chapter at the end of "Oktoberfest." He had included that second copy only in order to make use of some of its framing language for "The Invocation to the Fox." Other chapters which are listed were not finished, such as "Return"; or had more than one ending, such as "The Party at Jack's"; or were not sufficiently fitted into narrative context, such as "Chickamauga"; or were still only an assembly of disjunctive anecdotes or character sketches, such as the Book, "Utility Cultures, Inc." An examination of the material would lead most scholars to agree that Aswell had done an acceptable job of editing for commercial publication, even though his rearrangements and editorial decisions pushed the work toward the realistic novel and away from Wolfe's form, a form I have called elsewhere the literary thesaurus.[26]

However all this may be, I think that this exchange which Mr. Miehe's article has stimulated may indicate a need for a careful and detailed examination of Wolfe's manuscript and a full commentary on what it reveals: that is, what qualities or essentials, if any, have been lost in or distorted by the editing. Perhaps it might be accompanied by the re-editing of a small portion of the manuscript, a project that very well could prove valuable, even though a complete job would not be worthwhile. I certainly would like to see a study that goes considerably beyond the rather brief treatment I included in two chapters of *The Window of Memory* and that improves upon the conjectures I offered in the Appendix. Mr. Miehe's article, although it came to one wrong conclusion, would then have led to a worthwhile end.

Notes

1. "The Outline of Thomas Wolfe's Last Book," *Harvard Library Bulletin* 21 (1973), 400–401.

2. (Chapel Hill: University of North Carolina Press, 1962), pp. 425–37.

3. See the synopsis and outline of the "Doaks Book," as Wolfe called it, in *The Notebooks of Thomas Wolfe*, ed. Richard S. Kennedy and Paschal Reeves (Chapel Hill: University of North Carolina Press, 1970), pp. 929–36, and note the many correspondences to the Rough Outline.

4. Notebooks, p. 954.

5. Elizabeth Nowell (ed.), *The Letters of Thomas Wolfe* (New York: Charles Scribner's Sons, 1956), pp. 750–1.

6. *Letters*, p. 757.

7. Letter from Elizabeth Nowell to Thomas Wolfe, 11 May 1938. Houghton Library, bMS 1883.1 (477).

8. *Letters*, p. 764.

9. *Letters*, p. 765.

10. Houghton Library, bMS Am 1883 (832). [Plate I; cf. Plate III]. All quotations from the unpublished work of Thomas Wolfe are made by permission of Paul Gitlin, Administrator, The Estate of Thomas Wolfe, and by permission of W. H. Bond, Librarian of the Houghton Library, Harvard University.

11. Wolfe's hand is identifiable on the title sheets of bMS Am 1883 (1071) [Plate II(a)] and (869). Miss Jassinoff's hand is identifiable on many title sheets including bMS Am 1883 (969) [Plate II(b)], (910), (1115), (1123), (1113), p. 70.

Mr. Miehe has asserted in support of his theory that expressions such as "a variant" or "duplicate" in the Outline represent "terminology Edward Aswell as editor would easily use but quite untypical of any titling by Thomas Wolfe." Yet the title sheet of bMS Am 1883 (1071) shows the phrase "a variant" in Wolfe's hand, and several other title sheets typed on Wolfe's typewriter use "variant" and "duplicate"—see, for example, bMS Am 1883 (898) and (899).

12. Houghton Library, bMS Am 1883 (1337).

13. *Letters*, p. 758.

14. Notebooks, p. 991, footnote 16.

15. Houghton Library, bMS Am 1883.3 (84). Letter from Maxwell Perkins to Elizabeth Nowell, quoted in a letter from Elizabeth Nowell to Edward Aswell, undated, about 29 September 1938. Aswell abided by this restriction for *The Web and the Rock*, except for changes of characters' names, but he strayed from it in editing *You Can't Go Home Again*, presumably with Perkins' permission.

16. Miss Jassinoff was now a secretary in Miss Nowell's literary agency.

17. Houghton Library, bMS Am 1883.3 (84). References to the hurricane damage help to date this letter as of about 29 September 1938.

18. This copy of the Rough Outline is bMS Am 1883 (1336). [See Plates III and IV.]

19. As part of his argument, Mr. Miehe has stated, "The outline's typeface mirrors the typeface of manuscripts that are definitely the product of Edward Aswell's typewriter," implying that the Outline was typed on Aswell's typewriter. Although both typewriters are 12-pitch elite and both are troubled in alignment, there are distinctive differences. Aswell's typewriter was "out of motion," which caused all of its capital letters to strike perceptibly above the line. Also its letter "a" was very worn at the bottom; its "g" was worn or chipped at the bottom; and its "p" and "q" regularly fell below the line. The unidentified typewriter, despite its irregular alignment, shows none of these characteristics, except that the capital "W" strikes above the line. I should add at this point that one of Wolfe's title sheets, the one for "The Prologue," bMS Am 1883 (1092), appears to have been typed on this unidentified typewriter.

I am indebted to Joseph Dougherty of the Bundy Typewriter Company, Philadelphia, and to David Sautner and Edward Pfitzenmaier of the Suburban Office Equipment Company, Ardmore, Pa., for their advice and judgment.

20. These chapters are crossed out, presumably by Aswell, who wrote out the same titles just above "Im Dunkeln Wald." [Plate IV].

21. I did not know at the time that Aswell had been obliged to turn over Wolfe's three packing cases full of manuscript to Perkins, who was literary executor of the Wolfe Estate, and that he had available to him only the material Wolfe had given him on the evening of 17 May 1938.

22. See for example *Notebooks*, pp. 427–28, 461–63, 622–38, 844–58, 880, 884, 944–49, but especially pp. 929–36, which has many similarities to the Rough Outline, and 955–56, which is an abbreviation of it. Aswell, by the way, had no access to any of this material, for it reposed in the packing cases in the Scribner storeroom. The one exception is the synopsis entitled "A Statement of Purpose," *Notebooks*, pp. 938–49, which Perkins found and mailed to Aswell for his use.

23. Houghton Library, bMS Am 1883.3 (11), Letter from Edward Aswell to Maxwell Perkins, 5 October 1938; also the Perkins letter cited in footnote 15.

24. *Letters*, p. 758.

25. *Letters*, p. 764.

26. "Thomas Wolfe's Fiction: The Question of Genre," in Paschal Reeves (ed.), *Thomas Wolfe and the Glass of Time* (Athens: University of Georgia Press, 1971), pp. 1–30.

Part I

The Hound of Darkness
(1793-1916)

Book III

The Web and the Hound
(1906-1916)

Chapter

~~Caliban~~
(Three O'clock)

PLATE I:
A "Chapter" Title Page
(Note Broken "H"
in Fifth Line)
Houghton Library,
bMS Am 1883 (832)

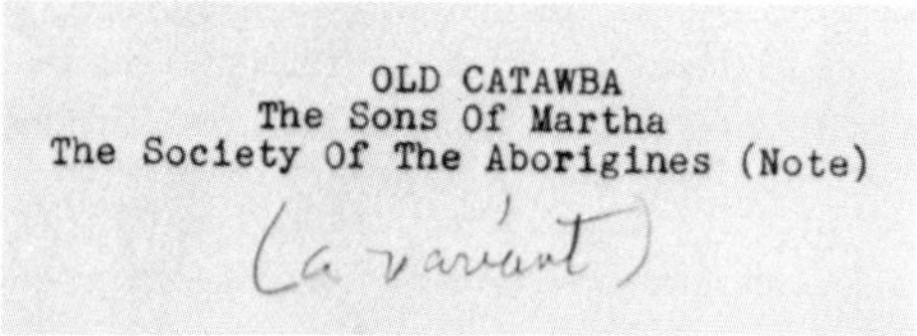
OLD CATAWBA
The Sons Of Martha
The Society Of The Aborigines (Note)
(a variant)

PLATE II(a):
A "Chapter" Title Page With
"A Variant" in Wolfe's Hand
(Remainder of Page is Blank)
Houghton Library, bMS Am 1883 (1071)

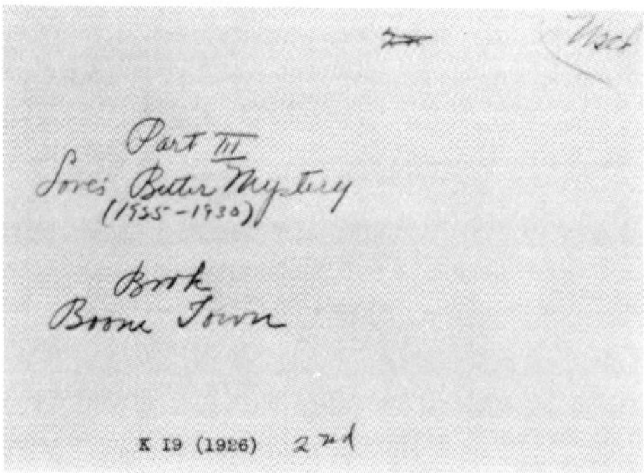
Part III
Love's Bitter Mystery
(1925-1930)
Book
Boone Town
K 19 (1926)

PLATE II(b): A "Chapter" Title Page with
Headings in Miss Jassinoff's Hand
(Lower Half of Page is Blank)
Houghton Library, bMS Am 1883 (969)

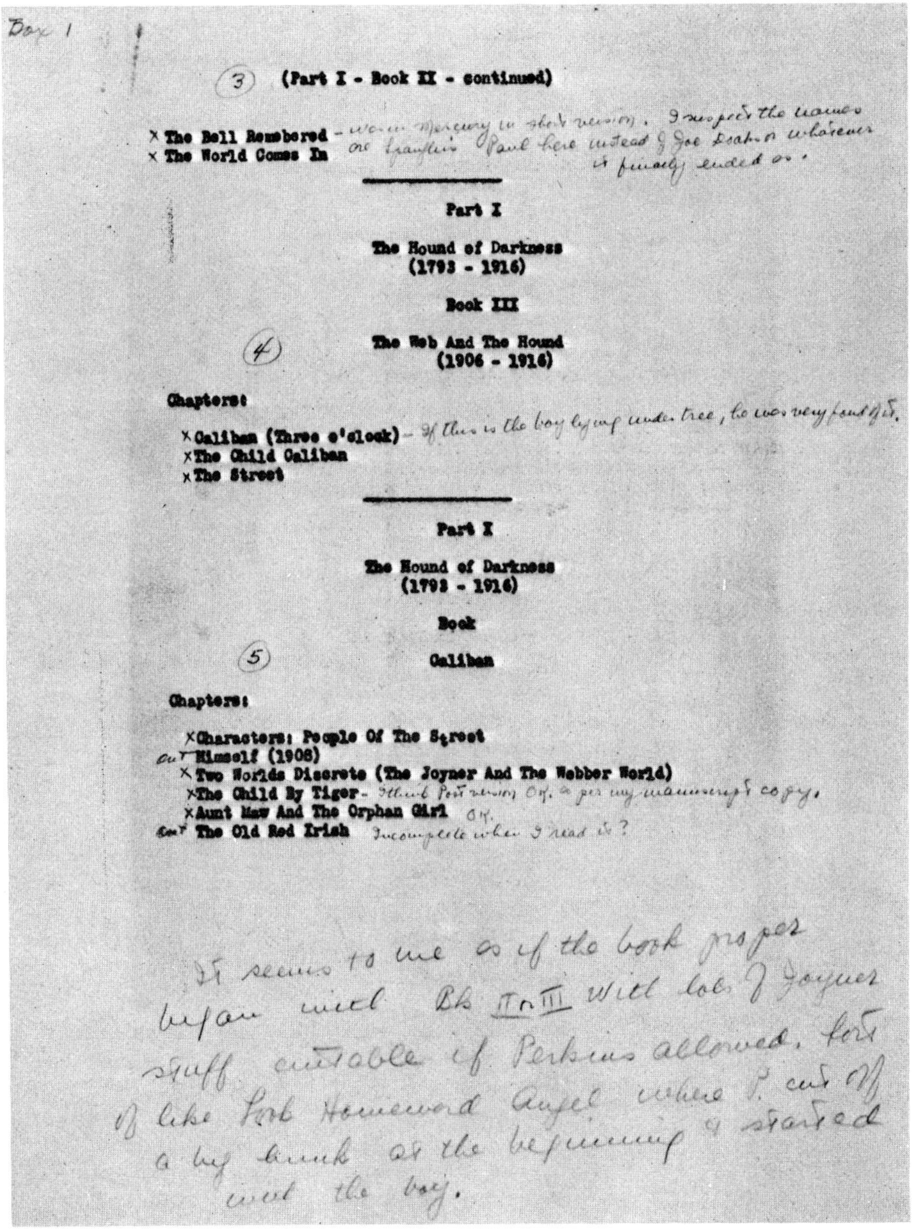

Box 1

(3) (Part I - Book II - continued)

× The Bell Remembered – was in Mercury in short version. I suspect the names
× The World Comes In are Franklin Paul here instead of Joe Seaton whatever it finally ended as.

Part I

The Hound of Darkness
(1793 - 1916)

Book III

(4) The Web And The Hound
(1906 - 1916)

Chapters:

× Caliban (Three o'clock) – If this is the boy lying under tree, he was very fond of it.
× The Child Caliban
× The Street

Part I

The Hound of Darkness
(1793 - 1916)

Book

(5) Caliban

Chapters:

× Characters: People Of The Street
Out Himself (1908)
× Two Worlds Discrete (The Joyner And The Webber World)
× The Child By Tiger – I think Post version OK. as per my manuscript copy.
× Aunt Maw And The Orphan Girl OK.
Out The Old Red Irish Incomplete when I read it?

It seems to me as if the book proper began with Bk II & III with lots of Joyner stuff suitable if Perkins allowed. Lots of like Look Homeward Angel where P. cut off a big hunk at the beginning & started with the boy.

PLATE III: A Page of the Rough Outline (Cf. Plate 1) with Comments By Miss Nowell at Right and at Bottom and Notes by Mr. Aswell at Left
Houghton Library, bMS Am 1883 (1336 [page 2])

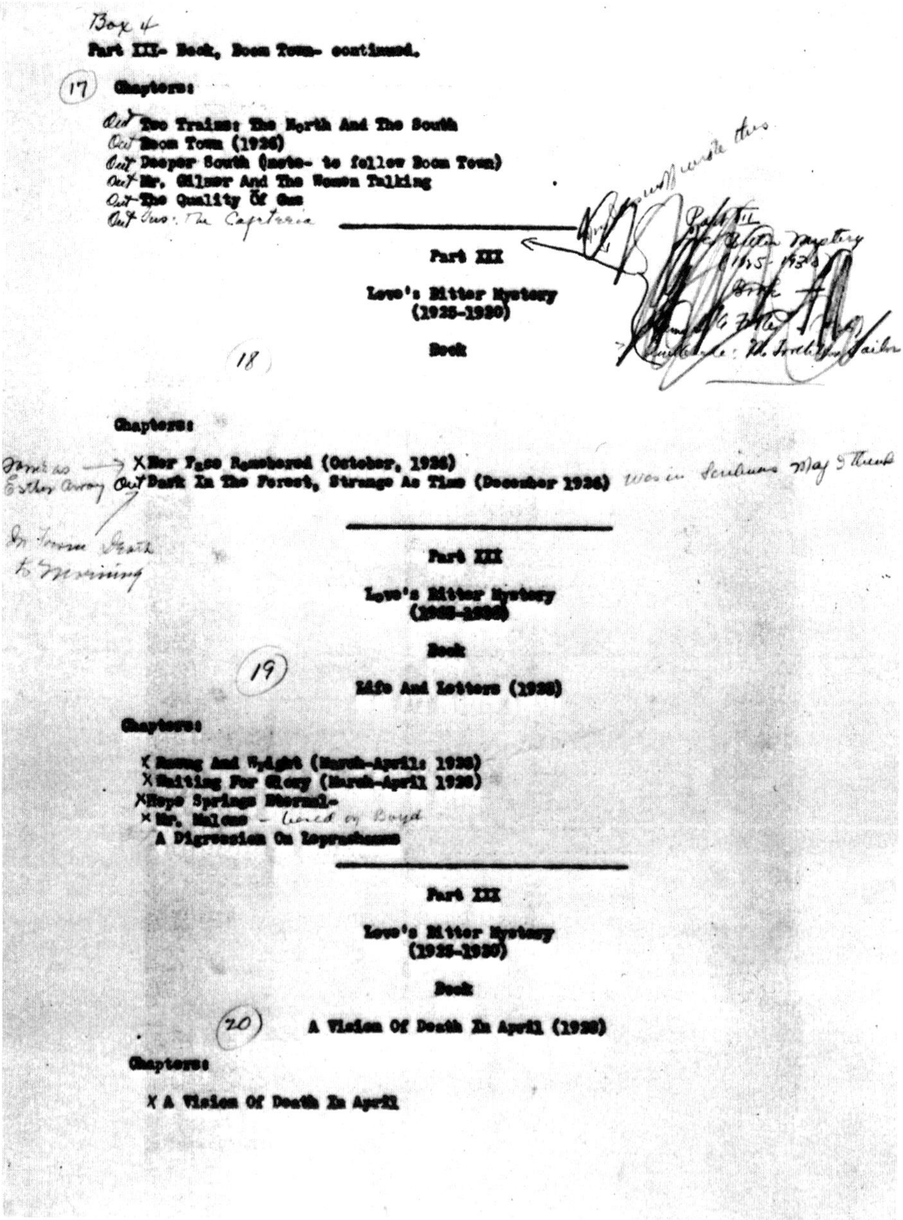

Box 4

Part III- Book, Boom Town- continued.

(17) Chapters:

Out Two Trains: The North And The South
Out Boom Town (1926)
Out Deeper South (note- to follow Boom Town)
Out Mr. Gilmer And The Women Talking
Out The Quality Of Gas
Out Ins: The Cafeteria

Part III

Love's Bitter Mystery
(1925-1930)

Book

(18)

Chapters:

Same as → X Her Face Remembered (October, 1926)
Esther away Out Dark In The Forest, Strange As Time (December 1926) Was in Scribners May I think

In Town Death to Morning

Part III

Love's Bitter Mystery
(1925-1930)

Book

(19) Life And Letters (1928)

Chapters:

X [illegible] And Wright (March-April: 1928)
X Waiting For Glory (March-April 1928)
X Hope Springs Eternal-
X Mr. Malone - loved by Boyd
A Digression On Leprechauns

Part III

Love's Bitter Mystery
(1925-1930)

Book

(20) A Vision Of Death In April (1928)

Chapters:

X A Vision Of Death In April

PLATE IV: A Page of the Rough Outline with Insertion by Miss Jassinoff at Upper Right
Houghton Library, bMS Am 1883 (1336 [page 8])

A Pebble in the Pool: Organic Theme and Structure in Thomas Wolfe's *You Can't Go Home Again*

Richard H. Cracroft*

And these tend inward to me, and I tend outward to them,
And such as it is to be of these more or less I am.
And of these one and all I weave the song of myself.

—Walt Whitman

I

Few serious readers will disagree with Frederick J. Hoffman's assertion that the works of Thomas Wolfe combine "an incredible mixture of the most impressive with the worst possible writing";[1] still, it has become all too easy and fashionable to criticize Wolfe's works adversely, and a closer look at both the works and their criticism makes it clear that critics have often failed to come to grips with Wolfe on his own terms. This imbalance is well demonstrated in the nearly universal critical attack on the apparent formlessness of *You Can't Go Home Again* (1940), the last of Wolfe's four massive, highly autobiographical novels. Henry Seidel Canby, for example, has flatly called the book "an artistic failure,"[2] and even such a kindly disposed critic as John Peale Bishop speaks of its "incoherent" writing and structure.[3] Similarly, Edward Wagenknecht finds the book "innocent of form,"[4] and B. R. McElderry, Jr., can write only of its "potential unity."[5]

A few lonely critical voices have been raised in defense of the structure of *You Can't Go Home Again.* Often, however, critics seem to evince the truth of Maxwell Geismar's claim that Wolfe, an infamously quantitative writer, has received only a chunk-style quantitative reading which does severe injustice to his artistic intentions and accomplishments in general and to *You Can't Go Home Again* in particular.[6] Seeing the four novels together as one great lump of formless prose, critics overlook the measured assessment of Joseph Warren Beach, who writes of Wolfe's works: "The only criticism that can fairly be made on the structure of these novels is that here and there details may be developed beyond what is necessary for the unfolding of the theme."[7]

Beach sees the basic form of *You Can't Go Home Again* as that of a tone poem or symphony. Through Wolfe's use of such form in the novel, Beach writes, "Every incident, every character can be accounted for in terms of . . . themes and their contrapuntal developments."[8] Eleanor Means Smith, in an unpublished dissertation on

*Reprinted from *Modern Fiction Studies*, 17, No. 4 (Winter 1971), 533–53.

Wolfe, expands Beach's musical metaphor into a convincing study in which she indicates that the author's apparent formlessness in this novel (and in the others as well) is a "deliberate attempt to capture and present the formless, chaotic quality typical of man's experience with life"[9] and that beneath this superficial formlessness lies a symphonic pattern which neatly and artistically harmonizes major and minor motifs into an encompassing unity.

Clyde C. Clements asserts that the novel is unified by symbolic patterns of reminiscence, progression, and projection,[10] but in imposing this kind of evolving symbolic unity on the novel Clements must necessarily neglect the impressive recurring interrelationships, the careful interweavings of theme and symbol throughout all of the seven parts which comprise the novel's tapestry. Indeed, so highly complex is the underlying structure of *You Can't Go Home Again* that an attempt to impose on the novel any structure other than that envisioned by Wolfe himself results in some kind of violation of the work's essential unity.

In a hitherto generally overlooked letter to his Harper's editor, Edward C. Aswell, Wolfe himself revealed that the pattern for his forthcoming work (which became *The Web and the Rock* and *You Can't Go Home Again*) was indeed progressive, dealing with "one man's discovery of life and of the world, and in this sense it is a book of apprenticeship." The book, he wrote, would be a "hopeful book" about discovery, "not in a sudden and explosive sense . . . , but of discovery as through a process of finding out."[11] But the novel was to have more than a simple progressive form, and Wolfe presents in this same letter his own vision of the novel's structure, a vision much closer to the symphonic pattern suggested by Beach than to the neatly ordered pattern advanced by Clements. Wrote Wolfe, with new objectivity:

> I have sometimes thought of the book as a series of concentric circles—that is, you drop the pebble in the pool—the Wilhelm Meister pebble or whatever we shall ultimately call him—but instead of pebble and pool simply in personal terms of pebble and pool, you get a widening, ever-enlarging picture of the whole thing—the pebble becomes important, if important at all, only in terms of this general and constant pattern of which it is the temporary and accidental stimulus. In other words, any other pebble would produce the same effect. The important thing is to tell about the thing itself, the thing that happens. The pebble, if you like, is only a means to this end. (*Letters*, pp. 713–14)

This becomes, then, the basic structure of *You Can't Go Home Again*: George Webber is "just an American who was looking hard at life around him, and sorting carefully through all the life he had ever seen and known, and trying to extract some essential truth out of this welter of his whole experience."[12] Thus, for the first time, wrote

Wolfe to Aswell, his hero becomes not a victim of circumstance, a romantic hero in conflict with, and in revolution against his environment, but a "kind of polar instrument round which the events of life are grouped, by means of which they are touched, explained, and apprehended, by means of which they are seen and ordered" (*Letters*, p. 714).

George Webber becomes the pebble in the pool, and as the circles radiate outward from the self, the point of impact, George as individual, artist, and Everyman, experiences a gradual metamorphosis from romantic solipsist to social realist, from youthful, selfish, rebel to mature and responsible adult.[13] The other favorite Wolfean metaphor, the web and the weaver (thus George *Webber*, *The Web and the Rock*, etc.) becomes appropriate, for in both the pebble-in-the-pool and the web images, the steady thrust or flow is outward in direction, increasing in dimension, yet always interrelated. In Wolfe, then, the movement is similarly from self to selflessness with complex interrelationships among his original, later, and ultimate footings. These images, which describe the basic structure of *You Can't Go Home Again*, reveal a sophisticated literary craftmanship which has been too often slighted and which merits closer investigation.

II

The fact that Wolfe did not live to complete *The Web and the Rock* and *You Can't Go Home Again* is germane to discussion of either work, for, as Aswell admits, had Wolfe lived the novels would have "turned out to be somewhat different from what they are."[14] At Wolfe's untimely death, however, it became Aswell's lot to transform the more than five-foot stack of typewritten manuscript into an approximation of the author's outlined intentions. Fortunately, before leaving New York on his fateful journey to Purdue and, later, the Pacific Northwest, Wolfe had taken care to arrange the manuscripts, bind them, and jot down a fourteen-page tentative outline of the projected work. Thus from the chaos of the unfinished manuscripts Aswell was able to shape, with less difficulty than he had imagined possible, the two novels and a book of short stories, *The Hills Beyond* (1941). As Aswell later wrote: ". . . the really incredible thing . . . was that once extraneous matter was removed, once the unfinished fragments and great chunks of stuff that did not belong in the books were taken out, the parts that remained fell into place and fitted together like the pieces of a jigsaw puzzle. It was simply amazing."[15]

Aswell notes that the manuscripts comprising *You Can't Go Home Again* were in such condition as to make it "a more satisfying book than its predecessor [*The Web and the Rock*]," but that it was necessary for him to fill in the gaps and provide continuity by writing a "few paragraphs as best I could to serve this purpose, drawing upon Tom's own words where they were available." These passages were then "printed in italics and set on pages by themselves in order to distinguish them from Tom's own text."[16]

However, Richard S. Kennedy's close textual study of Wolfe's manuscripts reveals that Aswell's hand intrudes more often into *You Can't Go Home Again* than has been suspected, for by that time the editor felt "free to play author with the manuscript." However, Kennedy considers Aswell's editorial changes valuable and notes that the editor's special contribution was rearranging the order of the work, which Wolfe had planned chronologically, even though it meant breaking up thematic blocks. Reorganizing thematically, Aswell "grouped up the scattered reactions to George Webber's book. He made the European trips into one. He placed the material about fame in the best possible sequence."[17]

In his thematic regrouping of the material, it is significant that Aswell did not sever the thematic links among the seven sections of the book. Indeed, though Aswell tidied up and rearranged the manuscript (which he would no doubt have done, *à la* Maxwell Perkins, even had Wolfe lived[18]), it is essential to realize that *You Can't Go Home Again*, despite necessary omissions of some fragmented chunks, and despite the reordering of the manuscript, remains *basically* as Wolfe envisioned it in his outline and statement of purpose.

Perhaps the chief reason that the novel retains its essential unity lies in the self-unifying method of writing which Wolfe employed. For although he saw his book as a rippling progression from the center of the circle outward, he, nevertheless, like a thoughtful observer on the shore, had the whole picture clear in his mind. Unlike those authors who write their works in a progression from the beginning to end, Wolfe "built" his novels by writing scenes which might occur at various points in the framework of the novel. Explains Aswell: "In this way he might cover within a month various unrelated events and characters widely scattered throughout the time cycle of his story. In this way, too, while writing the individual parts he was also working on the whole thing all the time."[19]

Such a method would have been impossible had Wolfe not been guided by a controlling purpose and organization that was "clear in his head right along."[20] Seeing the entirety of his work, Wolfe injected into the beginning, middle, and ending of the novel—no matter where Aswell finally placed them—interlocking thematic threads which contribute to the organic unity of its form. Aswell writes of this method: "Although Tom did not plan the various parts of his story as the published books which we know, he did plan the parts in themselves, and planned each part in relation to all the other parts. What is more, he planned the whole from first to last, and the whole was complete within him before he ever began to write."[21]

In May, 1938, Wolfe wrote his sister, Mabel Wolfe Wheaton, "my new book is all clear in mind, I know what it is all about from beginning to end, and the last few years I have done a lot of writing on it" (*Letters*, p. 734). This controlling vision of the work, exemplified in Wolfe's clear-cut statement of the central metaphors describing the book's form, in the careful (though tentative) outline of the work, and in the unusual method of writing which Wolfe employed, does much to explain why *You Can't Go Home Again* possesses an organic unity which permeates the work to a much greater extent than most critics have understood.

III

At the center of the pool is the pebble—George Webber. Until now, Webber, as himself in *The Web and the Rock* or as Eugene Gant in *Look Homeward, Angel* and *Of Time and the River*, has been concerned only with himself as an agonized and misunderstood artist in rebellion against a threatening society and a hostile universe. By the beginning of *You Can't Go Home Again*, however, Webber, squirming in his own private anguish, has begun to agitate the waters and start their slow, steady movement toward the distant shore.

Wolfe notes in his statement of purpose that in the first section of the book (now Chapter Five) this new Webber would be introduced as he enters a changeless Pennsylvania Railroad Station, the backdrop against which thousands of lives are constantly being "caught together for a moment, interfused and weaving." In Webber and this sea of humanity, Wolfe would introduce his recurring theme and structure: "the one and the many, the pebble and the pool" (*Letters*, p. 719). A closer look at a few of the numerous circles (or themes) through which George Webber passes in his odyssey from egocentric ("the one") to humanitarian ("the many") will demonstrate how well Wolfe has carried out his pebble-in-the-pool structure in *You Can't Go Home Again* and how thoroughly he has woven the threads of the web throughout the whole novel to make it a book surprisingly full of unifying echoes and haunting reminiscences which carefully foreshadow, from the first chapter of the book, Webber's ultimate position as chronicled by Wolfe. Such surging unity and organic interweaving may partially explain why the novel continues to impress readers (especially the more youthful ones) with its "that's-the-way-it-really-is" kind of psychological realism.

In the Station, and in Pullman car #K-19 which leaves daily for Libya Hill at 1:35 p.m., Wolfe presents one of the unifying themes of the book—changelessness. Throughout, ceaseless changes in the human condition take place against a backdrop which, like the sun and the seasons of Ecclesiastes, is immutable. The invariable cycle of the seasons and the eternal nature of the earth are emphasized among rich and poor, in Berlin, London, New York, Libya Hill, and Brooklyn. "Some things will never change," observes Webber; "Some things will always be the same. . . . Only the earth endures, but it endures forever" (p. 44). Much later in the book Webber is still chanting the same truth, but, typically, he has broadened his perspective: "The universe around us is the same," he says then. "Evil lives forever—and so does good" (p. 432).

And in the foreground, always in conflict with the changeless, is another unifying theme—man in his ephemeral madness. As early as Chapter Four, Wolfe introduces the ironically named "Security Distributing Corp.," its bustling change contrasting with its changeless warehouse and faceless employee who sits day after day, his face numb with an "impressive, immense, and formidable . . . stare," a stare symbolizing man's despair before the overwhelming insecurities of the universe (p. 41). Similarly, the Jacks's apartment building, with all of its solid-seemingness, is, in reality, "like a giant honeycomb," which shudders with the vibrations of the trains running far beneath it, the same trains which carried Webber to witness the equally hollow and insecure building boom of Libya Hill. Thus Mr. Jack, who "liked the feeling of security and power that great buildings gave him," is disturbed, in the midst of his reflection on the world's permanence and beauty, to feel a "trembling" in the earth (p. 152), the same trembling felt by Esther following the party (p. 318), a trembling which foreshadows not only the failure of Wall Street, but Webber's break with her and with his egocentric self, as well as the doom gathering about the hollow economic or political systems of Libya Hill and New York, or, later, London and Berlin.

Nothing human escapes change in *You Can't Go Home Again*, not even love, and early in the book Wolfe neatly foreshadows Webber's much later decision to break with Esther Jack. She queries whether he will love her forever, and Webber responds by showing her, in the street below, a panorama of brawling tailors, loud policemen, scurrying people, and screaming children acting out their feeble roles against a background of blue and vital sky, and budding trees. The clash between the calm permanence of earth and its "savage, foolish, violent, and mistaken" human inhabitants moves George to turn to Esther and murmur, shaken, "There's forever. . . . There's your forever" (p. 14).

Several critics have noted that Esther passes completely from the book following Webber's decision to leave her. However, many pages after the break, Wolfe threads in a reference to the affair with a final masterful touch presented through Randy Shepperton, who notices, on his visit to George's "stale" room,

> . . . a small green smock or apron, wrinkled as though it had been thrown aside with a gesture of weary finality, and beside it, half-folded inward, a single small and rather muddy overshoe. The layer of dust upon them showed that they had lain there for months. These were the only poignant ghosts, and Randy knew that something which had been there in that room had gone out of it forever—that George was done with it. (p. 377)

Thus, though moving outward in the pool of experience, George's present life remains fluidly and tenuously linked with his past.

George Webber's insecurity and loneliness as an artist had been all-consuming. But with these gradual insights into the insecurity and loneliness of others, he begins to master his habit of looking inward and commences, partially through his break with Esther and that which she and her crowd represent, to ride the ripples outward. Looking about him, he discovers "the vastness and loneliness of America" (p. 55), and it becomes "increasingly clear to him," he observes of Americans later in the book, "that one of the contributing causes of their complaint was loneliness" (p. 499). Pausing in his obsessive soaking up of experience long enough to digest this truth, he begins to discover America and Americans. He comes to realize, as did Wolfe, "what was for him the one available truth about this continent—that it is continued in himself."[22] This discovery provides Webber—and Wolfe—with a new objectivity, an objectivity not in the losing but in the expansion and extension of self to encompass all of America. Webber finds his own huge personal unhappiness as an artist reflected in the lives of his fellowmen, and he begins to gain "essential perspective and detachment" (p. 555). He is forced to rely less on his own impressions and feelings and more on the facts of the outer world; in short, he is forced to think.

In the flood of the great American Depression, Webber is caught up in a tide which sweeps the United States like "the fall of a gigantic boulder into the still waters of a lake. The suddenness of it sent waves of desperate fear moving in ever-widening circles throughout America"; and thereafter life "was not quite the same" (pp. 325–26). From this point on, the larger waters of America and the smaller waters of George Webber seem to merge, and he begins to identify his life and work with the life and work of his American brothers. He cannot, he finds, sit motionless in a rowboat while the waters about him are raging, and he begins, writes Beach, to give up his "intense and passionate concern for his own petty interests and designs in favor of an equally intense and passionate concern for the interests and designs of his fellow man and of all humanity."[23] He discovers that his own personality is but a microcosm of society[24] and that he was not, as Muller points out, "actually singular, that his prized individuality was not the sum of his differences from others, and that even the qualities that distinguished him were valuable chiefly because of all that united him with his fellows."[25]

Moving ever outward, Webber is still strongly enough attached to self to feel the pull of another of Wolfe's unifying themes, the hunger for fame, a hunger, however, which he stresses is shared by his fellow Americans. Therefore, he sees, in his lyrical night vision from the lofty perch on the Rocky Mountains, a Negro youth dreaming of a world championship in the ring, a Southern lad dreaming of baseball greatness, and a Jewish boy studying to become another Einstein, and concludes: "So, then, to every man his chance—to every man, regardless of his birth, his shining, golden opportunity—to every man the right to live, to work, to be himself, and to become whatever thing his manhood and his vision can combine to make him—this, seeker, is the promise of America" (p. 508).

In his own disillusioning initiation to the taste of fame—which arrives simultaneously with the Depression—Webber is courted by wealthy men and amorous women, lion hunters who desire something for themselves (pp. 349–51). Later, in the symbolic Lloyd McHarg (Sinclair Lewis), George again sees fame—this time at its "zenith." For in the great-souled McHarg he realizes that fame is a sham which can only disrupt and corrupt the artist much as love had done, and in the terrible night drive through the mazes of English country roads, Wolfe portrays an exhausted and disillusioned McHarg lost in the chaotic, howling darkness, the Walpurgis Night of an unfeeling universe (p. 593). Fame, Webber decides, "had been an empty victory" (p. 726).

At the book's end, George himself emerges in Berlin as a truly famous man, but in his growth away from his own ego-centered universe he finds that he can face the lion-hunters with confidence, that though fame is a universally sought goal, it is not enough. He again moves outward, and this movement, notes Geismar, "is the final shedding of Wolfe's American individualism, the relinquishing of his own vain personality, the merging of the artist with his material: humanity."[26]

Thus, like the concentrically flowing ripples in the water, Wolfe's theme increasingly broadens to encompass humanity. As Webber looks about for understanding and to understand, he sees the world more clearly and becomes concerned with the "nameless ciphers who swarmed about him in the streets" (p. 499), fellow citizens in a complex social pattern. More and more his attention turns to the faceless swarms of Americans "with skins of tallow grey" (p. 468), and he probes the causes of their sterile lives.

One of the many "nameless ciphers" which thematically unify the book comes to life in death, as, in the foreground of a carefully described changeless universe, the pseudonymous suicide, C. Green, emerges from a brief newspaper clipping to become more than "life's little man, life's nameless cipher, life's manswarm atom, life's American" (p. 467), to achieve an entity in death, but only because he dared to violate the "principle of Blotterdom" (p. 478).

By the end of the book, however, Webber's circle has broadened beyond nationalistic boundaries and enables him to see similarities among the "nameless ciphers" of mankind. Thus Daisy Purvis, his London housekeeper, emerges from anonymity to portray the same "capacity for self-deception" typical in most willing victims of the blighted economic system. A vigorous defender of aristocracy, Mrs. Purvis has no sympathy for the poor, for whom she feels "nothing should be—or need be—done" (p. 529).

Webber's eye also falls on McHarg's friend, the Dutch Rotarian-Babbitt, with his tricky, amoral, selfish look, the look of "the race of small business men" everywhere—in America, England, Holland, or Germany—the look of Mrs. Delia Flood, Mayor Baxter Kennedy, or J. Timothy Wagner, all real estate "tycoons" of Libya Hill; or that on the visage of Mr. Paul S. Appleton III, president of the Federal Weight, Scales and Computing Company, or on the face of his meritorious disciple, Mr. David Merrit;[27] or those looks on the faces of the London liquor merchant or the vulgar German publisher, Karl Lewald. And in the faces of all these people engaged in perpetuating an inequitable system, Webber begins to discern a similar look—a look of fear and insecurity which often rips through the façade to reflect a seemingly universal inner misery, an "utter, naked, frantic terror . . . of men who know that they are ruined and are afraid to admit it, even to themselves" (p. 85).

By the end of the book Webber has broadened his horizon so as to see the evils of mankind's greed embodied in another system—the fascism of Nazi Germany—and the weakness and the greatness of mankind embodied in another nameless cipher, a refined C. Green—"old Fuss-and-Fidgit," the German-Jew apprehended by the Nazis on the Belgian border. In this masterfully written episode, Wolfe carefully relates the hapless German to the C. Greens of mankind by describing the death pall which hung about the compartment on the train as being like that which one feels when "A man has leaped or fallen . . . from a high building to the pavement of a city street" (p. 693). In the Jew's brave refusal, despite his own terror, to betray his new acquaintances to the Nazis, broader symbolic implications are evident, implications which become clear as the travelers say farewell "to humanity; not to some pathetic stranger . . . but to mankind; not to some nameless cipher out of life, but to the fading image of a brother's face" (p. 699).

As George Webber's new wave of consciousness pulsates outward, he realizes that this self-delusion has swept not only such as Frederick Jack, Mayor Baxter Kennedy (and, later, virtually the whole German nation), but has corrupted the struggling servants of the system as well. The policemen are grafters, the chauffeurs are swindlers, and all have the same gray unhappy faces (p. 188). But it is in the doormen and elevator operators in the Jacks's apartment building that Wolfe best embodies the attitudes of the have-nots towards the system. John Enborg, a kind of American Daisy Purvis, a defender of the old order, insists, for example, that the specially privileged people who live in the building must be "protected and preserved" (p. 198). His assistant, Herbert Anderson, is the new American, unquestioningly hopeful, materialistic, sensual, deluded. But it is a third, Henry, who portends evil for the system. A coercive union man, a dissatisfied American (with no more real warmth, notably, than "The Company's" Mr. Merrit), Henry prophesies that John will one day be killed by the system he is protecting (p. 209). After John and Herbert, the slaves of the old American capitalism, do in fact meet their deaths, it is a glowering and foreboding Henry who, with hatred in his heart, carries the privileged wealthy up in the elevator. Henry is contrasted with the corrupt newspaperman who, showing no concern with the deaths of the two elevator men, is interested only in the social standing of the apartment's beautiful inhabitants.

Webber thinks his way a bit further into the ever-widening ripple, sensing that America must discover its hollowness, just as he had discovered, for himself, the hollowness of love and fame and the lives of his fellows; America must realize that a "hollow pyramid of a false social structure has been erected and sustained upon a base of common mankind's blood and sweat and agony" (p. 321). He begins to foresee "a larger world than this glittering fragment of a world with all its wealth and privilege" (p. 320), that it is time to shatter the glittering façade, time for the dissatisfied Henry's of America. The old system was a lie which had become a part of American life (p. 502), a lie which was strangling America. The truth must out.

Webber sees that America must be as it was on the night of the fire at the Jacks's—where all were in the great courtyard together, rich and poor, and where, with the falseness of the society cleansed away, the Tammany Hall man and the aristocrat, the courtesan and the society queen, the Jew and the Gentile were all one common, wholesome humanity. In such a society the frantic Philip J. Baer becomes a comic figure as he scurries about, offering $10,000 to anyone who will remove his financial records from the burning building (pp. 296–97). On the equalizing level of the court, the common fireman, Baer's social inferior, can roughly push Baer and his false values aside. To maintain this healthy leveling, this equality, there must be a complete revision of the American society.

Like Whitman in *Democratic Vistas*, Webber, always reflecting Wolfe's own attitudes, sees clearly that the direction in which the country is heading sharply divides American ideals from American realities. Wolfe wrote to his sister in May, 1938, that America, "which is such a beautiful and wonderful country, has been taken away from the people to whom it should belong and given largely into the hands of a few of the exploiters" (*Letters*, pp. 760–61). Like Wolfe, Webber concludes that the ennui and sterility in the lives of Americans—and all men—have an economic basis. George sees America as side-tracked, and says to Randy Shepperton:

> "I'm thinking about America. . . . Sometimes it seems to me . . . that America went off the track somewhere—back around the time of the Civil War, pretty soon afterwards. Instead of going ahead and developing along the line in which the country started out, it got shunted off in another direction—and now we look around and see we've gone places we didn't mean to go. Suddenly we realize that America has turned into something ugly—and vicious—and corroded at the heart of its power with easy wealth and graft and special privilege. . . . And the worst of it is the intellectual dishonesty which all this corruption has bred. People are *afraid* to think straight—*afraid* to face themselves—*afraid* to look at things and see them as they are. We've become like a nation of advertising men, all hiding behind such phrases like 'prosperity' and 'rugged individualism' and 'the American way.' And the real things like freedom, and equal opportunity, and the integrity and worth of the individual—things that have belonged to the American dream since the beginning—they have become words, too. The substance has gone out of them—they're not real any more." (p. 393)

Webber concludes that in America there can be no compromise with privilege, graft, and easy wealth, and he prophesies abstractly that there are "stronger, deeper tides and currents running in America"; and Webber feels he must ride these currents (p. 321).

And as he catches a glimpse of the madness destroying America, George sees that the nation must join him in riding the current outward, that both must be aware of "the submerged and forgotten Helots down below" who support and nourish "the mighty princelings at the top" (p. 724). This vision of man's suffering helps Webber "to blot out the more personal and self-centered vision of the world which a young man always has" (pp. 724–25); it is, again, a unifying vision which imbues the novel from start to finish.

In Germany he sees the "poor ones of the earth, the humble ones of life," who wait, hopeful and self-deluded, for their savior, Adolf Hitler, to arrive and depart from the Olympic Stadium in Berlin. In England he mourns for the helpless, hopeless poor, the people "bogged in their misery, sucked down in a swamp of inherited wretchedness which is never going to get any better" (p. 530); he mourns for an England where the "big people" live off the system and where the "little people," the "race of gnomes," have starved for generations. He sees the inevitable "lifeless, opaque pallor" and the "dark and dead" eyes (p. 532) of the poor in spirit and flesh. "May God have mercy on us all" (p. 536), he cries.

But it is in Brooklyn and New York where George sees "the whole" chronicle of the earth," for South Brooklyn is "the universe" (p. 432) where faces with the usual "dead eyes and flesh of tallow-grey" front the harsh realities of spiritual and temporal poverty. He again turns the nameless ciphers into sterile lives of men hungry for friendship, recognition, and success—and the desolate lives of Mr. Marple the insurance man, Mr. Wakefield the Grand Army veteran, and the nameless waiter who wants to sell George a story plot, momentarily emerge from the grey masses. Beneath City Hall George watches homeless men enacting a struggle for survival over the ignoble spoils of a toilet stall, a scene of "indignity and sheer animal horror" which he contrasts violently, like Stephen Crane in "An Experiment in Misery," with the massive buildings a few blocks away wherein "a large portion of the entire world's wealth was locked in mighty vaults" (p. 414).

To Webber, England is lost; Germany is past recovery, but America is yet salvageable, for, he asserts frequently in the novel, the poor who live in the wasteland of American cities are filled "with an almost quenchless hope, an almost boundless optimism, an almost undestructible belief that something is bound to turn up, something is sure to happen. This is a peculiar quality of the American soul . . ." (p. 429).

IV

Webber shares this same peculiar, boundless optimism. It is central to *You Can't Go Home Again*, where "something" is ever "stirring in the earth" (p. 372) and where the tide is always flowing. Riding high on this crest of optimism, Wolfe, like Webber, begins to look about him to see what can be done, for, he concludes, the economic framework of America must be changed.

As Wolfe grew more famous he was increasingly called on for support by various political factions and parties, and his decision to remain aloof is reflected in the steps which Webber took to avoid parties and cliques, factions and isms, all of which "had accepted some part of life for the whole, some fragmentary truth or half-truth for truth itself" (pp. 262–63). He had to avoid entanglements, for his aim was to "sing America" (p. 263).[28] This, then, was his next significant rush forward, his next ripple outward from the center—the arrival at the social responsibility of the artist.[29] This social involvement does not come suddenly, however, for Wolfe has carefully woven foreshadowings of Webber's increasing social awareness throughout the text, and it is ever clear, as he wrote, that "I was coming more and more to feel an intense and passionate concern for the interests and designs of my fellow men and all humanity" (p. 725).

This merging with American society created in Wolfe a unifying force which brought order into chaos, and, for the first time, his theme and his society were one. Like that of Whitman, his personal epic struggle transformed into the larger, grander epic of America. But, unlike the earlier Whitman who sang the dawn of America, Wolfe felt he was the singer of an America at the crossroads, an America that must opt for life or death. In the larger world, still but a reflection of his own inner world, he found a concept of a *whole* world which seemed to justify his earlier self-concern, for he felt he was a refraction of everything in society. He thus found, in forgetting himself for the multiverse about him, in identifying himself with the myriad insecurities and doubts surrounding him, a singleness of purpose. In a very Christian sense, he fulfilled the ancient promise: ". . . he that loseth his life . . . shall find it." So, in December, 1936, this twentieth-century "singer of America" could write Maxwell Perkins of his new-found unity of self and purpose:

> I have at last discovered my own America. I believe I have found my language, I think I know my way. And I shall wreak out my vision of this life, this way, this world and this America, to the top of my bent, to the height of my ability, but with an unswerving devotion, integrity and purity of purpose that shall not be menaced, altered or weakened by anyone. (*Letters*, p. 587)

Still, this unity of purpose, this oneness with his subject, did not make Wolfe a Fourth-of-July chauvinist, for he saw the clear difference between his ideal America and the reality about him. Thus, when the Polish-American, Johnnie Adamowski, praises the United States as being the one spot on earth "where all is peace and freedom—where all is friendship—where all is love" (p. 675), Webber, painfully aware of America's many flaws, makes some mental reservations but adds his unifying refrain that "the essence of America's hope had not been wholly ruined, its promise of fulfillment not shattered utterly . . ." (p. 674).[30]

Throughout, Wolfe (and, of course, Webber) remains the arch dreamer of the American dream, a believer that the "*real* truth" of America, its "richness and undying power," lay beneath the evident outward staleness[31] that Sinclair Lewis and others had so readily attacked.[32] Wolfe's poetic transcendental vision of America is reflected often in all sections of *You Can't Go Home Again*, from his sweeping visions of the whole land from atop the Rocky Mountains to his numerous catalogs of the heterogeneous composition of American society and his soaring optimism throughout (and especially at the end) of the book. In unabashedly Sandburg-like language, his final speech at Purdue in 1938 demonstrates his positive vision: "The people! Yes, the people! The people that cannot ever be defeated or betrayed—the betrayed and the defeated people, the corrupted and the misguided people, the duped and superstitious people, the inert and the submissive people—but in the end, always the people!—just the people!—the rock bottom of the indivisible and everlasting people!"[33]

Spurred on by this millenial glimpse of the brave new world, Wolfe deplored the spiritual bankruptcy of his age. Never really in the Center of Indifference, he nevertheless moved with a convert's zeal toward the Everlasting Yea, and he had little patience with those feeble, egocentric souls who remained far behind him in the pool's center, in the self-consuming state of the Everlasting No. This Yea-Sayer, optimist, and believer felt that in himself he had known all of the despair and disease in modern America, but, "trailing visions of the abyss,"[34] he conquered self and flowed outward toward union with the dream of greatness which was his America. And if he could do it, he felt, so could others.

His antipathy for the Nay-Sayers of America and the world seemed to grow as he flowed towards the outer reaches of the pattern. And what he most despised in those who denied America's promise was "their attitude of acceptance, . . . their complaisance about themselves and about their life, their loss of faith in anything better" (p. 260). This acceptance of the death of the dream, of the evils of the system which he assails throughout the novel, moves him to revile, in a letter, the "lost generationers, the bitter-bitters, the futility people, and all other cheap literary fakes sicklied o'er with a pale coat of steer-shit. . . ." He warns of the "futility boys and girls, the sterility lasses, the elegant mockers, the American T. S. Elioters. They are a low but vilely cunning lot of bastards," and he cries, in a typical Wolfean sweep through time and space, for the positivism of Christ, Coleridge, Socrates, Dostoievsky, and, anticlimactically, Jeb Stuart and Davy Crockett.[35]

You Can't Go Home Again is threaded with Nay-Sayers, and Wolfe is consistent in condemning them wherever they appear. Those who passively accept the system, such as New York's John Enborg and Herbert Anderson, London's Daisy Purvis, and Libya Hill's Sam Pennock and Randy Shepperton, all fall under Wolfe's condemnation, but not nearly so much as the better educated, more thoughtful Nay-Sayers like the newspaperman who would sell his brother for a story (p. 309) or Franz Heilig, the sensitive German intellectual, who, at last, reveals "a depth of cynicism and indifference which was greater than George had ever before suspected" (p. 652). In England Webber meets McHarg's friend, Rickenbach Reade, a debunking author who has retreated from life much like that "race of futilitarians," the expatriate Americans in Paris, "to whom nothing was left except an encyclopaedic sneer—a sneer at anything American" (p. 610).

Other Nay-Sayers appear briefly: Hunt Conway, Foxhall Edwards' friend of "the lost generation" (p. 715); Haythorpe, the aesthete turned homosexual and suicide; Collingwood, the Humanist turned Communist; and Spurgeon, teacher of American Democracy turned "devoted leader of the intellectual Communists" (pp. 409–10). Or the negative bevy of young sophisticates with whom Webber roomed during his first year in New York, debunking intellectuals who were "sorry about a great many things and people" from Shaw to O'Neill to Galsworthy and developed a "niggling and overrefined aestheticism which was pallid and precious," and detached from life, and destructive to imagination and creativity (pp. 720–21). All of these Nay-Sayers seemed to express a right to special privilege, an exemption from the human laws governing others, the same totalitarianism of spirit which was evident elsewhere in the self-deceiving businessmen of Libya Hill or New York. These people had not yet accepted what Webber was to discover in surging out from himself—"the true power and talent of selfless immolation" (p. 722), the key which would unlock the gate to the new America.

Webber is saddened to find this same negativism in two of his most admired friends. The first, Stephen Hook, is a sensitive writer who presents a cold and bored front, yet who is really, like Wolfe, sick with the fear, wonder, and fascination of life (p. 300). Superior to the Lawrence Hirshs, the Lily Mandells, the Jack Abramsons, and the Amy Carltons of Esther Jack's circle, he had, nevertheless, been "hooked" by the Nay-Saying decadence of his surroundings. Hook is like Judge Rumford Bland, of Libya Hill. Both are talented and sensitive, yet both see that society will have none of them unless they compromise their gifts. They do.[36] He becomes a solemn caution of the potential direction Webber's own career and attitudes could take should he not change his course. Without hesitation, Hook joins the crowd of the degenerate wealthy who hover about Piggy Logan's disgusting exhibition much as the duped riverside dwellers flock to see "The Royal Nonesuch" of Huck Finn's nefarious raftmates.

In Foxhall Edwards, Webber's editor (and fictional equivalent of Maxwell Perkins), George sees the most devastating manifestation of the pessimistic spirit, for Edwards has, of all the characters, the most to offer the realization of the American dream. Thus his tragedy is greatest. Fox is none of the "tatesy-watesy, hicksy-picksy, wilsony-pilsony, . . . sneer-puss fellows" (p. 485), but a "*hopeful* fatalist" (p. 734), the embodier of the pessimism of Ecclesiastes, one of Wolfe's favorite books. But "Fox really has no hope that men will change, that life will ever get much better." He knows the forms will change, but the changes will create new problems. He will waste no hope on the hopeless, for he has the "tranquil fatality of calm acceptance" (p. 493). Unlike Webber, when Fox sees how things are going in America, he whispers, "Too bad! . . . We should have *had* it! We were just beginning—we should have had it fifty years ago, as Rome had it, and as England had it! But all this turmoil came too soon—we didn't have it long enough! Too *Bad!* . . ." (p. 498).

Webber's answer to Edwards is woven throughout the optimism of *You Can't Go Home Again.* Although it may be as Edwards and his fellow-Nay-Sayers claim, says Webber, he must disagree. Americans must, he writes, deny fatalism and feed our souls on the poetic vision of America, which is, Wolfe wrote to Sherwood Anderson, the "only way actually it can be seen."[37] With the same mysticism found in Whitman, Sandburg, Masters, Hart Crane, and Benét, Webber-Wolfe, with a radiant broom thatched with patriotic and philosophic optimism, sweeps his American dream clean of Nay-Sayers.

You Can't Go Home Again reflects the optimism of several Yea-Sayers: The simple faith of Nebraska (Bras) Crane, the baseball great who refuses to be affected by the insecurities which surround him and returns to the earth for his living; the positive life and attitude of Mr. Katamoto; or the faith of Else von Kohler, Webber's Berlin mistress, who remains unaffected by the bitterness surrounding her (p. 658); and the hope and faith of the American poor, who believe the dream, who hope amidst despair. But it is George Webber himself who is the center of affirmation; it is Webber who remains unaffected by incidents which could have turned him into a bitter individual; it is Webber who represents the spirit of America.

As Else von Kohler bids farewell to George, she says, in her German accent, "You are religious man. You are artist. And the Artist *is* religious man" (p. 658) and whispers "Be great one that I know. Be religious man" (p. 664). This is, then, one of the outermost circles which George has attained by riding the crest of the ripple from the center of his being. He has been converted to a new religion, and the essence of his belief "is that man's life can be, and will be, better, that man's greatest enemies . . .—fear, hatred, slavery, cruelty, poverty, and need—can be conquered and destroyed" (pp. 737–38). George Webber has come a long way from home.

He has come to realize that philosophy and growth are fluid or organic, that he and all men are "Time's plant" (p. 739) who outgrow the old forms and cells and honey-combs which must be destroyed. And the people, the "deathless, undiscovered, and immortal people," must live (p. 741). For the Nay-Sayers represent death-in-life, while the natural, healthy organism must represent growth-in-life.[38]

From Germany, Webber, like Wolfe a Germanophile,[39] learns of the dark and atavistic greed and evils of the past. Webber, too, had fed in a transcendental manner on the "single selfishness and compulsive greed" (p. 472) of the past; he had occasionally and naturally desired to reverse the outward flow of the ripple, to return to the center of the web. But he now determines to root out Germany and his own atavistic yearnings from his soul and turn to the past-less America to sing a new song of the future, an abstract future unaffected by the outmoded forms of the past (p. 611). He thus rejects that individualism which he felt was rooted in primitivism and turns from self and man's elemental past toward a new freedom in a new world.

V

In a sense, Wolfe and Webber had gone home—home to the American dream and thereby found a unity in their lives. For Webber there is no longer a dichotomy between "Man-Creating" and "Man-Alive." They have become one—the social man is the creative man, and Man-Alive must triumph over the "shrugs and sighs and shakings of the head" (p. 738). Wolfe and Webber become prophets of a bright new world, not heralds of doom. "I believe that we are lost here in America," Webber cries, but, he affirms, "I believe we shall be found. And this belief, which mounts now to the catharsis of knowledge and conviction is for me—and I think for all of us—not only our own hope, but America's everlasting, living dream" (p. 741).

This is the positive, nebulous message of the future, a future embodied in Wolfe's phrase "You Can't Go Home Again," the spiritual conviction which informs the whole book, a phrase which, wrote Wolfe, "crystallized a feeling, a conviction, a discovery that I had been slowly coming to for years."[40] It again emphasizes the forward thrust of the central metaphors of his book—the outward circling ripples and the ever-increasing web; for, though the outermost circles or strands are closely related to the previous rings or threads, the wave never narrows, never returns to the point of the pebble's impact, and the spider in its spinning never returns to the center of its web. So it is with Webber, who finally refuses to look back at all. So must it be, he claims, with America. So it is with the structure of *You Can't Go Home Again.*

Wolfe has numerous flaws, but one of those flaws would not seem to be formlessness or lack of unity in the complex ripplings and weavings of *You Can't Go Home Again.* But whatever his flaws, Wolfe's infectious "shout of affirmation on the side of the angels"[41] makes him the continued spokesman for a vital America as he breaks from singing of a lost youth to chanting America's future. Time and again he demonstrates in his last novel that, as his friend Hamilton Basso wrote, whenever Wolfe "digs through to what he is after, he is magnificent in a way few American writers have been."[42]

Americans who insist on shrugging Wolfe off, or forgetting what he did and tried to do, "will be," claims J. B. Priestly, "smaller, older, closer to death."[43] For in spite of his abstractions, he achieves, throughout the novel, a dynamic philosophy which affirms, with Goethe, that while human growth is like a drunken beggar on horseback, "What was important, perhaps, is not that the beggar was drunk and reeling, but that he was mounted on his horse, and however unsteadily, was *going somewhere*" (p. 7). From Chapter One (where this statement first appears) through Chapter Forty-Eight of *You Can't Go Home Again,* this is Wolfe's recurring, hopeful message to a jaded, skeptical, and cynical world.

Notes

1. *The Modern Novel in America, 1900–1950* (Chicago: Henry Regnery Co., 1951), p. 169.

2. Quoted in Elizabeth Nowell, *Thomas Wolfe: A Biography* (Garden City, N.Y.: Doubleday & Co., 1960), p. 257.

3. "The Sorrows of Thomas Wolfe," *The Collected Letters of John Peale Bishop*, ed. Edmund Wilson (New York: Charles Scribner's Sons, 1948), p. 137.

4. *Cavalcade of the American Novel from the Birth of the Nation to the Middle of the Twentieth Century* (New York: Holt, Rinehart & Winston, 1952), p. 410.

5. *Thomas Wolfe* (New York: Twayne Publishers, Inc., 1964), p. 103.

6. Introduction to *The Portable Thomas Wolfe*, ed. Maxwell Geismar (New York: Viking Press, 1950), p. 6.

7. *American Fiction, 1920–1940* (New York: Russell & Russell, 1941; 1960), p. 205.

8. Beach, p. 205.

9. "Wolfe's Unfinished Symphony: A Study of Form in the Novels of Thomas Wolfe," unpublished doctoral dissertation (University of Wisconsin, Madison, 1948), p. 18.

10. "Symbolic Patterns in *You Can't Go Home Again*," *Modern Fiction Studies* 11 (1965), 286–96.

11. Elizabeth Nowell (ed.), *The Letters of Thomas Wolfe* (New York: Charles Scribner's Sons, 1956), p. 711, Feb. 14, 1938. Hereafter all references to this volume will be included in the text and abbreviated as *Letters*. Wolfe also pointed out in this letter that the book would conclude that the home of "every one of us is in the future; there is no other way." He also notes that the book "might almost be called 'You Can't Go Home Again."

12. *You Can't Go Home Again*, introduction by Edward C. Aswell (New York: Harper & Brothers, 1940; 1941), pp. 410–11. All citations from this book will be given in the text hereafter by page number alone. Harper's published Wolfe's three posthumous works. Wolfe broke with Charles Scribner's Sons, his original publishers, about a year before he died.

13. See Richard Walser, *Thomas Wolfe, An Introduction and Interpretation* (Cambridge: Harvard University Press, 1950), p. 4.

14. Edward C. Aswell, "Note on Thomas Wolfe" in *The Hills Beyond* (New York: New Avon Library, 1944), p. 214. Indeed, Wolfe saw the whole manuscript as comprising one novel. He had no concern for the publisher's dilemma, and he left it to the publisher to divide the novel up into proper volumes, when the time came. Aswell conjectures that the final novel as Wolfe had projected it might well have gone into as many as five or six separate volumes.

15. Aswell, "Note on Thomas Wolfe," p. 209. Hereafter: Aswell.

16. Aswell, pp. 213–14.

17. *The Window of Memory: The Literary Career of Thomas Wolfe* (Chapel Hill: University of North Carolina Press, 1962), p. 403.

18. It was a fact of Wolfe's life that his encyclopedic vision and his voluminous outpouring of words made him subject to the stabs of the editorial pencil. And Wolfe was most sensitive about it. When Bernard DeVoto wrote in his now-famous review of *The Story of a Novel* that Wolfe's works received their final shape "not from the artist's feeling for form and artistic integrity, but from the office of Charles Scribner's Sons," he bruised Wolfe's sensitivity in such a way that an eventual

break with his long-time friend and Scribner editor, Maxwell E. Perkins, would assuage the pain. See "Genius Is Not Enough," *Forays and Rebuttals* (Boston: Little, Brown & Co., 1938), p. 328.

19. Aswell, p. 210.

20. Aswell, p. 206.

21. Aswell, p. 202.

22. Bishop, p. 129.

23. Beach, p. 203.

24. See Edwin Berry Burgum, "Thomas Wolfe's Discovery of America," *The Novel and the World's Dilemma* (New York: Oxford University Press, 1947), p. 302.

25. Herbert Muller, *Thomas Wolfe* (Norfolk, Conn.: New Directions, 1947), p. 9.

26. Maxwell Geismar, *Writers in Crisis: The American Novel*, 1925–1940 (Boston: Houghton-Mifflin Co., 1947), p. 231.

27. Wolfe's discussion of "The Company" in mock religious terms is a minor masterpiece. Originally published as "The Company" in *New Masses* for January, 1938, Wolfe struck out at the treatment of his brother-in-law, Ralph Wheaton, by the National Cash Register Company. Wheaton was fired because of the drop of business in his territory. The story in *New Masses* has even more booster talk, slogans, and cliches, although, as Kennedy points out (p. 369), Wolfe finally omitted the most Rabelaisian of the lot: "Let Federal Service You." Despite its appearance in *New Masses*, the story has no distinctively Communist flavor. In fact, Wolfe was not a Communist sympathizer. See footnote 28.

28. He especially avoided Communism. He called himself a "social democrat," that is, a man who believes in "socialism and communized socialism and in democracy but not in individualized democracy. I do not believe in the abolition of private property, in the class warfare, or in the so-called dictatorship of the proletariat. . . . I do not think there is any great 'Communist danger' in America at the present time. But I do think there is a grave Fascist danger, and it is with Fascism that I am concerned" (Kennedy, p. 370). He often battled with Perkins over politics. Perkins was an anti-New Deal Democrat and compared their views as being like those of Erasmus, who favored compromise, and Luther, who was the man of revolution. Wolfe favored taking strong action. See Kennedy, pp. 364–65.

29. Wolfe pondered long on what to do about his social responsibility. He wrote to Donald Ogden Stewart in 1938 that his social responsibility first struck him one day after reading a letter from a friend on art, love, and beauty. Looking out the window, Wolfe saw a man digging in a garbage can for food. From that time forth, he wrote, "I have never felt the same way about love or art or beauty or thought they were enough" (Kennedy, p. 364, from an unpublished letter written about February, 1938). By the time of his Purdue speech in May, 1938, Wolfe was insisting that the function of the artist cannot be discussed "without reference to its social implications." (See *Thomas Wolfe's Purdue Speech*, "Writing and Living," ed. from dictated and revised typescript with an introduction and notes by William Braswell and Leslie A. Field [Purdue University Studies, 1964], pp. 53–54.

30. As early as November 8, 1928, Wolfe wrote, in a letter to Aline Bernstein, of his concern for the direction in which America was heading. Mourning the defeat of Al Smith at the polls, and the ascendancy of the Ku Klux Klan, the Anti-Saloon League, the Rockefellers, the Hoovers, and the Coolidges, Wolfe wrote, "My part of America is not beaten four to one" (*Letters*, p. 150). Many of his letters reveal the duality in his feelings for America; thus he wrote to Sherwood Anderson, in 1935, of the "terror and mystery and ugliness and beauty" of his native land (*Letters*, p. 472).

31. *Letters*, p. 306. To Perkins, August 29, 1931.

32. Wagenknecht, p. 144.

33. *Thomas Wolfe's Purdue Speech. . . .*, p. 72.

34. Geismar, *Portable Wolfe*, p. 6.

35. *Letters*, p. 273. To Alfred S. Dashiell, November, 1930. Note that in this group of Nay-Sayers Wolfe included academicians as well. He often lambasted (as did Aswell, in his "Note") the academic world. See, for example, *You Can't Go Home Again*, pp. 457–58, 554, 732; also see his treatment of Piggy Logan's decadent critics, pp. 723–24.

36. Early in the novel Wolfe wrote of Judge Bland: "Perhaps he was the key to the whole tragedy. Perhaps Rumford Bland had sought his life in darkness not because of something evil in him—though certainly there was evil there—but because of something good that had not died. Something in the man had always fought against the dullness of provincial life, against its prejudice, its caution, its smugness, its sterility, and its lack of joy. He had looked for something better in the night. . . . Was he one of the lost men—lost, rejected, his energies unused, the shoulder of his strength finding no work to bend to—because what he had to give of hope, intelligence, curiosity, and warmth had found no place there, and so were lost?" (pp. 144–45). Significantly, it is Bland who first introduces Wolfe to the truth which he threads throughout the book—"You Can't Go Home Again."

37. *Letters*, p. 656, September 22, 1937. At this time Wolfe and Anderson had a quarrel which apparently was never made up.

38. See Smith, p. 19.

39. Wolfe was widely read by Germans. His work was well translated by German poet and novelist Hermann Hesse.

40. *Letters*, p. 730, March 7, 1938. Elizabeth Nowell, Wolfe's agent, describes, in her biography of Wolfe, that he received the phrase from Ella Winter, Lincoln Steffens' widow, after a wildly disputatious party at the home of Sherwood Anderson. She wrote to Miss Nowell of the incident: "He started telling me of his horror of going back to his home and what he had found there, and I just said, 'But don't you know you can't go home again?' He stopped dead and then said, 'Can I have that? I mean for a title? I'm writing a piece . . . and I'd like to call it that. It says exactly what I mean. Would you mind if I used it?' I laughed and told him that I didn't 'own' it any more than I'd own any other thought. . . . But he was violently excited. Later he . . . asked if I'd have any objection, any objection whatever, if he used it for the title of a book." (From Ella Winter to Elizabeth Nowell, p. 410 in *Thomas Wolfe, A Biography*). Adds Nowell: "From that time on Wolfe was so delighted with the phrase 'you can't go home again' that he was almost obsessed by it" (p. 410).

41. Pamela Hansford Johnson, *The Art of Thomas Wolfe* (New York: Charles Scribner's Sons, 1963), p. 131 (first published in England as *Hungry Gulliver*).

42. "Thomas Wolfe: A Summing Up," *The New Republic*, Sept. 25, 1940, p. 423.

43. *Literature and Western Man* (New York: Harper & Brothers, 1960), p. 440.

You Can't Go Home Again: Wolfe's Germany and Social Consciousness

Leslie Field*

In his four large novels and two collections of stories, Wolfe dwelled on a few themes, which, in *The Story of a Novel*,[1] he pointed out had been *central* to his writings: his various concepts of time, the "Where Now?" motif, and man's search for a spiritual father. In the speech he gave at Purdue University in 1938,[2] he said that these earlier themes were no longer crucial. Entries in his notebooks[3] and letters[4] echo this assertion. He noted that as a beginning writer he had been too egocentric, too much the sensitive artist divorced from his environment. Late in his young life he saw the need for looking outside of himself, for looking at the political, social, and economic world, and for trying to understand it, assimilate it, and somehow to bring it into his own writing. This movement away from narcissism he attempted in his last novel, *You Can't Go Home Again*.[5]

In many ways *The Web and the Rock* is fictionalized autobiography with protagonist George Webber playing Thomas Wolfe, as were the first two books with the earlier counterpart, Eugene Gant. But in *The Web and the Rock* Wolfe seems to be moving outside himself to a new social awareness, a new social consciousness of people and institutions that are not simply projections of Thomas Wolfe.

With *You Can't Go Home Again*, Wolfe goes even farther in this direction. Episodically, the novel's protagonist involves himself with a variety of people, places, and ideas. Early on George Webber resumes his life with Esther in New York. He awaits publication of his first novel. He returns home for a visit and has a reunion with a boyhood friend, Nebraska Crane, a professional baseball player. He meets Judge Rumford Bland, a usurer whom he used to know. He ruminates on all that has gone wrong in the town he grew up in. Then he returns to New York. Wolfe has chapters on the Jack family in their fashionable New York apartment. A party featuring Piggy Logan and a fire at the Jacks's assume symbolic proportions as Wolfe contrasts the haves and have nots in depression United States.

Further episodes involve George's trip to England and Germany. In England he has a wildly kaleidoscopic time with Lloyd McHarg, supposedly fashioned on Sinclair Lewis, and on his last trip to his beloved Germany George sees the face of evil in the Nazis who lionize him, preen for the Olympic Games, and smash in the heads of Jews on the side streets of Berlin and Munich. "I Have a Thing to Tell You" (which initially appeared as a separate piece in *The New Republic*)[6] is a poig-

*Reprinted from H. G. Jones, ed., *Thomas Wolfe of North Carolina* (Chapel Hill, N.C.: North Caroliniana Society, 1982), pp. 5–20. North Caroliniana Society Imprints No. 6. © 1982 by The North Caroliniana Society, Inc.

nant picture of man's inhumanity to man, the Nazi persecution of the Jew. Finally we have "Ecclesiasticus" and the "Credo," on which the book ends.

Some of Wolfe's finest expressions of social awareness emerged in *You Can't Go Home Again.* Much of this social awareness or social consciousness involves Wolfe's attitude toward Germany and the Jews. Was Wolfe anti-Semitic? In a very real sense his fiction and especially his letters and notes do reveal bigotry and prejudice. Moreover, in his seven trips to Germany he discovered in himself a strong affinity for Germans and Teutonic culture—long before he discovered his America. Yet in "I Have a Thing to Tell You," which reappeared as a climactic epiphany in the last part of *You Can't Go Home Again*, Wolfe sees the evil behind the mask of Germany, and senses at once that anti-Semitism and humanity are incompatible.

George Webber, having returned to his beloved Germany as a famous author, is now on a train leaving it once more. At Aachen, the last stop before the border, he and other travelers in his compartment are shocked that one of their fellow passengers—a nervous little man, whom George had privately called Fuss-and-Fidget—had been seized by the authorities. The rumor circulates that he is a Jew caught trying to escape with all of his money. As the terrified little man tries to persuade the officers to let him go, he is led past his traveling companions, his eyes glancing at them for just a moment. But he does not betray them by showing in any way that he knows them, and they board the train, leaving him behind on the platform. "He looked once, directly and steadfastly, at his former companions, and they at him. And in that gaze there was all the unmeasured weight of man's mortal anguish" (*YCGHA*, p. 699). Wolfe wrote this in the 1930s, some time before the rest of the world took seriously the plight of the Jew, and well before one heard the terms *final solution*, *collective guilt*, and *The Holocaust.*[7]

Wolfe was gaining in knowledge and sensitivity, but his perception that "you can't go home again" did not break his spirit; indeed, strangely enough, it heartened him. Life is change, he felt, and therefore we can improve it. His final credo, in the last pages of his novel, is no defeated whine or whimper. The loss of false illusions, he said, is only the way to new belief. Here is Wolfe's conclusion:

> I believe we are lost here in America, but I believe we shall be found. And this belief . . . is . . . not only our own hope, but America's everlasting, living dream. I think the life which we have fashioned in America, and which has fashioned us . . . was self-destructive in its nature, and must be destroyed. I think these forms are dying, and must die, just as I know that America and the people in it are deathless, undiscovered, and immortal, and must live.
>
> I think the true discovery of America is before us. I think the true fulfillment of our spirit, of our people, of our mighty and im-

> mortal land, is yet to come. I think the true discovery of our democracy is still before us. And I think that all these things are certain as the morning, as inevitable as noon. . . . Our America is Here, is Now, and beckons us, and . . . this glorious assurance is not only our living hope, but our dream to be accomplished. (*YCGHA*, p. 741)

Thus does Wolfe's long, posthumous work end optimistically as a celebration of America that he knew and loved. He saw the face of evil all around him but he insisted in his fictional letter to Foxhall Edwards/ Maxwell Perkins that "we must deny it all along the way."

Richard Kennedy in *The Window of Memory* does a remarkably comprehensive analysis of the ambience for *You Can't Go Home Again.* In a section called "A Political Awakening: I Have a Thing to Tell You," Kennedy details a chronological and psychological context for this period of Wolfe creativity. Kennedy sums up this way: For most of his life, Wolfe was not a politically minded person. Even though he had been to Europe, including Germany, a few times, "he knew more about European restaurants than about European social problems."[8] In short, Wolfe's attitudes toward Germany and his knowledge of the German political system had been superficial up to about 1935. He had had "casual contacts" with Germans, resented some of the arrogance he observed among them, and dismissed samples of German materialism as vulgar Babbittism. But still Wolfe "had come to love Munich and the southern Germanic people of Austria. In his writing he began to identify his father's country in southern Pennsylvania with a Germanic cleanliness, generosity, and vitality."[9]

But when Wolfe went to Germany in 1935, he saw a change: Nazism and evil had begun to seep into the very fibre of the German soul.[10] Kennedy goes on to acknowledge that "*I Have a Thing to Tell You* is a well-defined mark in Wolfe's career in both thought and composition. In order to purge himself of guilt for having been deceived by the veneer of Nazism, Wolfe acknowledges the claim of human brotherhood with a strength that his self-centered individualism had not allowed to emerge before."[11]

That which now appears as Wolfe's last publications is significant ideologically, aesthetically, and bibliographically. Over the years much has been made of the posthumous Wolfe works. Most recently John Halberstadt, writing in the *New York Review of Books* and the *Yale Review*,[12] raises the big question once again: Who put together Thomas Wolfe's posthumous books? He argues that what we have today in *The Web and the Rock*, *You Can't Go Home Again*, and *The Hills Beyond* is as much the creation of Aswell, Wolfe's last editor, as it is of Wolfe. Maybe more. Perhaps. I don't wish to explore that controversy now. Suffice it to say that before Halberstadt, Kennedy, Holman, Field, Reeves, Rubin and others pointed out in one way or another that the Wolfe in these posthumous books is not the Wolfe who wrote *Look Homeward,*

Angel. Creative and perhaps even freewheeling editing have given us twice as much Wolfe fiction as we would have had had we relied solely on the material Wolfe saw into print before he died. Some of this editing may be akin to what we now associate with *Billy Budd* or *The Mysterious Stranger.* That is, a well-meaning attempt by editors, in this instance Edward Aswell, to give us a text that we otherwise would not have had. Or it may be a shoddy bit of editorial commercialese. Time will tell.

However, a central fact does remain: Wolfe's *Look Homeward, Angel* was written in a subjective, romantic vein. As a beginning writer he worked introspectively and egotistically—very much from within. Later, in the 1930s, like Whitman, he used autobiography to move from the *I* to America, Europe, and the cosmos. His letters, notebook jottings and statements, plans for his forthcoming books in the 1930s were often repetitious, fuzzy, ill-defined. But a common denominator does emerge: In this period Wolfe was conscious that he wanted to move away from his earlier subjective mode of writing typified by *Look Homeward, Angel.* He was moving on to something else. And that something else was a sense of social consciousness, objectivity, and a belief in "you can't go home again" in all of its ramifications.[13]

In Wolfe's *Notebooks* we have ample evidence that he had been worrying about his new direction for some time. For example, in a section called "Political and Social Notes: 1937–1938," Wolfe darts back and forth as he considers dictatorship, socialism, democracy, and other forms of government. In a piece called "A Spanish Letter," which he never mailed, Wolfe wrestled with many forms of government, including Fascism. In a somewhat revised form this material was included in Chapter 38 of *You Can't Go Home Again* (*Notebooks*, pp. 901–14).

In typically rambling fashion Wolfe covers much ground in his "Spanish Letter." First he goes back to his roots, North Carolina, and his hard-working stone-cutter father, the solid conservative outlook of his family, then to his own lyrical writing and juvenile conflicts with his environment, his early limited view of the artist and his society, his breaking away from his romantic egocentric artistic view of life, his ultimate break with his locale:

> You can't go home again—back to your childhood, back to the father you have lost, back to the solacements of time and memory—yes, even back to art and beauty and to love. For me, at any rate, it is now manifest that they are not enough. And I do not think that this be treason. . . . (*Notebooks*, p. 904)[14]

Wolfe went on to say in his long letter that he had left his home in North Carolina, had wandered the streets of Brooklyn, had written much, had visited Germany, for which he felt a special love, had gone back to New York, and then had returned to Germany. Finally, he said, he discovered that Germany had changed. Germany was still golden, and he was embarking upon a glorious career, but something was wrong. He met friends, saw signs, felt something. And ultimately he saw a picture of Germany that he had never seen before: He began to see and feel and experience "the full horror" of that which had never before been part of life.

> This was the picture of a great people who were spiritually sick, psychically wounded: who had been poisoned by the contagion of an ever-present fear, the pressure of a constant and infamous compulsion, who had been silenced into a sweltering and malignant secrecy, until spiritually they were literally drowning in their own secretions, dying from the distillations of their own self poison, for which now there was no medicine or release. (*Notebooks*, 907)

Wolfe still felt in 1935 that the German people had a noble heritage. As difficult as life was then, they still reached out in order to share cultures of the past and those around them in the present. He saw that the Germans were still immersed in literature and the arts. But Wolfe also sensed that even this semblance of the old Germany was rapidly disappearing.

> Everywhere about me, as time went on during that spring and summer of 1935, I saw the evidence of this dissolution, this shipwreck of a great spirit, this miasmic poison that sank like a pestilential fog through the very air, tainting, sickening, blighting with its corrosive touch, through fear, pressure, suppression, insane distrust and spiritual disease, the lives of everyone I met. It was, and was everywhere, as invisible as a plague, and as unmistakable as death; it sank in on me through all the golden singing of that May, until at last I felt it, breathed it, lived it, and knew it for the thing it was. (*Notebooks*, p. 909).

Wolfe returned to Germany one last time, in 1936, and he noted that "the pestilence of the year before had spread and deepened" (*Notebooks*, p. 909). It was the time of the Olympic Games in Germany, and Wolfe described in great detail the magnificence and pageantry of the games, which signified the power and preeminence of Germany. And then he contrasted this with the other spectacle—

> . . . great displays of marching men, sometimes ungunned but rhythmic, great regiments of brown shirts swinging through the streets; again, at ease, young men and laughing, talking with each other, long lines of Hitler's bodyguards, black-uniformed and leather-booted, the Schutz-Staffel men, stretching in unbroken lines from Leader's residence in the Wilhemstrasse up to the arches of the Brandenburger Tor; then suddenly the sharp command, and instantly, unforgettably, the liquid smack of ten thousand boots as they came together, with the sound of war. (*Notebooks*, p. 913)

Thus did Wolfe see the complete corruption of his beloved Germany, his second home. And it sickened him as he realized with a sorrowful heart that he could not go home again.

By February, 1938, Wolfe had apparently roughed out the contents of what was to be the novel we know as *You Can't Go Home Again.* The long synopsis or statement of purpose, although designed for Edward Aswell's eyes, was not seen by Aswell until after Wolfe's death. As we know, much controversy still exists concerning whether Wolfe's posthumous publications were well-served by his editors at Harper's.[15]

At any rate, Wolfe's "Statement" talks of a book which he plans to be a "process of discovery." He says:

> . . . the whole book might almost be called "You Can't Go Home Again"—which means back home to the father one has lost, back home to romantic love, to a young man's dream of glory and of fame, back home to exile, to escape to "Europe" and some foreign land, back home to lyricism, singing just for singing's sake . . . —back home to the escapes of Time and Memory. (*Notebooks*, p. 939)

Wolfe goes on to say that he is planning a "hopeful" book, an optimistic view of life. Moreover, he intends this to be "the most objective book that he has ever written, and he also intends . . . [paradoxically] for it to be the most autobiographical" (*Notebooks*, p. 939). In this long statement Wolfe speaks of himself as author in the third person. It gives him a chance to stand at some distance from himself as he describes the self he once was, the self who wrote an earlier fiction such as *Look Homeward, Angel.* It gives him an opportunity to expound once more on his *use* of autobiography:

> Autobiographically, therefore, he [the protagonist] should bear perhaps about the same relationship to the life of the author, as Wilhelm Meister bears to the life of Goethe, or as Copperfield bears to the life of Dickens: as to the story itself—the legend—it should bear about the same relation to the life of the author . . . even perhaps as Don Quixote bears to the life of Cervantes—although this book is perhaps more in the vein of satiric legendry than the book the author has in mind. (*Notebooks*, p. 942)

Leo Gurko points out that "the subject matter [of *YCGHA*] is aggressively sociological, at times grimly so. The two great experiences of the 1930s—the depression and the rise of the Fascist empires—are more vividly present than were earlier contemporary events in the preceding novels."[16] Gurko says this book may very well be Wolfe's "depression novel." Moreover, he goes on, "An instructive view of Wolfe in his last stage can be gained by comparing *You Can't Go Home Again* with *The Grapes of Wrath*, another depression novel. . . ."[17] Although Gurko sees great differences between the two books, he does posit some striking parallels that are intriguing:

> The two novels wonderfully reflect the two movements of the thirties: the contraction at the start and the expansion at the end. One can say that Rose of Sharon offering her milky breast to the starving man on the last page of *The Grapes of Wrath* is a metaphor of the sentiments expressed in Wolfe's credo on the last pages of *You Can't Go Home Again.*[18]

Wolfe's experiences, his life in the South and the city, his observation of aesthetes and the wealthy, and the vivid impressions he had of the depression, progressively molded and enlarged his critical awareness of life outside himself. He gained a new insight into American society and into man himself; but he needed further experiences for the maturation of his social consciousness: Germany conveniently provided him with these. Wolfe himself recognized that the way to find America was to leave it.[19] Oddly enough, his sojourns in Europe—especially in Germany—led him by a straight path to an augmented awareness of America.

Wolfe's feeling about Germany up to perhaps 1936, or even 1937, parallels his expression in "Dark in the Forest, Strange as Time" (in his *From Death to Morning* collection): that is, an almost mystical feeling of kinship for Germany and the Germans, to which the Germans seemed instinctively to respond. Wolfe's novels were popular in Germany both with the critics and the reading public.[20] In 1935 German cultural life was highly controlled by the Nazis, and Wolfe's appeal was not to the Nazis, "but in spite of them."[21] In the mid-thirties there existed a potent and dangerous underground current, "Die Stillen im Lande," generated by people of all classes and professions who, in disgust with the party principles of National Socialism and the inclusion of these values in contemporary German letters, quietly and unobtrusively rebelled by turning to American and British literature.[22] It was to this responsive and sensitive group that Wolfe appealed. Wolfe became a legendary figure in Germany during his 1935 visit. His appeal lay, by and large, in the "implicit romanticism" of his early works.[23] To the Germans he symbolized an era "when great writers were great men. Something of the angel and the demon in him . . . gave back to the intellectual and creative people of Berlin a sense of their past, of the dignity and power and freedom of a mind not under stress."[24] Wolfe, quite naturally, was influenced by this German enthusiasm, and his final awareness of the sickness of Germany hurt all the more because of the warmth and love the Germans had bestowed upon him and because he had so loved his dark Helen.[25]

Those who knew Wolfe seem to agree that in 1935 he did not or could not recognize what was happening to Germany. Ledig-Rowohlt (depicted as Franz Heilig in *YCGHA*) recalls that, during Wolfe's 1935 trip to Germany, their conversations were primarily unpolitical. And, says Rowohlt, Wolfe was carried away by the adulation of his German friends to the extent that "his political skepticism was still glossed over by joy at his literary success; and besides, he loved Berlin more than any other European capital."[26] Wolfe in 1935 was so bewitched by his German fame that he was not then overly critical of the Nazis, accepting "surface impressions" of Hitler's Germany.[27] Wolfe's 1935 mood has been explained as a "state of delirium" induced by personal experiences. *Of Time and the River* had just been published and proclaimed a success. Wolfe's exuberance over this good fortune released months and years of pent-up anxiety, and "everything . . . [took on] the proportions of a gigantic and infinitely beautiful dream." His trips to Germany heightened this euphoria. He left this land of magical dark beauty "with many of his illusions intact, though some were wavering."[28] In a letter to Maxwell Perkins, in which he describes his impressions of Germany in 1935, Wolfe tells of the changes he has witnessed in the Germans. He is hurt, puzzled, and somewhat mystified by the metamorphosis which he recognizes connotes only evil. But, Wolfe warns, this evil is not isolated: it affects the entire world: "But more and more I feel that we are all of us bound up and tainted by whatever guilt and evil there may be in this whole world and that we cannot accuse and condemn others without in the end coming back to an accusal of ourselves."[29] He describes with heartfelt pain the German towns overrun with marching soldiers, contrasting this image with a picture of the sun "shining all day long and the fields the greenest. . . ."[30] Thus, there were creeping in on Wolfe in 1935 incipient doubts about Germany, and the next year he returned there, soberer, "eager to learn what lay beneath the surface of Nazi success and effectiveness."[31]

Publicity of international events and figures was permitted in Germany in 1936 because of the Olympic Games being held there that year. Wolfe's German publisher shrewdly used this opportunity to publicize Wolfe and his novels, although Wolfe "made no secret of what he thought of Hitler's activities." The aura of secrecy and intrigue in Germany that year engulfed even Wolfe. He became attracted to a blonde artist who later made an unflattering drawing of him, which Wolfe indignantly berated as giving him a "Schweingesicht." Then, according to Rowohlt, Wolfe in all seriousness suspected that the blonde had been bribed by the Gestapo to caricature him. Rowohlt explains this ludicrous situation: "Lately he [Wolfe] had come across so many frightening details about the National Socialist regime that he, too, began to suffer under the weight of personal mistrust and political suspicion."[32] And Wolfe even suspected his publishers of machinations against him because in 1936 his novels were not selling as well in Germany as they had earlier.[33]

Actually, Wolfe was quite concerned that year with the "Dark Messiah," Hitler. He had seen Hitler at the games, and from Martha Dodd, the daughter of the American ambassador to Germany, he had received information about Hitler which made him more informed about

Hitler's deeds than the Germans were. Wolfe, says Rowohlt, had no optimistic illusions in 1936 about Germany and feared more mischief was inevitable; and "he realized bitterly that everywhere the men of good will were being oppressed by the men of power, and that Hitler was unleashing nothing but evil in the world."[34] Wolfe learned much from Rowohlt. With the American, Rowohlt discussed personal troubles and pressing social problems, such as the infringement of civil liberties by the Nazis. "Through my own example," Rowohlt tells, "it became particularly clear to him how much the tyranny of National Socialism forced us to abandon our individual rights," how much the German people were being pushed into the position where communication among them was difficult.[35]

Rowohlt encouraged Wolfe to write a novel, not as a propagandist but as a novelist appealing "to the conscience of mankind." However, recalls Rowohlt, Wolfe merely smiled, and indicated that because he loved mankind above all else "he would be obliged to be political in such a book,"[36] the "book" being the story/essay he called "I Have a Thing to Tell You." At least one thing is certain about this story: it showed that Wolfe had resolved his emotional and intellectual difficulties about Fascism by 1937, for "I Have a Thing to Tell You" is a categorical repudiation of Nazism; and Wolfe, writing to a friend, claimed that the story showed his break with the Reich.[37]

Though the story was a worthwhile, timely, and necessary revelation of the ills of Nazism, Wolfe endangered his friends, particularly Rowohlt, whom he depicted as Franz Heilig. Few readers of Rowohlt's *American Scholar* article on Wolfe's last stay in Germany will be unmoved by Rowohlt's description of his emotions in 1937 when Martha Dodd suggested that he read *The New Republic*. Reading "I Have a Thing to Tell You," he was instantly aware that Wolfe had transcribed their conversations "with phonographic exactness," and had rendered Heilig's biographical data correctly as Rowohlt's. The rending thing for Rowohlt was that Wolfe had pictured Heilig "with all the inner contradictions that the tactical juggling of those years involved and that he, as an American, simply could not understand." Wolfe, though, probably understood that he was endangering the lives of his friends as well as his own position in Germany, but felt that he must place truth and integrity foremost. Rowohlt describes the situation as follows: "Here indeed, a writer had seized on an outstanding political situation, had 'written what he had to write,' and had made his appeal to the conscience of mankind."[38]

Rowohlt had warned Wolfe that the Nazis would blacklist his books if he wrote anything politically tinged against Nazism. As predicted, his books were banned by the Nazis until it was decided "that the circulation of *The New Republic* was not such as to foment any considerable anti-Nazi sentiment."[39] It is ironic that Wolfe, whose appeal to the Germans for so long lay in the "implicit romanticism and unpolitical humanism" of his earlier works, whose novels, the Germans felt, "stood apart from national and international issues of the day and operated in a non-political frame of reference that was neither Nazi or anti-Nazi,"[40] should have his books blacklisted for several months because he offended the sensibilities of the Nazis by finally writing a story with unguarded and intentional political overtones which hardly sanction National Socialism.

The change which 1936 Germany wrought in Wolfe is reflected in the basic attitudes he held late in life and subsequently espoused in the fiction published posthumously. *You Can't Go Home Again* is Wolfe's most politically minded work. A convincing argument has been made that the basis of his earlier works was "vitalism"[41]—that is, an attitude which does not "express itself in social or political terms," an attitude which emphasizes life as "an all-pervasive force," which expresses itself through feeling rather than "theoretical application." It is a type of Nietzschean will to power, "a wish to overpower, a wish to overthrow," to expand, absorb, dominate everything. Compare, for instance, Eugene Gant's Faustian desire to know and have everything with George Webber's later view to see the similarity between Nietzsche's and Wolfe's "vitalism." The young Wolfe, also like Nietzsche, has contempt for the masses or "manswarm." Wolfe had considered himself an individual superior to and above the masses, who lack vitality; but he admired the Munich beer-hall crowd, for to him they were a vital collective entity; and the Olympic Games, with their "collective vitality" impressed him. But when Wolfe became aware of the evils in Germany—racism, worship of force, antiintellectual suppression of truth—he related these evils to the qualities he found in himself and his own work. Realizing that Nazism is atavistic, he rejects similar primitivistic, vitalistic tendencies, concluding that man cannot return to sub-rationality; and therefore he must repudiate his own individualism. This repudiation of vitalism must bring about a recasting of personality. Wolfe must now give his brain complete control; his "critical intelligence" must constantly be in the fore. That is, he must now become a thoroughgoing socially conscious thinker and writer. Wolfe had indeed assumed a heavy artistic role. For the remainder of his short life he would faithfully adhere to this stance in his fiction. But he refused to sacrifice his imagination on the altar of fact. Thus did he become obsessed with the translation of "fact" into the "substance of poetic truth."[42]

Wolfe's social criticism may seem naive, superficial, and emotional, but Wolfe was attempting to mature, to develop a social consciousness, and to temper the emotional extravagance, the prejudices of his earlier works with "critical intelligence." The lack of "movement and color, individuality and magnificence" in *You Can't Go Home Again* and *The Hills Beyond* compared with his earlier writing is perhaps a result of Wolfe's inhibition of vitalism in these later works in favor of a cooler and more critical objectivity.[43] Before 1937, for example, he could write in his notebook a vindication of Hitler's government because in Germany "you are free to speak and write that you do not like Jews and that you think Jews are bad, corrupt, and unpleasant people. In America you are not free to say this" (*Notebooks*, p. 829). But in 1937 he could write in "I Have a Thing to Tell You" a tragic, sympathetic story of the German-Jew, "Fuss-and-Fidget."[44] This objective treatment of a Jew—who is not characterized as a Jew or described with stereotyped adjectives which (barring a few special exceptions) Wolfe normally attributes to Jews—is remarkable in comparison with Wolfe's earlier depiction of Jews.[45] And it does not seem too farfetched to say that Wolfe seems to have grown in stature, temperamentally and artistically, because he was able in this story to depict a Jew sympathetically and objectively. The border incident, then, is for Wolfe the final piece of the puzzle which he needed to formulate a creed and a positive attitude.

Wolfe was now unflinchingly aware of the evil in man: Hitler was a "recrudescence of an old barbarism," the atavistic propensities in man springing out. Racism, worship of brute force, suppression of truth, resort to lies, myths, contempt for the individual, anti-intellectualism, belief in blind faiths and obedience—"each of these fundamental elements of Hitlerism was a throwback to that fierce and ancient tribalism" which made the Teutons destroy the Roman civilization. "That primitive spirit of greed and lust and force had always been the true enemy of mankind" and still is, Wolfe concludes, not only in Germany, but in America, wherever the ruthless "dog-eat-dog" philosophy is sanctioned. Recognizing the evil atavistic tendencies in mankind and in himself, he firmly believes that man, if he is to be saved, cannot go home again—and this summation of his experiences was the most difficult value judgment he had ever made or had to face (*YCGHA*, pp. 705–706).[46] And at the pinnacle of his development of social consciousness, he finds—significantly enough—that he must reject Fox's credo:

> All of this makes the paradox of our great difference as hard and strange as the paradox of our polarity. And in this lies the root of trouble and the seed of severance. Your own philosophy has led you to accept the order of things as they are because you have no hope of changing them; and if you could change them, you feel that any other order would be just as bad. In everlasting terms—those of eternity—you and the Preacher may be right; for there is no greater wisdom than the wisdom of Ecclesiastes, no acceptance finally so true as the stern fatalism of the rock. Man was born to live, to suffer, and to die, and what befalls him is a tragic lot. There is no denying this in the final end. *But we must, dear Fox, deny it all along the way.* (*YCGHA*, p. 737)

His final credo, expressing a belief in man's ultimate ability to conquer the enemies of greed, lust, atavism, is genuine philosophy and faith, even though many insist that Wolfe reaches an impossible conclusion. It is a culminating faith, its pinnacle based on critical evaluation of the town, the metropolis, the wealthy, the masses; on a critical observation of the consequences of the depression and Nazism; and a value judgment arrived at by a man striving for and finally reaching a social consciousness.

Notes

1. Thomas Wolfe, *The Story of a Novel* (New York: Charles Scribner's Sons, 1936).

2. William Braswell and Leslie A. Field, eds., *Thomas Wolfe's Purdue Speech: "Writing and Living"* (West Lafayette, Indiana: Purdue University Studies, 1964).

3. Richard S. Kennedy and Paschal Reeves, eds., *The Notebooks of Thomas Wolfe*, 2 vols. (Chapel Hill: The University of North Carolina Press, 1970). All subsequent references will be to volume 2 of this edition and will be indicated by *Notebooks* parenthetically in the text.

4. Elizabeth Nowell, ed., *The Letters of Thomas Wolfe* (New York: Charles Scribner's Sons, 1956).

5. Thomas Wolfe, *You Can't Go Home Again* (New York: Harper and Brothers, 1940). All subsequent references will be indicated by *YCGHA* parenthetically in the text.

6. See *YCGHA*, pp. 691–99, which is a modification but substantially the same material as "I Have a Thing to Tell You," *The New Republic*, 10, 17, 24 March 1937, pp. 132–36, 159–64, 202–07. See also C. Hugh Holman, ed., *The Short Novels of Thomas Wolfe* (New York: Charles Scribner's Sons, 1961), pp. 235–78.

7. To capture the same time frame and the factual context Wolfe alludes to fictionally, see especially Arthur D. Morse, *While Six Million Died: A Chronicle of American Apathy* (New York: Random House, 1968), and Walter Laqueur, *The Terrible Secret: Suppression of The Truth about Hitler's Final Solution* (Boston: Little, Brown and Company, 1980).

8. Richard S. Kennedy, *The Window of Memory: The Literary Career of Thomas Wolfe* (Chapel Hill: The University of North Carolina Press, 1962), p. 325.

9. Kennedy, p. 326. See also *YCGHA*, p. 728 and *Purdue Speech*, p. 69. Significant material concerning Wolfe's German experiences and his attitudes toward Germany appears fictionally throughout books VI and VII of *YCGHA*. The factual source for this material in a variety of forms appears in the following: *Notebooks*, pp. 901–19; *Purdue Speech*, pp. 67–78; and in Nowell's *Letters*, pp. 459–63 ff. See also Elizabeth Nowell, *Thomas Wolfe: A Biography* (Garden City, New York: Doubleday and Company, Inc., 1960), pp. 120–27 ff.

10. Kennedy, pp. 328–32.

11. Kennedy, p. 332.

12. See John Halberstadt, "Who Wrote Thomas Wolfe's Last Novels?" *The New York Review of Books*, XXVIII (March 19, 1981), 51–52; see also John Halberstadt, "The Making of Thomas Wolfe's Posthumous Novels," *The Yale Review*, 70 (Autumn 1980), 79–99; Eliot Fremont-Smith, "Wolfegate: Of Time, the River, and Fraud." *The Village Voice*, February 25–March 3, 1981, pp. 35, 37; Edwin McDowell, "Paper on Thomas Wolfe Stirs Debate on Scholarship VS Privacy," *The New York Times* (Mon., April 6, 1981), p. 17; Richard S. Kennedy, "The 'Wolfegate' Affair." *Harvard Magazine*, 84 (September-October 1981), 48–53, 62.

13. See especially *Purdue Speech*, pp. 89ff.

14. In various forms this material and other *Notebooks* entries dealing with Wolfe's concepts of "you can't go home again" appear in *YCGHA*, pp. 704–43, and in *Purdue Speech*, Appendix I, pp. 89–116.

15. See Halberstadt, note 12. Halberstadt claims that his dissertation on Wolfe "may not leave the library at Yale in either its book or microfilm form, "but if it were permitted to see the light of day, he might prove that Wolfe's posthumous novels were "not really written by Wolfe in the usual sense but were predominantly the work of . . .Edward Aswell."

16. Leo Gurko, *Thomas Wolfe: Beyond the Romantic Ego* (New York: Thomas Y. Crowell Company, 1975), p. 137.

17. Gurko, p. 154.

18. Gurko, pp. 154–55.

19. See *The Story of a Novel*, p. 30.

20. See William W. Pusey, III, "The German Vogue of Thomas Wolfe," *The Germanic Review*, XXIII (April 1948), 137–48; Kurt Pinthus, "Culture Inside Nazi Germany," *The American Scholar*, IX (Autumn 1940), 490; and Martha Dodd, *Through Embassy Eyes* (New York: Garden City Publishing Co., 1940), pp. 89–91.

21. Pusey, p. 140.

22. Pinthus, p. 490.

23. Pusey, p. 141. It is interesting to note that the quality for which the Germans admired Wolfe—Romanticism—is the same for which many American critics have rejected him. Years ago Edmund Wilson succinctly summed up the attitude of American critics: "I have never written about Thomas Wolfe, because I find him completely unreadable. I know that he has talent, but his writing is too verbose for me—I admire compactness and terseness—and his swollen imagination is very uncongenial to me. I found last year in Germany that he was enormously popular over there—he is, I suppose, writing in the tradition of German romanticism, but this does not endear him to me."—Edmund Wilson, letter to the present writer, 19 April 1955.

24. Dodd, pp. 90–91.

25. See C. Hugh Holman, *The Loneliness at the Core: Studies in Thomas Wolfe* (Baton Rouge: Louisiana State University Press, 1975), p. 151.

26. Heinrich Maria Ledig-Rowohlt, "Thomas Wolfe in Berlin," *The American Scholar*, XXII (Spring 1953), 189–91.

27. Pusey, p. 142.

28. Dodd, pp. 91–94.

29. Roger Burlingame, *Of Making Many Books: A Hundred Years of Reading, Writing, and Publishing* (New York: Charles Scribner's Sons, 1946), p. 325. Although in his book he does not mention to whom and on what date this letter was written, Mr. Burlingame informed me that Wolfe wrote the letter to Maxwell Perkins on 23 May 1935. To my knowledge, this letter does not appear in any collection of Wolfe or Perkins letters.—Roger Burlingame, letter to the present writer, 18 July 1955.

30. Burlingame, pp. 325–26.

31. Dodd, p. 94.

32. The material in this paragraph comes from Rowohlt, pp. 194–95.

33. Rowohlt, p. 198.

34. Rowohlt, p. 196.

35. Rowohlt, p. 197.

36. Rowohlt, pp. 196, 199.

37. Thomas Wolfe, letter to Dixon Wecter, 5 March 1937. See *Letters*, p. 614.

38. Rowohlt, pp. 200–01.

39. See George R. Preston, Jr. *Thomas Wolfe, A Bibliography* (New York: Charles S. Boesen, 1943), p. 71.

40. Pusey, p. 141.

41. See Bella Kussy [Milmed], "The Vitalist Trend and Thomas Wolfe," *Sewanee Review*, L (July-September, 1942), 306–24. Note that here and elsewhere in this paper Kussy's definition of "Vitalism" is employed; this paragraph is in effect a summary of Kussy's most helpful study.

42. See especially the *Letters*, p. 751, and the *Purdue Speech*, pp. 54ff.

43. Kussy, p. 323.

44. See note 6.

45. See Paschal Reeves, *Thomas Wolfe's Albatross: Race and Nationality in America* (Athens: The University of Georgia Press, 1968), pp. 39–85. Reeves analyzes Wolfe's "Jews" in five categories: "student, businessman, elite society, lover, and symbol."

46. See also John Miller Maclachlan, "Folk Concepts in the Novels of Thomas Wolfe," *Southern Folklore Quarterly*, IX (December 1945), 175–86. Maclachlan evaluates Wolfe's observations and conclusions in the light of *kulturgeist*.

Fame and the Athlete in Wolfe's Fiction

John L. Idol*

Ever since his undergraduate days at the University of North Carolina, when for a time he considered becoming a sportswriter,[1] Wolfe never lost his interest in athletics as one of America's most expressive activities. His Eugene Gant dreamed of becoming a famous athlete, achieving in one of his fantasies the status of Yale's greatest fullback.[2] An older Eugene, sounding like Walt Whitman chanting one of his catalogues, celebrated America as

> the place of the crack athletes and of the runners who limber up in March; it is the place of ten-second men and great jumpers and vaulters. . . . It is the place of baseball players, and the easy lob, the soft spring smackings of the glove and mit, the crack of the bat; it is the place of the batters, fielders, and pitchers, of the nigger boys and white, drawling, shirt-sleeved men, the bleachers and the resinous smell of old worn wood. . . . It is the place of the fighters, the crafty Jewish lightweights and the mauling Italians, Leonard, Tendler Rocky Kansas, and Dundee.[3]

A far more graphic rendering of America's involvement in athletics oc-

*Reprinted from the *Thomas Wolfe Review*, 5, No. 2 (Fall 1981), 38–43.

curs somewhat later when Eugene, visualizing the whole contest, recalls his dead brother Ben's job of posting at a newspaper office the story of a World Series game as the play-by-play report came over the wire:

> The batter stands swinging his bat and grimly waiting at the plate, crouched, tense, the catcher crouched, the umpire bent, hands clasped behind his back, and peering forward. All of them are set now in the cold blue of that slanting shadow, except the pitcher who stands out there all alone, calm, desperate, and forsaken in his isolation, with the gold-red swiftly fading light upon him, his figure legible with all the resolution, despair and lonely dignity which that slanting, somehow fatal light can give him. (*T/R*, pp. 202–03)

As this catalogue and vivid description show, Wolfe knew that one of the most vital threads in the fabric of American life was athletics. In time, when he turned to his Webber cycle, he would examine two athletes closely and trace their fortunes as they pursued their careers. Placed together with George Webber, they would serve the thematic function of paralleling, in their rise to fame, the climb of George Webber to renown. Their manner of handling the winning and losing of fame would provide a thought-provoking object lesson for George Webber. The aim of this paper is thus to show how the behavior of two athletes, Jim Randolph and Nebraska Crane, both enabled Wolfe to reveal something essential about the fabric of American life and to present further evidence concerning the emptiness of fame.

Early (1930–1931) in his planned shift from Eugene Gant to Monk Hawke as his new protagonist,[4] Wolfe began thinking of bringing a baseball player into his stories about America. By 1938, the place athletics would assume in his fiction had been much enlarged. How large that place would likely be becomes apparent in Wolfe's plan for an article on sports for his agent, Elizabeth Nowell, an article that Wolfe thought could develop into "a piece about America" (*NB*, *II*, 924). Instead of writing an article, he ultimately saw the novelistic potential of the material, material gleaned from his attendance of baseball games and wrestling matches in Asheville, his adventures as a sports spectator and friend of athletes at Chapel Hill, his witnessing of the Dempsey-Firpo fight, his regular habit of seeing the Yankees or Dodgers a few times each season, and his visit with Arthur Mann, a sportswriter, to a baseball writers' dinner in New York.[5] The material relating to football and boxing he gave to his depiction of Jim Randolph; that concerning wrestling and baseball, to Nebraska Crane.

> To the gangly, awkward Monk Webber, Jim Randolph was a man who had done brilliant and heroic things, and he looked the part. It seemed that he had been especially cast by nature to fulfill the most exacting requirements of the writers of romantic fiction. He was a Richard Harding Davis hero. . . . His beauty was conformed by a real manliness, his physical perfection by a natural and incomparable grace,

> the handsome perfection and regularity of his features by qualities of strength, intelligence, tenderness, and humor that all the heroes of romantic fiction can counterfeit but do not attain.[6]

Just as he was without equal on the Pine Rock College campus for his bearing and heroic adventures, he had no match there in athletic ability. Powerful and graceful as a race horse or panther, he had won legendary status as a collegiate football and baseball player and had played semi-professional baseball under an assumed name (*W/R*, p, 177).

His most glorious day as a football player came in Pine Rock's defeat of archrival Monroe and Madison, a team Pine Rock had lost to for nine years in a row. Following a scoreless first half, Pine Rock sprung its leading runner, Randolph, free at the midpoint of the third quarter. "Pacing out to the right, behind the interference, weaving and pawing delicately at the air, [Randolph] found his opening and shook loose, around the end, for a run of 57 yards to a touchdown" (*W/R*, p. 185). His dash was to bring the only points of the game, and that scamper and that game were

> the apex of Jim Randolph's life, the summit of his fame. Nothing that he could do after that could dim the glory of that shining moment. It was a triumph and a tragedy, but at that moment Jim, poor Jim, could only know the triumph of it. (*W/R*, p. 185)

Randolph's glorious feat occurred on the Thanksgiving before the nation plunged into World War I. Romantic hero that he was aspiring to become, Randolph rushed to enlist and, after training, saw action in France, where he was wounded. Back at Pine Rock, and though still a sick man, he played basketball, but "there was something lacking, something had gone by." Never again would he be the athlete he once was. Indeed, Wolfe wrote, "it would have been better for him had he died in France. He had suffered the sad fate of men who live to see themselves become a legend" (*W/R*, p. 186). His age, wounds, and the disillusioning experiences of the war and its aftermath brought an end to Jim's hopes for continued athletic prowess. He had probably become "a member of what the intellectuals since [the War] have called "the lost generation" (*W/R*, p. 186).

If Jim had himself lost his hold on slippery fame, he was nonetheless still to pursue it vicariously by becoming a sportswriter in New York and by gathering around him a few of the young men, including Monk, who had idolized him at Pine Rock. These young men "represented the lost past to him. They represented his lost fame" (*W/R*, p. 250). His participation in athletic events appears in the depth of his involvement in the classic bout between Firpo and Dempsey. Jim was assigned the job of covering the activities at Firpo's camp, where he quickly developed sympathy for the Wild Bull of the Pampas.

Jim came, finally, to understand that bickering collegiate admirers and his projection of his own need for fame upon the shoulders of younger athletes were not pillars upon which to build his fame. In fact, "the period of his fame was past. . . . He now lived in a world of bitter memory" (*W/R*, p. 268). To escape those memories and to live the life of a romantic hero, he asked for an assignment in South America. He failed, in short, to lay firm hands on fame in New York. That deed would be accomplished by another athlete, a part-Cherokee baseball player named Nebraska Crane, and by Monk Webber, a novelist.

Nebraska and Monk had grown up sharing a love for wrestling and baseball. Nebraska's father, a police captain, had once wrestled professionally. Even when nearly fifty years old he sometimes entered the ring against local challengers. During one season in Libya Hill, he "met the whole series of sinister antagonists—Masked Marvels, Hidden Menaces, Terrible Turks, Mighty Swedes, Demon Dummies, and all the rest of them" (*W/R*, p. 48). Their other interest in sports, baseball, led to different ends, Monk becoming an admiring spectator, Nebraska turning his love of the game into a career. He rose to national acclaim by playing in the big leagues in New York, where his name "had been emblazoned in the paper everyday."[7]

While Crane had been climbing to the majors, Monk had attended college and later had struggled to establish himself as a writer. Upon returning from his first European voyage, Monk found a headline in the *Herald* leaping out at him: "Crane Slams Another Homer." Monk instantly felt "a strong desire to see Nebraska again and to get back in his blood once more the honest tang of America" (*Y/C*, p. 87). A telephone call to Nebraska led to a happy reunion, during which time Monk learned that his friend was beginning to feel his age after seven years at the top.

> "But, good Lord, Bras, you're all right! Why, the way you got around out there today you looked like a colt!"
>
> "Yeah," Nebraska said, "maybe I looked like a colt, but I felt like a plough horse." He fell silent again, then he tapped his friend gently on the knee with his brown hand and said abruptly: "No, Monkus. When you been in this business as long as I have, you know it." (*Y/C*, p. 61).

Despite his complaints, Nebraska the next day banged another homer.

For a period of four more years, Nebraska enjoyed the praise of devoted fans and teammates. When Monk next saw him, Nebraska was suffering from a pulled tendon and was on the disabled list. They met on a train heading for Libya Hill, to which Monk was now returning as a famous writer following the publication of his first novel, a widely celebrated work. Nebraska, now just thirty-one years old, was going home for a visit during his convalescence. He talked with Monk about the impending end of his playing career. Monk protested that Nebraska was much too young to think of quitting. Exhilarated by his fresh taste of fortune and fame, George could not understand Nebraska's "quiet resignation," for seemingly Nebraska was a man speaking of "a ready acceptance of defeat." Monk then realized that the Cherokee blood of his friend might offer an explanation, for from the Cherokees he had inherited a "cheerful fatalism" that "had always been the source of his great strength and courage" (*Y/C*, p. 64).

Unlike many fellow Libya Hillians on the same train, Nebraska, a man as close to nature as he is fatalistic, refuses to catch the land-speculation fever raging among the town's leading citizens. Three hundred acres of land to retire to and to raise tobacco on will be enough for him, he says. He lacks the slightest urge to gamble on making a fortune. Nor does he need to be nourished by the blandishment of fame. His inward strength requires no retinue of idolaters. He needs no adulation to remind him of his athletic prowess. To Monk's question about whether he could be content to live the unglamorous life of a farmer, Nebraska replies,

> "Huh? Satisfied?" Nebraska turned to him with a puzzled look. "How do you mean?"
>
> "I mean after all you've seen and done, Bras—the big cities and the crowds, and all the people shouting—and the headlines, and the World's Series—and—and—the first of March, and St. Petersburg, and meeting all the fellows again, and spring training—" (*Y/C*, p. 65).

What Nebraska had already learned about fame, Monk, now unable to fathom the wisdom of his old friend's easy dismissal of it, would learn again and again as he tried to enjoy the lionization his writing talent brought him. Another writer, Lloyd McHarg, had to teach him again the lesson Nebraska had for him. McHarg's hectic life and incurable suffering from "that infirmity of Noble mind" showed Monk unmistakably the hollowness of fame.

Much later, in a confessional mode, Monk confided to Foxhall Edwards, his editor and friend, the chief goals of his youth, Love and Fame.

> Love and Fame. Well, I have had them both.
>
> You told me once, Fox, that I did not want them, that I only thought I did. You were right. I wanted them desperately before I had them, but once they were mine I found that they were not enough. And I think, if we speak truth, the same thing holds for every man who ever lived and had the spark of growth in him. (*Y/C*, p. 723).

Eventually, Monk saw that his pursuit of love and fame had partially blinded him to a rot developing in America. When he recognized the nations' enemy, one of mankind's oldest, "single selfishness and compulsive greed (*Y/C*, p. 742), he virtually reasserted the values implicit in Nebraska's return to the soil, to a manner of life before America had lost its vision and before the selfish and greedy enemies of the country "stole our earth from us, destroyed our wealth, and rearranged and despoiled our land" (*Y/C*, p. 742).

Through his brief study then of how athletics formed one of the many threads of American life, Wolfe clearly saw how strong was the lure of fame, how slippery it could be, how worthless it was compared to other goals a person might set for himself and his nation. In his ultimate decline to single selfishness, Jim Randloph had become confused and lost. But Nebraska, as Wolfe conceived him, stood for the unspoiled America, "strong, simple, full of earth and sun" (*Letters*, p. 722).

Thus in the matter and form which the Webber cycle was taking before Wolfe's death, his two athletes would be developed as strongly contrasted figures and would touch upon Monk's growth and goals in significant ways. When Monk truly realized the emptiness of his youthful goals, he was prepared to say,

> By then life's weather had soaked in, although I was not fully conscious yet what seepings had begun, or where, in what directions, the channel of my life was flowing. All I knew was that I was exhausted from my labor, respiring from the race, conscious only, as is a spent runner, that the race was over, the tape breasted, and that in some measure I had won. (*Y/C*, p. 726).

These words appear in the Webber cycle, as arranged by Edward Aswell, after Monk has met McHarg and has experienced the wondrously warm acclaim which Monk's novel won in Germany. In view of the thematic development of the novel, Aswell placed them well. For by this point in the development of Monk's thought, the world of Jim Randolph, Lloyd McHarg, and Adolf Hitler is wrong, destructively wrong. Monk now more clearly perceived that Nebraska, the resilient part-Cherokee Indian baseball player offered, through the model of his life and ideals, something America needed.

No longer consumed by his overweening desire for love and fame, Monk would undertake the role of exploring the nation's diseased soul and of advocating more virtuous living. Randolph's case was a strong reminder of a diseased, lost soul. The healthy soul was Nebraska's. With men of such simple faith and firm principles lay one of the hopes of America. Wolfe came, at last, to set before his readers a polarity of values expressed through his characterization of two athletes, both of whom reflect and project a part of America, past, present, and future. In sum, Wolfe, with sensible assistance from Aswell, gave every sign of having woven his athletes expertly into the developing thematic patterns of the projected Webber cycle.

Notes

1. Richard Walser, *Thomas Wolfe Undergraduate* (Durham, N.C.: Duke Univ. Press, 1977), p. 104.

2. Thomas Wolfe, *Look Homeward, Angel* (New York: Charles Scribner's Sons, 1929), p. 493. Subsequent references to this novel are given in the text under the abbreviation *LHA.*

3. Thomas Wolfe, *Of Time and The River* (New York: Charles Scribner's Sons, 1935), pp. 157–58. Cited in the text as *T/R.*

4. Thomas Wolfe, *The Notebooks of Thomas Wolfe,* ed. Richard S. Kennedy and Paschal Reeves (Chapel Hill: Univ. of North Carolina Press, 1970), II, 517. Cited as *NB.*

5. Thomas Wolfe, *The Letters of Thomas Wolfe,* ed. Elizabeth Nowell (New York: Charles Scribner's Sons, 1956), pp. 720–21. Cited as *Letters.*

6. Thomas Wolfe, *The Web and The Rock* (New York: Harper and Brothers, 1939), p. 175. Cited as *W/R.*

7. Thomas Wolfe, *You Can't Go Home Again* (New York: Harper and Brothers, 1940), p. 57. Cited as *Y/C.*

The Plays

Thomas Wolfe's *Welcome to Our City*: An Angry Young Southerner Looks Back

Phyllis H. Lewis*

In May, 1923, Thomas Wolfe, then a student in the playwriting workshop of Harvard Professor George P. Baker, wrote in a letter to his mother this scathing criticism of his hometown:

> What I shall try to get into their dusty little pint-measure minds is that a full belly, a good automobile, paved streets, and so on, do not make them one whit better or finer,—that there is beauty in this world,—beauty even in this wilderness of ugliness and provincialism that is at present our country, beauty and spirit which will make us men instead of cheap Board of Trade Boosters, and blatant pamphleteers.[1]

The attitude reflected in these words had largely been formed during infrequent visits to Asheville while Wolfe was a student at Chapel Hill and later Cambridge. What probably gave particular force to this censure, however, was his absorption in his new play, titled *Niggertown*, later renamed *Welcome to Our City*,[2] in which he treated the themes of material progress and commercialism in a setting based on his perceptions of his hometown.

In rather typical fashion, *Welcome to Our City* demonstrates the sense of outrage and cynicism prevalent among sensitive young writers of the 1920's, but in some exceptional moments the play goes beyond mediocrity in revealing particular conflicts facing the South as it struggled to reconcile economic and social demands of the present with the traditions of its past. The late C. Hugh Holman has pointed out that Wolfe "belonged loosely with the New South School, which saw in industrial progress the key to a new and better life and believed that

*Reprinted from the *Thomas Wolfe Review*, 8, No. 1 (Spring 1984), 20–26.

the South must emerge from its retreat to the past into the reality of the modern world."[3] Holman argues further, however, that Wolfe had more in common with the group of traditionalist writers known as the Nashville Agrarians than he was willing to admit. He recognized, for example, the detrimental effects of industrialism and man's continuous need for transcendency. His works beckon us time and again to re-examine our spiritual roots with the hope of finding therein a clue to the inexplicable present. *Welcome to Our City* scrutinizes especially the South's memory of its own past and suggests that there may have existed formerly, in the abstractions dear to the Southern mind, an ordering principle that the advocates of purely material progress have unwisely abandoned.

The play is set in Altamont, a small Southern mountain town, recognizable as the locale of *Look Homeward, Angel.* The year is 1922, and Altamont, like the rest of America, has begun a spree of speculation and expansion. In ten scenes, the action presents a conflict between whites and blacks for possession of a tract of valuable inner-city property. Inspired by the influx of tourists and new residents, the town boosters have designed an urban renewal plan to impress the wealthy classes attracted to Altamont by the healthful mountain air and natural scenery. To carry out this plan, the Altamont Development Company must gain control of the central section, which offers the most advantageous site for new construction. Ironically, this section, never prized before the boom period, is the home of Altamont's black population.

When the play begins, the resident Negroes have already been notified by their white landlords that they must leave their homes. Most are resigned to leaving peacefully; trouble arises, however, when a property owner among them, a black physician named Johnson, refuses to sell his fine old house. Johnson's resistance pits him against an aging aristocrat, William Rutledge, who has personal motives for aligning himself with the town developers. The house had formerly belonged to Rutledge's father, who had been a slaveholder and a prominent citizen in the community. Rutledge had inherited the place from his father's estate, but because the Civil War had devastated the family's resources, he had to sell it when he was still a young man. Now a successful lawyer, Rutledge wants to reclaim it as a memento to the honor and dignity of his family. As the play progresses, Johnson becomes almost convinced to sell his house to Rutledge, but just before the hour for closing the deal, he discovers the son of his rival, Lee Rutledge, attempting to seduce his daughter Annie. Aided by a rabble-rouser from the North, Johnson incites the other Negroes to riot against the whites. The State militia is called out and several people are killed, including Johnson himself and an old Negro man who has taken no part in the conflict. The coveted house is completely destroyed by fire.

In the disparate motives of the characters who struggle for a single parcel of land, Wolfe has set up a polarity between the value system of antebellum Southern society and the creed of what had by 1922 begun to be termed the New South. At one extreme is Will Rutledge—sentimental, scholarly, professedly humanitarian, but just a little superfluous in this bustling city. On the other side are the moderns, represented by the booster-types, politicians, and merchants who promote progress and economic growth. These include Preston Carr, the Governor of the State; Henry Sorrell, president of the Altamont Development Company, and Joseph Bailey, secretary to the Altamont Board of Trade.

Unwilling to take sides himself, Wolfe often appears cynical about the efficacy of either set of ideals. Furthermore, by teaming the traditionalist Rutledge with the progressivists in a common effort to accomplish distinct purposes, Wolfe comments negatively on the ability of a society to progress so long as greed and egoism are the prevailing impulses. In contrast to the others, Rutledge suavely diverts attention from his baser motives by focusing on the idealistic aspects of his venture. He joins the realtors' development scheme to reclaim a family heritage, not to make money. Seen from another angle, though, his goals—to overpower a Negro man's will and to purify a shrine to White Supremacy—are as reprehensible as the narrow economic interests of the town developers. At least, they make no pretense about their reasons for wanting the Negroes removed. The area is an eyesore, a blight upon the city, and to attract the moneyed classes who can bring prosperity to the white population of the town, they must eradicate the blacks quickly and efficiently.

Though their methods unite them, differing attitudes toward the Rutledge ancestral home, which is the central symbol of the play, clearly distinguish the motives of the two groups and emphasize opposing views of Southern experience. The first reference to the house occurs in Scene 2 when Bailey, Secretary to the Board of Trade, speaking to Reeves Jordan, a newcomer to the city, points to the "old Rutledge home," which stands on the very summit of the town in the middle of the Negro district. A literary man, Jordan expresses considerable interest in the "fine old house"—it represents, he says, "feudalism—something we call the Old South." In his almost apologetic response, however, Bailey makes it clear that nostalgia for the past has no place in the current plans for the town's future.

These two views continue to be contrasted in the pairing of William Rutledge and Henry Sorrell in Scene 3. To Rutledge, the house represents the means for reviving an appealing way of life while to Sorrell its existence in the heart of the planned development area merely obstructs the desired changes. At one point Rutledge tries to communicate to Sorrell his sense of the importance of his mission:

> Yes, Sorrell, for we are buying back a kingdom today, my friend. We are buying back a treasure of memories and romance, so delicate, so

> rare, so far removed from this obscene push, that I almost hold my breath when ever I think of it. It's not dead! It's not dead! It sleeps—the one thing I yet dream of (Sc. 2).

The outcome of Rutledge's plan to recapture the past supports the conclusion that the past is actually the present—that there never has, in fact, been any change and probably never will be. The very nature of his design is structurally suspect. When asked by his wife about his intentions concerning the old homeplace, Rutledge admits that he cannot bear to return there to live, but he does not offer in substitution any real use for it. Perhaps he will give it to his son Lee at his marriage, he adds almost in afterthought, to pass on to his descendants. With dramatic irony, this resolution begins to form in the father's mind at the moment that Lee is acting out the old corruption of former generations. Having intruded into the Johnson home, he has approached the Negro girl Annie for sexual favors. Upon discovery of this, the girl's father has become enraged and the events are set into motion that will destroy Rutledge's dream forever. In this way the house becomes finally a reminder of something lost, but more importantly, the clue to recognizing that the trappings of the Old South had never signified more than an ideal. At this point, as Lee, the son and heir, returns to the place of his father's birth, the vision of the Old South melts into that of the New South. Insubstantial dreams shape behavior on both sides, and one is no more culpable or successful than the other. The conflagration and strife at the end of the play efface all hope for a return to a former time, and the animosities between rival groups seriously mar the prospects for a happier future.

Besides Rutledge, two other characters—Henry Sorrell's father, a veteran of the Civil War, and Amos Todd, an "Uncle Tom" among the blacks—demonstrate the futility of carrying on the externalities of a defunct social order. Dependent upon his son for a living, Old Sorrell comes into the real estate office one day to collect his allowance. Angered by his rejection by the younger generation, he gestures to his peculiar wound and complains, "I was good enough to go all through the Civil War and git a bullet hole in the roof o' my mouth big enough to stick yore fist through—but I ain't good enough now to be treated decent when I come to my own son's office." The younger Sorrell responds unsympathetically, "But the Civil War was over fifty years ago. We're living in different times today" (Sc. 3).

Like Sorrell and Rutledge, Amos Todd is an anachronism in his day. A shoe repairman by trade, Amos has found a way to make an adequate living and to exist peacefully among whites by accepting the narrow confines of his inferior social place. Loyal and humble, he actually prefers the servant role because it provides a buffer against a world he cannot understand. This false sense of security blinds him, though, to portents of disruption in his comfortable existence. While other blacks grow wary of their relations with whites, Amos retreats into a longing for a former time when life for Negroes seemed happy and protected. When finally the violence breaks out between the races, Amos is unprepared to act to save himself. As the rioting moves closer to his shop, his grandson warns him to flee, but the old man merely retorts, "I ain't gwine to budge, de white folks ain't got no grudge agin me" (Sc. 10). Shortly afterwards, he is killed when a stray bullet flies through his shop window.

By satirizing those who mistakenly believe in the continued validity of specious ideals, Wolfe shows his opposition to any attempt at romanticizing the Old South. On the other hand, he strongly rejects the crass methods of the New South proponents who have proceeded ruthlessly to shove the region into the industrial age. Whereas he renders Rutledge and Amos Todd with occasional sympathy, he ridicules the boosters, politicians, and clergy who have moved into their positions of power and wealth, not through any superiority of intellect or sensitivity of spirit, but by a well-developed pragmatism and a firm sight on the goal of economic prosperity. They represent, in Wolfe's view, the ominous direction of the modern South as the region prepared to compete commercially with other areas of the country.

Several scenes in the play show especially Wolfe's disapproval of the methods and ideals of the new class of aristocrats. When Henry Sorrell meets his old schoolteacher McIntyre, Sorrell, eager to reveal his success, disparages his teacher's classical learning. Comparing himself with those who made high marks in Latin and Greek, he boasts, "I suppose I'm doing about as well as those that took all that stuff. . . . I don't believe most of those fellows amount to much anyway" (Sc. 3). When the whole tribe of philistines gather for a society ritual at the Altamont Country Club, their chatter characterizes the vapidity of their minds. They discuss, for example, the new direction of higher education, which emphasizes instead of the humanities "the practical value of training"; that is, "the dollars and cents advantage." They prate about the "great recreational value of the fine arts," of ways "to sell people the idea of culture," of putting "the whole thing on a paying basis" (Sc. 4). Throughout this scene not a redeeming quality emerges.

Epitomizing the hypocrisy of the society, Governor Preston Carr, a fatuous, silly, pompous caricature of a human being, is singled out by Wolfe for special ridicule. Full of platitudes, Carr eagerly becomes the center of any group, with his boasts of the great things the State has accomplished and the greater things to come. One scene shows him in elaborate pantomime as he prepares for bed. He removes all that cosmetic art has provided—toupee, false teeth, shoe-risers, shoulder pads, braces, abdomen supporter; when he finally kneels to say his prayer, he seems "no more than a small pudgy and rather terrified boy." The effect is comic; yet in stage directions Wolfe implies a sinister element about the success of such a person. He has become successful through "an absolute and unscrupulous will to get what he wants most," and he has shown that "he will pander, bargain, compromise and cheat, and never lose the smile from his face" (Sc. 7).

In addition to exposing the artificiality of modern business and politics, Wolfe satirizes the modern church. Sorrell, for example, advises young Lee Rutledge that "church membership is a business asset these days, and you can't afford to overlook it" (Sc. 3). In a demonstration of the insensitivity of the clergy to human problems, the Reverend Smallwood ignores the sound of approaching rioting as he repeates the inane jargon of his profession. The dissenting Negroes, upset because they are being turned from their homes, are, in his words, "poor, strayed sheep" (Sc. 9).

In *Welcome to Our City* Wolfe has condemned the basic ideologies of both groups of his characters—the ones who romanticize the Old South and the others who worship material progress. The play confirms the lack of wisdom in looking upon a distorted view of the past to ameliorate the problems of the present or to shape the future. It also rejects bare faith in economic prosperity as a panacea. Wolfe's tone is mostly hostile, cynical, and satiric as he propounds the premise that real progress cannot be measured in concrete terms.

Occasionally, however, his bitterness and anger subside to reveal his strong belief in the dignity of man and the hope for a sustaining unity of spirit. This mood becomes especially apparent as William Rutledge accepts the reality of his present and the awful significance of his abortive attempt to glorify a sordid past. Becoming convinced of his distance from his son and indeed from his whole world, Rutledge grows in his awareness of the need for something outside himself to order his life and to bind him to others. The apex of his development as a character occurs at the end of the play as he watches his son Lee, dressed in the uniform of the modern soldier, shoot and kill his rival Johnson. In the background the old mansion is ablaze. Stricken by sorrow for all, Rutledge embraces his son and with these words seals their mutual bond of guilt: "We are joined in this blasted and deserted place—but we are joined" (Sc. 10).

This poignant expression of human solidarity could easily have been spoken by any of Thomas Wolfe's American contemporaries just after the end of the First World War, but its setting here has special relevance to the circumstances of the South in the early twentieth century as the region still struggled with the extinction of traditions and absolutes in the face of massive social and economic change. Rutledge becomes the spokesman for the sense of loss and defeat experienced by the modern Southerner. He pursued his dream of owning the property of his ancestors because it had vaguely represented for him the means of reaffirming significance and focus in his life. In comparison, the money-crazed schemes of the town developers appear petty and sterile. In some of Rutledge's final words, Wolfe clearly shifts the balance of sympathies toward the believers and the dreamers; despite the imperfections of the old system, he seems to be saying, there had been then the recognition of man's need to seek beyond the concrete world a centrality that is now disparaged. Expressing his unhappy awareness, Rutledge concludes, "There is nothing to die for. . . . And we have not even a hell left that we can go to" (Sc. 2). His position emphasizes the intensity of the loss of order for the twentieth-century Southerner, capable now of viewing the history of his land with some objectivity but still influenced by family and place to feelings of nostalgia and regret. Lost in a maze of confusion and guilt, Rutledge at one point summarizes the peculiar position of his people, "We lose what we have never had. And that . . . is the greatest loss" (Sc. 6).

Notes

1. C. Hugh Holman and Sue Fields Ross, eds., *The Letters of Thomas Wolfe to His Mother* (Chapel Hill: UNC Press, 1968), pp. 42–3.

2. Until this decade the only publication of this play was an abridgement, in the October, 1957, issue of *Esquire*. The complete typescript is part of the Wisdom Collection in the Houghton Library of Harvard University. Wolfe left two versions—the one he prepared in 1922 and 1923 with the title "Niggertown," produced by the 47 Workshop as "Welcome to Our City" [Harvard Univ. Library, *46AM-7 (11), (12)], and a revised and expanded form that he submitted to the Neighborhood Playhouse in 1924 in hope of securing a commercial production (Harvard *46AM-7 (13), 14). Scene numbers in this study refer to the latter version. The shorter version, edited by Richard S. Kennedy, was published by LSU Press in 1983.

3. C. Hugh Holman, *The Loneliness at the Core: Studies in Thomas Wolfe* (Baton Rouge: Louisiana State University Press, 1975), p. 117.

Thomas Wolfe's *Mannerhouse*

Jerry L. Rice*

The idea for *Mannerhouse* came to Wolfe very early in his Harvard career. In a letter to his mother probably written in 1920, he relates the story of a Southern aristocratic family impoverished by the Civil War and eventually destroyed by the new order that grows out of the reconstruction period. The family is to represent the entire Southern aristocracy. And their house is to be "the symbol of the old South, the

*Reprinted from the *Thomas Wolfe Review*, 6, No. 1 (Spring 1982), 25–34. © 1982 by the University of Akron, Akron, Ohio.

old aristocracy being torn down, to make place for the new, productive order."

Wolfe is often vague and general when he sets forth a new play idea. He is often able to tell what he wants to accomplish, but not how he is going to do it. In this letter, however, he outlines the complete plot of his play, names and describes all of the major characters, details the setting and the action; and even quotes some of the dialogue. There is certainly nothing indecisive about this early plan. Wolfe explains in this letter that the whole idea came to him in a flash and that he worked out the details of the play within three hours. The germ of the plot grew out of an incident related by his father. This genesis is important, for it shows Wolfe beginning with story and characters rather than with a message or a problem. In writing *Welcome to Our City*, Wolfe started with a desire to display the greed of his hometown; the story and characters came later.

The outline of this new drama is found in the same letter in which Wolfe recounts the plot of "The Mountains," a very conventional piece. It is not surprising, then, to find that the plans for *Mannerhouse* are rather traditional. Even though it was not completed until after the radical *Welcome to Our City*, the dramatist retained the original format. Thus, Wolfe was not firmly committed to the unusual staging techniques employed in *Welcome to Our City*. When the story allowed it, he was quite content to return to the more common form of drama.

Wolfe concludes the descriptions of his play with his usual enthusiasm, saying, "Well, I have the stuff for a fine play here. . . . I'm so fired up by it that I'm rushing doing [*sic*] at a tremendous clip." The fire must have been extinguished almost as quickly as it was ignited, for the idea was not mentioned again until May 1921, when Wolfe wrote his mother that Baker was anxious for him to complete the play, "the first act of which he [Baker] had last year, and liked." According to another letter Wolfe wrote to his mother in March 1923, Baker had still seen only the first act. During the three years which had passed since he had been fired up by this idea, the dramatist had evidently done no work on it. In this last letter, Wolfe mentioned his plans to complete *Mannerhouse* and enter it with *Welcome to Our City* in a Workshop contest. Again he lost interest in the project. After he had left Harvard and had started teaching at New York University, he wrote his mother that he had "a prolog, two acts, and part of the third finished." Thus, the idea for *Mannerhouse* was with Wolfe during most of his Harvard years; but, for some reason, he never really settled down to work with it until he was ready to leave Cambridge.

When he did finally begin intensive writing, however, his faith was as strong as ever. In a fragmentary letter tentatively dated July 1923 (but which might have been written after he left Harvard), he wrote,

"I think my play 'The House' will 'pack a punch' for it is founded on a sincere belief in the essential inequality of things and people, in a sincere belief in the necessity of some form of human slavery . . . and it deals . . . with the one period in our history that believed these things and fought for them and was destroyed because of its belief in them." In this statement, Wolfe shows a change in emphasis. The original play was a simple story of the Southern aristocracy. In this new plan, Wolfe shows a concern for the slavery issue. Because of this shift in emphasis, he moved the time of the play back to the start of the Civil War rather than its conclusion.

In 1924 the dramatist took the still uncompleted manuscript to Europe, where it was stolen. The theft was evidently just the blow he needed to goad him on, for he then vowed to rewrite it in two weeks. And in sixteen days he had a completed first draft. Thus, after many years of procrastination, false starts, and delays, Wolfe finally forced himself to settle down to the business of writing *Mannerhouse*. It is curious that he postponed the work on this piece so often. It is true he expresses excitement in his letters; but each enthusiastic account of his plans for this drama is followed by a period of silence, often lasting for more than a year. This indifference prevailed even after *Mannerhouse* was finished.

In its final form, *Mannerhouse* opens with a powerful prologue in which we see Ramsay's slaves building the House. Their work is interrupted when a minister comes to welcome Ramsay, a Southern gentleman, to his new home and to pray for his Negroes. Ramsay indicates that the laborers are to kneel down for this blessing. One giant black, obviously a leader, realizes the significance of the minister's incantations and refuses to kneel. Ramsay knocks him down, and the minister prays. His supplication states the thesis of slavery in *Mannerhouse:*

> Oh God, we beseech Thee, be merciful to us . . . and to these wretched heathen whom Thou hast delivered unto our care; vouchsafe that we may be kind and just and temperate in our dealings with them, and that we may lead them with Thy love, from the dark forest. Thou hast made men, O God—likewise hast Thou made masters—Thou has put Thy mark and Thy injunction on both. . . . And these Thou has delivered unto us. Hear us and answer us, O God, so that in time these souls which have lived in error may be brought to light, That through Christ's love and blood and sacrifice upon the Cross, the souls of these savages may all at length be saved. (pp. 10–11)

This belief in the divine providence of slavery forms the basis of Ramsay's life. As a result, the war becomes more than a commercial venture where the wealthy fight to protect their property. After the minister exits, the giant Negro attempts to kill Ramsay. The gentleman prostrates him with the butt of his gun. When the slave recovers, he drags himself away; and Ramsay says, "It is well. He was strong before; now he will be faithful" (p. 15). At the end of the prologue, the giant falls to his knees before Ramsay, who says, "It is the first time a king has kissed my hand. What he has done the others must do. I will be king in my own right. . . . My God! Is this, then, how a prayer is answered? . . . Oh then, our cause is one, God" (p. 16). The curtain closes to the sound of the savage chants of the Negroes and of a church bell ringing in the distance. Thus, Wolfe establishes a powerful religious motivation for the subsequent action. The slaves have become a divine trust; and the war, then, can become a crusade for a holy ordinance. In addition, the dramatist provides an explanation of Ramsay's character. The prologue reveals the birth of a king and his kingdom. Without this scene all of Ramsay's subsequent speeches would sound like the simple rantings of a pompous egoist.

Act I opens on the eve of the war. The scene is inside the completed house as the Ramsay family and their peers celebrate the coming march to battle. As in Wolfe's original plan for this play, Ramsay (now a general) has two sons. The older, Ralph, is a copy of his father. Eugene, the younger, is the poetic voice of truth, a combination of Hamlet, Cassandra, and Oscar Wilde. Despite the identical names, the hero of *Mannerhouse* is not the autobiographical Eugene of *Look Homeward, Angel.* Eugene Ramsay does occasionally speak for the dramatist, but he is a much more fictionalized character than is Eugene Gant. Wolfe's description of the original hero fits the character of the final version of the play. He says that "Eugene, the younger, is filled with bitterness and broods in his heart because his father and brother will not wake up and realize that they are making no efforts to avert ruin." The rest of the characters think he is a coward as he ridicules the war and the stupid allegiance to a romanticized past that is leading them to the slaughter. Even his mother is blinded by the philosophy. When she cries that she is giving a husband and two sons to the cause, Eugene replies with typical sarcasm:

> EUGENE. Pardon me, Mother, but aren't you being a little too generous—shall I say extravagant with your gifts? . . . after all, it is my life you are giving, isn't it?
>
> MRS. RAMSAY. Ah, Gene, I would offer my own gladly, but we women can only wait.
>
> EUGENE. Very trying, I'll admit, Mother, but comparatively safe. To be quite frank, Mother, I have a sort of proprietary interest in my own hide which you so generously are offering up to the careful inspection of an enemy who will not hesitate to shoot it full of holes. (p. 39)

And so Eugene mocks the hypocrisy of the entire Southern tradition. He scoffs at his father's illusion that these soldiers are gentlemen in the romantic tradition, knights protecting a kingdom, crusaders in defense of Truth. Even so, Eugene dons the regimental uniform to follow his father.

Meanwhile, Porter, one of Ramsay's tenant farmers, pleads for the release of his own son from the army, explaining that the boy is needed to work the farm and adds that this war is not the poor man's fight. The general is shocked by this "unworthy and dishonorable request" p. 52). In a grandiose gesture of disdain, Ramsay promises to sign the land and the house which Porter occupies over to him as payment for the boy. Prideless, Porter accepts.

At the end of the first act, the men march off to war. And "somewhere within the house . . . there is a displeasing sound—the sound of a single large drop of water which somewhere forms, swells, develops, and falls at length with an unvarying and punctual monotony" (p. 82).

An interlude between the acts depicts the jubilant marching of the soldiers to war and their stumbling retreat.

In Act II the conquered heroes return to the House. Ralph has been killed, the army has been "defeated, but not beaten" (p. 98), the aristocracy has been impoverished, while Porter has made steady financial gains with his land. And the general finds his empire crumbling; all his slaves, except the giant Tod, have deserted him. The scene closes with the sound of the drop of water falling again.

The second part of this act is the death scene of the General a few months later. Since no specific malady is mentioned, we assume that the old man is succumbing to the effects of having his kingdom destroyed. His last duty is to see that the House continues. So he sells it to Porter, thus signing away Eugene's rights. It is obvious that Eugene would not have perpetuated the House, but Ramsay fails to explain why he thinks that Porter will. The General dies, and the scene ends with the sound of mighty wings beating in the distance.

In Act III, some years later, Eugene returns, posing as a carpenter so that he can help Porter raze the house. Margaret, the girl-next-door who has loved him all this time, tries to take Eugene away, but insisting that he has one more job to complete, he sends her home to wait for him. Eugene then attempts to help tear down the house, but he cannot strike a blow against it. Instead, he attacks Porter, who has been goading him on. The other carpenters lead Eugene outside, where, Samson-like, he wrenches one of the giant columns from its decayed base. It falls on him, pinning him to the floor. He calls to the Negro inside, "Tod! Tod! Oh, I have failed! Tod! Here was a House. It was by you begun; by you it must be ended" (p. 182). The servant leaps into the room and is attacked by the carpenters and Porter. Porter stabs Tod, who "makes no resistance, but when the man is done, sinks slowly forward upon him, and breaks him in his mighty grip" (p. 182). All the men are trapped inside the room as the walls tumble down on them. The curtain falls to the sound of the crashing house "followed by silence save for the faint far ending of a waltz which dies upon the wind; save for a merciless little drop of water which somewhere swells, develops, and falls at length with punctual, unvarying monotony" (p. 182).

One can see from this outline that *Mannerhouse* is as packed with expressionistic symbolism as was *Welcome to Our City*. A critic reviewing the published play for *The New Republic* said it is "frequently top-heavy with a symbolism which misses absurdity only because the scale is grand." It may miss absurdity, but it certainly does not miss ambiguity. Wolfe often fails to indicate what the symbols are supposed to represent. In addition to the representational importance of the Ramsay family and the House itself, the dramatist includes such devices as the drop of water, the beating of wings, and the ostentatious uniforms of the soldiers. At the first sound of the drop of water, the General says, "Do you hear, Tod? Water is falling somewhere in the house. There is a leak. Find it and stop it" (p. 82). It is not clear what this leak is supposed to represent or why Tod must be the one to stop it. The stage directions say that "The Negro begins to circle the room, in a foiled search, with great strides . . . until at length he is circling the room like a great hound, making baffled, snarling noises in his throat" (p. 83). This is very histrionic, but not very illuminating. If Wolfe wants the leak to represent a specific weakness in a specific facet of the aristocracy, he certainly does not indicate it in the text. The wings beating at the death of the General, on the other hand, are so obvious that an audience would probably find them absurd.

Between these two extremes lies Wolfe's use of the army uniform to represent the sham of the war. He finds the plumes of the soldiers' hats particularly effective for this. Eugene sees in these feathers all the superficiality of the General's cause; later, when Eugene returns from the war as a defeated soldier, the stage directions indicate that "there is subtle mockery in the angle at which he wears his incredibly battered hat, with its soiled, awkward plume" (p. 98).

The farrago of symbols is not, however, the only weakness in *Mannerhouse*. Another fault comes from the fact that Wolfe is not certain what the major theme is. We have seen that he originally thought to relate the story of the fall of an aristocratic family; later, he wanted to show his belief in the necessity of slavery. Still later, after it was completed, Wolfe explained the meaning of *Mannerhouse* in a letter probably to Miss Alice Lewisohn of The Neighborhood Playhouse. He wrote, "My play tries to express a passionate belief in all myth, in the necessity of defending and living not for truth—but for divine falsehood. . . . It contains the first complete expression of that thing that has fascinated and terrified me since I was a child. Are we alive or dead? Who shall tell us? Which of the people in this play are ghosts, and which are living?" Thus, at one time or another, Wolfe held four totally different ideas about the dominant theme of this piece; and Eugene seems to be the spokesman for all of them. But it is often difficult to be sure whether his speeches are commenting on the necessity for divine falsehood, the question of reality and illusion, the slavery issue, or the inevitable ruin of his family. The other characters seldom attempt to grasp what Eugene talks about. Either they understand him implicitly and ignore him, or they pay no attention to his banter because it is incomprehensible. Eugene is a Hamlet-type character whose speeches have all the madness of Shakespeare's hero. But without Hamlet's reasons for feigning madness, Eugene seems genuinely insane. So the character of the hero demonstrates another weakness in the play. Neither his own philosophy nor his interrelationships with the other characters is entirely clear.

In addition, the character of Margaret is not clearly defined. In the original plan she was to provide the love interest. At the final curtain she and Eugene were to walk down the path away from the House, towards a new life. And as they left, they were to hear the sound of hammering and realize that "a castle is being torn from it's [*sic*] foundation, a mansion of the past is falling before the inexorable call of To-morrow." In the new ending she leaves Eugene alone in the House. But it is her ghostly voice calling from the deep recesses of the mansion that urges Eugene to pull the pillar from the porch. This climax is theatrically more spectacular, but it forces the already shadowy figure of Margaret even further into the background. And Margaret certainly is shadowy. Eugene calls her "Ghost," tells her she is not real, and speaks to her as if she were dead. By the time he sends her away in the third act, she herself is unsure of her existence. So perhaps Eugene just imagines that Margaret's voice calls to him before he starts to tear the house down in the spectacular climax. Margaret's presence in the play is never quite clear.

The theatrical ending exemplifies another weakness which we have already seen in Wolfe's dramas. Again he depends on the special-effects men and his own stage directions to do the job that his dialogue should have done. The crashing conclusion achieves most of its power through artificial auditory and visual effects. The actors have few important lines, and their action is simply designed to complement the technical spectacle.

Wolfe's dependence on stage directions is visible in the strictly narrative description for the opening scene. One paragraph from the three pages of directions is enough to establish the point:

> SCENE: Upon a hillside in the South two hundred years ago. A primitive landscape is in the process of conversion. Here, on top, where the hill is round, and before it slopes away to the East, a clearing has been made in the dense undergrowth of young pine, oak, chestnut, and laurel. It is early summer, but in that warm lush wooded place, the brown and fragrant needles of the pines yet carpet the earth. (p. 1)

This is not a stage direction; it is a descriptive vignette. As will be seen later, this kind of writing cannot be used as a guide for designing a stage setting.

In spite of these weaknesses, however, there are moments of extremely powerful drama. We have seen that the prologue is such a moment. In addition, there is a brilliant travesty on the aristocracy in a scene where both General Ramsay and Major Patton, his friend and neighbor, go to great lengths in their efforts to ignore the defeat of their social class. The Major, with all the delicacy of a foreign ambassador, admits that he is "temporarily a bit hard pressed" (p. 124). The General begs to be allowed to help him and discovers that he himself is "out of ready currency . . . at the moment!" (p. 125). Ramsay insists on writing a check, only to remember that his account is overdrawn. He solves this problem saying, "However, I shall simply give you the check, and you may fill in the date as soon as I make a deposit" (p. 126). The Major writes an I.O.U. in which he agrees to repay the loan just as soon as he is able. No money has changed hands, and none is likely to. But both gentlemen have retained their pride.

The scenes between Ramsay and Porter also are generally effective. There is no obscurity in the dialogue, simply a portrayal of two different worlds. Wolfe contrasts Ramsay's pompous speeches on dignity, honor, and tradition with Porter's illiterate rants on the practical facts of life. Because of these extremes, each character is both pitiable and admirable; and the scenes between them are fine examples of delineation through dialogue.

Moreover, Wolfe's dialogue is often poetically concise and yet pregnant with meaning. The following scene between Mrs. Ramsay and Bynum, a slave who left Ramsay when the law freed him, demonstrates this:

> MRS. RAMSAY. And why are you here now?
>
> BYNUM. To see de Marse.
>
> MRS. RAMSAY. You have no master, Bynum—you have deserted him. Perhaps the time will come when you will be sorry for the way you have treated your good master, the master who was always so kind to you.
>
> BYNUM. Yas'm.
>
> MRS. RAMSAY. Until that time Bynum, never show yourself around this house again. Really, I don't see how you can look us in the face . . .
>
> *The Negro Bynum goes off with straggling steps. She looks after him, striving hard to control her wounded pride and curiosity. Recalling him with an impulsive cry.*
>
> Bynum!
>
> BYNUM. Yas'm.

MRS. RAMSAY. Why did you go?

BYNUM. Why I don't know, Mis' Mary. I reckon it was 'case we knowed we could. (pp. 90–92)

With these few lines and the simple action, Wolfe has forcefully shown the abysmal gap between the belief that slavery was divinely ordained and the inherent desire of man to be free. These moments of powerful theater are, however, too few and too far apart to suggest that *Mannerhouse* is a great play. Its production history suggests that it is not even a good play.

When Wolfe returned from Europe in the fall of 1925, he submitted *Mannerhouse* to the Theatre Guild. Again he was faced with weeks of silence, until he finally wrote a letter demanding the return of the manuscript. The Guild's play reader replied that *Mannerhouse* was momentarily due to be voted on by the board of selection. So Wolfe agreed to let them keep the play until they reached a decision.

Meanwhile, Professor Koch had suggested that Wolfe take his play to Sheldon Cheney of the Actors' Theatre. In addition, the playwright sent copies to The Neighborhood Playhouse and the Provincetown Players. So he began the job of "peddling" his work among the theatrical companies of New York. But Wolfe was not a peddler. In a letter to his sister, Mabel Wolfe Wheaton, he explained, "My greatest deficiency is a total lack of salesmanship. . . . I never sent my plays to more than two or three managers and if I got no answer within a month I wrote insulting letters demanding their return." And so his attempts to sell the play were unsuccessful.

It is not clear whether Wolfe or the production companies lost interest first. None of the people involved make any further comments on this piece. Wolfe set sail for Europe in June 1926; and, in July, he wrote to Mrs. Roberts that he had begun work on a novel. Wolfe never again expressed any desires to be a dramatist. Thus, the last chapter of his career in the theater is strangely undramatic. When he submitted *Mannerhouse* to the Neighborhood Playhouse, he wrote the customary letter telling the director what the play meant to him. That letter ends simply: "Read it carefully, Miss Lewisohn. Certainly men have felt like this, but I have never seen it expressed." After that, Wolfe, the dramatist, was silent. There were no vitriolic letters of defense. There were no tortured cries over scenes that should be changed. There were, in fact, no suggestions for changes; for apparently there were no negotiations. The drama was mysteriously dropped. And Wolfe started work on *Look Homeward, Angel.*

He didn't forget the play entirely, however; for he devoted a chapter in *Of Time and the River* to a reading of it by Eugene, the hero of the novel. In the narrative, *Mannerhouse* is the title of a play which Eugene has written. This chapter provides a unique opportunity to see the novelist's later attitude towards his own play. Wolfe sounds like a drama critic as he points out the features of the good scenes and the faults of the bad. He writes that "The scenes between the hero and his father . . . were good; . . . as were those between the hero and Porter. . . . But the scenes between the hero and the girl were less successful: the character of the girl was shadowy and uncertain—a kind of phantasmal combination of the characters of Roxane in *Cyrano*, and Ophelia" (p 545). He concludes that *Mannerhouse* "was made up both of good and bad . . . it was marked by the varied influence of . . . Shakespeare, Chekhov, Shaw, Rostand, the Bible" (p. 549).

Wolfe, as the omniscient author, tries to be objective in his analysis of the play. For the most part, he is successful, albeit somewhat sentimental. Describing the prologue, he concludes, "This was a fine scene, and should have been beautiful and moving on the stage" (p. 549). And Wolfe seems to grow a bit nostalgic about his offering. But curiously there is no hint of bitterness connected with the play. In the context of the novel, Eugene is content to read the manuscript to his friends; he has no particular desire to have it produced. Perhaps Wolfe here is rationalizing the failure of the real play by implying that he, like his fictional counterpart, made no effort to sell it to any theater companies. On the other hand, Wolfe could have used this fictional incident to satirize and ridicule the directors of the theater groups he had actually dealt with. He often did this in his writing, as in the descriptions of Professor Hatcher's playwriting classes or The School for Utility Cultures in this same novel. But the novelist is content to read and discuss the play, then forget it. This seems to be what Wolfe did in real life. Compared to his comments about his other dramas, Wolfe's comments on the finished offering amount to an apathetic silence.

When *Mannerhouse* was published, in 1948, it received mixed critical comments. Most of the critics viewed it as a curiosity. An affirmative estimate from the New York *Herald Tribune* said "it is interesting to have it in print at last, because it is the work of an artist who for all his egocentricity and rhetorical excesses had distinct affinities for the dramatic form. . . ." The reviewer for the *New Yorker* also recognized dramatic talents in *Mannerhouse*. Neither of these, however, was able to give it unqualified praise. The negative comments can be represented by the *New York Times* reviewer, who says that "it is rarely a better-than-average sophomoric philosophical melodrama." George White Graice, of *Theatre Arts*, passes it off as "so much lingual fancy-work." Most of the critics, however, recognized some moments of power. Thus, *Mannerhouse* was thought to be at best an indication of what Wolfe *might* have accomplished in the theater, at worst a fine reason for him to have changed to the narrative form.

The New York Times announced that a theater group called New Stages was planning a New York production of *Mannerhouse*. But no record or comment about such a product is to be found in the usual bibliographical sources. There is, in fact, no indication that the play has ever been done in the United States.[1]

In Germany, however, there have been two productions of it. Gustaf Gruendgens, one of West Germany's most important directors, produced *Herrenhaus*, a translation by Peter Sandberg. The first time, it was offered at the Schauspielhaus in Duesseldorf November 12, 1953; and "on the opening night there were enthusiastic ovations and fifty curtain calls." A second production, in the Deutsche Schauspielhaus of Hamburg on January 26, 1956, was "hailed as a major theatrical event of the season." The success of the play represented the success of both Wolfe and Gruendgens. It is obvious that Wolfe's piece could not have been brought to the stage without some careful adapting. For example, the literary quality of the opening stage directions, as we have seen, presents a problem in scenic design. Of course, one could create a set that would fulfill the various requirements of Wolfe's directions; but that would mean the loss of fine prose writing. Gruendgens recognized the literary power of the playwright's descriptions of the scene and the impossibility of recreating it visually. So he used the unorthodox technique of having an actor read the opening stage directions. Gruendgens' production then, is a combination of the narrative prose and the dramatic elements of *Mannerhouse*. It represents, of course, a compromise. But, then, the play itself is a compromise, Wolfe's last compromise with the dramatic medium.

Behind all of Wolfe's work with this piece, we have seen an attitude of comparative indifference. Moments of extreme enthusiasm over it were countered by long periods when he apparently ignored it completely. Wolfe spread the writing over a period of four years, and then he rewrote it in two weeks. He sent copies of it to four different theater groups, and he wrote a couple of letters about it. Then he mysteriously let the matter drop.

This vacillation indicates two things about *Mannerhouse*. The fact that he took so long to write it shows that Wolfe was not nearly as fired up about it as he thought he was. He began serious work on it after the failure of *Welcome to Our City*. But by that time he had become thoroughly disgusted with the red tape connected with Theater. In the April 1924 letter in which he completely rejected *Welcome to Our City*, he wrote, "My love of the theatre has grown: my dislike of most of the people I have met who are concerned with the theatre has grown, also." He recounted his frustrations in his attempts to get the Guild to read his play and concluded that "a mere course in play-writing is not enough. There should be a sister course in peddling, auctioneering, servility, fawning, licking, and whining—a kind of sales-course you know."

I believe this attitude governed his attempts to sell *Mannerhouse*. By the time he returned from Europe, he had already thought of writing something other than drama; and he was in no mood to enter into any long frustrating negotiations with the Theatre Guild over a play that had never been extremely important to him anyway. Thus, *Mannerhouse* represents an indifferent final attempt in the drama. The play itself is a mixture of good and bad dramaturgy, brilliant and ambiguous dialogue, and typical Wolfean narrative prose.

Notes

1. Although no *commercial* production of *Mannerhouse* seems ever to have been staged in the United States, there has been at least one university production of it. On May 5, 6, and 7, 1949, for its fiftieth anniversary, the Yale Dramatic Association presented this play (editor's note).

The Short Fiction

"An Angel on the Porch" and *Look Homeward, Angel*

Guy Owen*

Many readers who encounter Thomas Wolfe's "An Angel on the Porch"—one of his best short stories—are often misled into thinking they are reading a chapter of *Look Homeward, Angel.* For example, it is reprinted in *The American Tradition in Literature* with a note indicating that it later appeared as Chapter XIX of the novel, nowhere suggesting that Wolfe re-shaped and extensively revised the material from the novel.[1] Mabel Wolfe Wheaton also refers to it as a chapter from *Look Homeward, Angel.*[2] And Wolfe himself is misleading here, for in *You Can't Go Home Again* he wrote of his alter ego George Webber's euphoria in having his first novel accepted: "Rodney's [*Scribner's*] Magazine, too, had become interested in the young author and was going to publish a story, a chapter from the book in their next number."[3]

One recalls the often repeated story of the meeting when Max Perkins and Wolfe were going over the massive manuscript of the novel before launching into the painful and arduous task of revising it. When they came to this episode in which Gant sells the angel to mark a young prostitute's grave, Wolfe blurted that he knew the material was too strong and would have to come out. " 'Take it out?' Perkins exclaimed. 'It's one of the greatest short stories I have ever read!' "[4]

As we know, "An Angel on the Porch" did appear in the August 1929 issue of *Scribner's Magazine* as "The first work of a new writer about whom much will be heard this fall,"[5] two months before *Look Homeward, Angel* was published. But before turning the story over to the magazine's editors, Wolfe must have realized that, in spite of Perkins' confidence, his manuscript was not really a conventional story, or at least not a remarkably good one. Very few chapters of novels can be printed without some revision, and Wolfe's was no exception. He set to with his customary zeal for re-working a manuscript, and it is,

*Reprinted from the *Thomas Wolfe Newsletter*, 4, No. 2 (Fall 1980), 21–24. © 1980 by the University of Akron, Akron, Ohio.

I think, interesting and instructive to note the substantive changes he made in it and to suggest the reasons for them.[6]

The most important revisions were made at the beginning of the story—though significant changes occur on every page of "An Angel on the Porch." In looking over Chapter XIX, Wolfe must have noted that the scene began undramatically, taking place in something of a vacuum. More importantly, Elizabeth, the bawdyhouse madam, was not introduced until almost two and a half pages into a seven-and-a-half-page chapter. What to do?

Wolfe wrote a new opening for "An Angel" in which Queen Elizabeth is introduced in the very first line, along with Oliver Gant and his tombstones, which establish the mood of the story. He also created suspense and conflict in the second sentence with " 'There goes the Queen,' said Gant, stopping their debate" (p. 205). The slabs of death and the simpering angel are brought forward here from the sixth page of Chapter XIX,[7] setting up an immediate tension with the fountain in the square, Wolfe's symbol of life, which is introduced in Chapter XIX before the images of death. Interestingly enough, Wolfe has Elizabeth observe here almost exactly what Oliver Gant had noted as a young man in Baltimore: ". . . turning her candid stare upon smooth granite slabs of death, carved lambs and cherubim within the shop, and finally an angel poised upon cold phthisic feet, with a smile of soft stone idiocy, stationed beside the door. . ." (p. 205). This combines phrases from page 4 and page 264 of the novel.

Then, realizing the need for a more sharply defined setting, he swiftly sketched in Gant's marble shop, economically employing details and one whole paragraph from the earlier Chapter IX,[8] careful to omit young Eugene, who was the observer there. (Incidentally, he would return to some of this material in "The Four Lost Men."[9])

Any reader who compares the two openings will recognize the effectiveness of Wolfe's revision. Moving Queen Elizabeth forward, together with the symbolic angel, makes the story's opening far more compelling, as well as being easier to get into. After establishing at once that Gant and Elizabeth had been lovers, which the novel does not do, Wolfe could then pick up the first page of Chapter XIX, which introduces Gant, Jannadeau, and Altamont's square—though no city or state is named in "An Angel."

But even here he makes several important changes. For one thing, with the addition of "That proud and sensual flesh was on its way to dust" (p. 206), he lets the reader know immediately that Gant is dying. He also points up the symbolism of the angel—not at all clear in Chapter XIX, though it is established as early as the second page of the novel—by adding that Gant's stiffened hand had once carved "so cunningly the dove, the lamb, and cold joined hands of death (but never the soft stone face of an angel)" (p. 206), echoing from the novel: "He never learned to carve an angel's head" (p. 4). With these revisions the second page of "An Angel" is clear to a reader who has not read the novel.

In addition to writing a new first page, Wolfe omitted almost all of the second page of Chapter XIX, for reasons that should be obvious. Because he did not want to clutter up his story with too many characters, he cut out Helen and her young friend who kisses Gant, effective as this little flashback is. Besides, by keeping the young "virgins" and their drugstore admirers, he had already established the important contrast of youth and age, innocence and experience.

Having made the cut, Wolfe obviously needed a new transition, which he kept simple and effective. Retaining the tag from the deleted scene, he wrote a brief paragraph: "Gant looked and saw. His thin mouth was tickled by a faint sly smile. He wet his thumb quickly" (p. 206). Then back to the present and the argument with the Swiss watch repairman, before Elizabeth's return to purchase the angel for the grave of Lillian Reed. Here he adds that the madam was "bound homeward for her latticed terrace" (p. 207), apparently recalling the bawdyhouse Eugene visits much later in Exeter: "The Negro rapped gently at the latticed door. There were always latticed doors. Why?" (p. 407).

As indicated earlier, Wolfe was prepared to drop this whole episode from *Look Homeward, Angel.* One would be surprised, then, if he did not tone down the rather sensational scene for the readers of *Scribner's.* As a matter of fact, he does in two different places. Elizabeth calls the dead prostitute's hard-hearted father a "bastard" twice in Chapter XIX. This is changed to "old devil" and "dirty old crook," which makes less obvious the combination of the gutsy and the sentimental in the madam. More important, in the novel Wolfe has Elizabeth say of the deceased prostitute, " 'She went like that—one hemorrhage right after another, *down here!*' "*She tapped her abdomen*" [italics added]. "An Angel" leaves out the italicized words, an omission which blurs the implication that the young woman died from a bungled abortion. However, these seem to be the only changes Wolfe made for the sake of propriety.

There are, to be sure, numerous other minor changes or additions, but they are for stylistic reasons or for clarification. For example, after a reference to Cynthia, Wolfe adds, "the name of his first wife." After Gant says that he had spoken to Lillian Reed only recently, Wolfe writes for the sake of irony: "He convinced himself permanently that this was true." This he borrows from Gant's earlier reaction to the death of Jim Bowles: " 'I was talking to him the day before I went away,' he lied, convincing himself permanently that this was true" (p. 72). Other changes are decidedly minor: an extra adverb cut in one instance and added in another; *pleasantly* changed to *cheerfully* to avoid repetition; *regarded* changed to *looked* for the sake of parallelism; *shocked* changed to *startled* apparently because Wolfe felt it was more evocative, using it twice on one page of "An Angel." A few other sentences are rewritten for the sake of euphony. In one instance, however, Wolfe should have let well enough alone: he changed "There was laughter from the square" to "There was from the square laughter."

Although the repetition of the slabs of death and the symbolic angel serves beautifully to stitch "An Angel" together (they are not so used in Chapter XIX), Wolfe might have omitted some of the repetition in the story. For instance, Jannadeau probes into "the entrails of a watch" in the first paragraph, then later "into the viscera of a watch." In shifting his material around, Wolfe was not always careful enough in re-writing it or dropping it entirely. (Incidentally, the reader of "An Angel" loses one devastating bit of irony; that is that Elizabeth, Gant's former lover, shares the name of his wife, whose love of property Gant loathed, while here he praises the madam for her wise investments!)

To sum up, "An Angel on the Porch" is not simply a chapter from *Look Homeward, Angel,* in spite of what both editors and author have written.[10] It is a meticulously revised and re-shaped version of Chapter XIX, plus a re-written page from Chapter IX, as well as remembered details and phrases from Chapters I, VII, and XXIX. A study of Wolfe's numerous changes reveals him struggling with the form of the conventional short story. No one should question the worth of his efforts, for the result is a mature work of art, far superior as a story to any of the "stories" in *From Death to Morning.*

Notes

1. See the footnote on page 1360 of *The American Tradition in Literature,* 4th ed., II, edited by Sculley Bradley, Richmond Croom Beatty, E. Hudson Long and George Perkins (New York: Grosset & Dunlap, 1974).

2. Mabel Wolfe Wheaton, with LeGette Blythe, *Thomas Wolfe and his Family* (Garden City, N. Y.: Doubleday, 1961), caption on photograph, opposite p. 169.

3. *You Can't Go Home Again* (New York: Grosset & Dunlap, 1940), p. 20.

4. A. Scott Berg, *Max Perkins: Editor of Genius* (New York: E. P. Dutton, 1978), p. 131).

5. *Scribner's Magazine* 86 (August, 1929), 205. All subsequent references will appear in the text.

6. There were also dozens of changes in punctuation, italics and capitalization that were probably made by a conservative editor at the magazine. In addition, several of Wolfe's long convoluted sentences were broken up, making them easier to read.

7. *Look Homeward, Angel* (New York: Random House), p. 264. All subsequent references will appear in the text.

8. *Look Homeward, Angel,* p. 100.

9. *From Death to Morning* (New York: Grosset & Dunlap), p. 120.

10. C. Hugh Holman wrote, "An Angel on the Porch" . . . had been drawn directly out of *Look Homeward, Angel* in *The Loneliness at the Core: Studies in Thomas Wolfe* (Baton Rouge: Louisiana State University Press, 1975), p. 59.

Thomas Wolfe's "Chickamauga": The Fact and the Fiction

John S. Phillipson*

1 THE BACKGROUND

Writing to Hamilton Basso on July 13, 1937, Thomas Wolfe said that in eight weeks that spring he had produced six short stories, including "Chickamauga," "one of the best stories I ever wrote." Subsequently turned down by the *Saturday Evening Post*, *The American Magazine*, *Harper's*, and *Scribner's*, it finally appeared in *The Yale Review* for Winter 1938, and it was reprinted in *The Hills Beyond* (New York: Harper's, 1941).[1]

Wolfe got the story almost by accident. When he was returning home in April of 1937 after an absence of seven years, he stopped off at Burnsville, a mountain town thirty-eight miles northeast of Asheville, to visit Westall kin (his mother's family) and phone Mabel (his sister) to see whether coming home was "safe."[2] The booth (if not the phone) from which he called still stands today inside the famed Nu Wray Inn, established in 1833 by a family named Smith and, since the Civil War, operated successively by the Ray and Wray families.

Today the Inn continues to serve its home-style meals to a widespread clientele and to rent its bright, cheery rooms to travelers. Room 17, where Wolfe stayed, today contains twin beds; in 1937 it housed a double bed, according to Rush Wray, present operator of the Inn, who recalls Wolfe's visit. It was on this occasion that Wolfe got from John Westall, his great-uncle, then ninety-five, the story that became "Chickamauga." Mr. Wray remembers Wolfe's excitement at the time as he spoke of the notes he had taken during his conversation with the old soldier and of his hopes for an excellent story from them.

"He told about it all so wonderfully and in such pungent and poetic language," Wolfe wrote to Basso, "such as so many of the old country people around here use, that I couldn't wait to get back to New York to begin on it. My idea was simply to tell the story of a great battle in the language of the common soldier—the kind of country mountain boy who did so much of the fighting in the war."[3] In July, when he was living at the rented cabin near Oteen, just outside of Asheville, he had been back to New York and had written the story.[4]

Brothers Ivan and Bruce Westall still live in Burnsville and remember the story-telling proclivities of their grandfather. "Grandfather didn't talk the way the speaker does in the story, though," says Bruce. "He was very precise and careful; he never said 'hit' for 'it.' " Grandfather Westall, "a carpenter and mica-trimmer by occupation, was a Bible scholar whose

*Reprinted from the *Thomas Wolfe Review*, 6, No. 2 (Fall 1982), 9–22. © 1982 by the Univ. of Akron, Akron, Ohio.

reading was chiefly the Bible, encyclopedias, and the *National Geographic*," says Ivan. "He was a short man, perhaps 5' 6", always immaculate."[5] In his later years he continued to play the fife, as he had done in his youth, and he added the recorder. "To the end," say the brothers, "his mind was as clear as it could be. There was no sign of senility." He spent his final years with his daughter Laura, who died thirty years later, in 1967. In the years following the Civil War, according to Census records, he fathered ten children and farmed. His wife died in 1921.

The Toe River Valley, where John Westall was born and to which the narrator of "Chickamauga" traces his ancestry and his own birth, covers the southern part of Yancey County, in the shadow of Mount Mitchell, the highest peak east of the Mississippi. In this region, atop a lesser summit, stands Westall Cemetery, in a clearing of perhaps 200' square. A narrow dirt road winds to it from a two-lane macadam road about ten miles southeast of Burnsville. The well-kept family cemetery reminds the visitor of that more famous necropolis at Grover's Corners, NH. Open sky. Greenery. Mountains. Silence. Peace. No sign below marks the turnoff for the winding ascent about a half-mile from the beginning of the Pisgah National Forest. John Westall's marker, a short, narrow column of what appears to be sandstone, shows weathering in the years since his death in November, 1937. It lists only his name and Civil War record.

Bruce Westall calls "absolutely false" the belief that his grandfather married his best friend's fiancee after the war, as does the narrator in the story. (Jim Weaver, the narrator's friend, dies at Chickamauga.) Mr. Westall also thinks the death of Jim—in fact, that whole character—a bit of Wolfean imagination.[6] If old John Westall commented on this story, we must assume that when Wolfe came back to Asheville in the summer of 1937, he brought with him from New York a typescript of it that he showed to the old soldier. (Could he have stopped a second time at Burnsville?) Since John Westall died in November of that year, he could not have seen the story in print, for it was not published until after his death.

Wolfe gave his narrator in "Chickamauga" the speech patterns of an uneducated mountaineer, perhaps reflecting the speech of his great-uncle as a young soldier some seventy-five years before.[7] We should beware, however, of associating the narrator too literally with Wolfe's relative. The narrator probably is a composite of mountain folk; certainly the story gave Wolfe a chance to reproduce mountain talk, just as in "Only the Dead Know Brooklyn" he reproduced Brooklynese.[8]

2 THE FICTION

On his nineteenth birthday, August 7, 1861, the unnamed narrator of "Chickamauga" tells us, he and his best friend, Jim Weaver, walked some twenty miles to Clingman to enlist in the Confederate Army, setting out at 7:30 a.m. and arriving before noon. The narator tells us that he was born at the Forks of the Toe River in 1842, the same place that his listener's grandfather was born in 1828. That the listener's great-grandfather and the narrator's father were the same—Bill Pentland—establishes the kinship as that of great-uncle (as in real life). Wolfe regularly uses the name *Pentland* for his mother's family, the Westalls.

By 3 p.m. the two young men had joined the 29th North Carolina Regiment of infantry, and the narrator was not to see home again until the war was over. Although he had expected to be with Lee's Army of Virginia, the young soldier actually was sent to oppose the Union forces in Kentucky and Tennessee. Here is our first suggestion of a major motif of the story: things often turn out differently than we expect. After two weeks in Clingman, the recruits drill in Altamont (Asheville) for two months—"right up and down where Parker St. now is," all open fields then.

In late October, the company moves out to the nearest rail head, eighty miles distant, at "Locust Gap."[9] The route is explicit: "up the Fairfield Road along the river up past Crestville, . . . across the Blue Ridge there, and down the mountain" to Old Stockade; then on to Locust Gap, the whole trip taking three and one-half days. Here again is the expectation-actuality motif: "We thought we was goin' off to have a lot of fun. If anyone had knowed what he was in fer or could a-seed the passel o' scarecrows that came limpin' back barefoot and half naked four years later, I reckon he'd a-thought twice before he 'listed up." From Locust Gap they travel by train to Richmond, where they learn they are being sent West, and the rest of the war they spend in the West and South.

In Tennessee and Kentucky there are skirmishes and raids during the remainder of the fall and the ensuing winter, and the soldiers discover hunger and "hard marchin' in the cold and wind and rain." In February of 1862 they almost participate in the relief of Fort Donelson: seven miles away, with sunset coming on, they fall out to rest and hear five cannon shots announcing surrender of the fort to Grant.

Much later in the war they fight in the strange battle of Stone Mountain—strange because in it "one side never fired a shot" yet won a victory (by rolling boulders upon the ascending foes). And in April of 1862 they fight in the Battle of Shiloh. After Shiloh, there is no more joking: from then on, there is fighting to the end. Jim, wounded at Shiloh, uses a two-month furlough to visit Martha, the girl he fell in love with just about the time he joined the army. He dies at Chickamauga.

Wolfe's narrator now relates how "Old Rosey" (Gen. William S. Rosecrans, a commander of the Army of the Cumberland) stalked the Confederate forces through Tennessee all during the spring and summer of 1863, driving them out of Shelbyville and Tullahoma, following them as they fell back across the Cumberland. In July the Confederates are in Chattanooga. Despite rain-softened roads, Rosecrans pushes his troops across the Cumberland Mountains in August and by early September is again in full pursuit, so close now that as he enters Chattanooga on September 8, the Confederates are exiting from the city's other end, to take up a position along the Chickamauga Creek. Thinking he has the Confederates in retreat, according to the narrator, Rosecrans sends Alexander McCook south to head them off. Going too far south, however, McCook finds himself and his men cut off from Gen. George H. Thomas and the rest of the Northern forces. A battle is inevitable.

On September 17, says the narrator, he and his comrades in arms were in position on the Chickamauga, their backs to Lookout Mountain and the creek; the next day, the Northern forces took their position in the woods opposite, on a rise, "with Missionary Ridge behind them to the east." The narrator now describes the battle, which began "upon our right at ten o'clock" (on Sept. 19, 1863). Later he heard (he tells us) that the battle began when the Federals coming down to the creek met some Southerners under Forrest (Nathan Bedford Forrest) and drove them back. During the ensuing day-long fighting, the narrator participated in four charges. At 2:30 p.m., the Confederates broke through the Federal right and went on beyond the widow Glenn's, where Rosecrans was quartered, driving the Northern forces across the Lafayette Road and taking possession of that road until driven back.

Control of that road, "Bloody Lane" it came to be called, alternated between Northern and Southern forces all the day, and fighting continued for "an hour or more" after night had fallen. Meanwhile, the woods had caught fire, and nurses and stretcher-bearers moved through the remaining trees and stumps to bring out those still alive whom they could reach.

On the second day, each side knew where the other was; the Confederates knew that the battle would be upon their right—on Rosecrans's left, with Thomas in charge of this left flank. The Confederates attacked at 10:30 a.m. At 2 p.m., Longstreet, according to the narrator, seeing a gap in Wood's position on the right, poured through it with five brigades that "broke their line and smashed their whole right." The result was a Northern rout so great that Rosecrans, the narrator says, was swept along with his men as they streamed into Rossville on the way into Chattanooga.

But Thomas, still there on the left, "turned and fell back along the Ridge and put his back against the wall thar, and he wouldn't budge." Then the battle recommenced, with the men of the twenty-ninth charging up the ridge "five times, I think" (one of the few places in his story where the narrator admits uncertainty about an event) before darkness fell. By the time of the last charge, just at nightfall, the Confederates were being forced to take ammunition from their dead, having none themselves. It is in this final charge that Jim is killed. Morning finds the Northerners gone and the Confederates "in possession of the field." Chickamauga, says the narrator in a final appraisal, was not only "the biggest fight that I was ever in" but also "the bloodiest battle anyone has ever fought."[10]

3 THE FACTS

The 29th North Carolina Regiment of infantry contained two John Westalls—John B., a musician (fifer) of Company B, and John D. of Company K. Both came from Yancey County, in the hill country of western North Carolina, above Asheville. Because the middle initial of Wolfe's aged relative was "B" (for *Baird*), the fifer of Company B is our narrator—to the extent that one identifies the narrator of any story with a specific living person. We shall see that strict identification of this kind is undesirable and, at times, impossible.

John B. Westall enlisted in Co. B of the 29th Regiment at the age of nineteen on July 3, 1861, as a private.[11] His actual birth-date was Aug. 12, 1842. He surrendered in Alabama May 4, 1865, and was paroled in Mississippi May 9. In 1903 he filed a pension claim as a result of a liberalized pension law in 1901 and was granted a fourth-class pension of $30 a month for the wound in the left hand that he suffered July 3, 1864, in the Atlanta campaign.[12] He married Mary M. Hollifield in 1866, who predeceased him.[13]

Records for the 29th North Carolina Regiment are among the slimmest of all regiments in this state. The roster for it "is based primarily on the North Carolina Roll of Honor, prisoner of war records, pension applications, and variety of miscellaneous records. Information was also gained from . . . postwar histories, cemetery records, and records of the United Daughters of the Confederacy. No muster rolls were located" for Co. B.[14]

Co. B was raised in Yancey County and enlisted on July 3, 1861. Its captains at various times were William B. Creasman, David M. Ray, and Daniel W. Angel. Similarly over the years the 29th Regiment had two colonels, Robert Brank Vance, and William B. Creasman, and two lieutenant-colonels, William C. Walker and James Marion Lowry. There were no Maj. L. C. McIntyre, Col. Leander Briggs, or Capt. Bob Saunders (names given by the narrator) in the 29th regiment. It would have been easy for Wolfe to get the names of the actual regimental officers had he wished to do so for historical accuracy. The 29th North Carolina Regiment of Infantry was officially formed Sept. 24, 1861, with ten companies, A-K, constituting it. (The letter "I" was not used.) Brig. Gen. Robert B. Vance ("Colonel Vance" above), in *Histories of the Several Regiments and Battalions from North Carolina in the Great War 1861–1865*, edited by Walter Clark, says: "This regiment was organized at

Camp Patton, Asheville, N.C., in the summer of 1861."[15] This agrees with the narrator's statement that he and his fellow enlistees drilled at Asheville.

His ensuing account, however, of the company's movements to September of 1863 does not accord with those of the 29th Regiment in actuality. The twenty-ninth was not at Fort Donelson or Shiloh, and there was no Battle of Stone Mountain, although in the Battle of Atlanta, July 22, 1864, fighting occurred within a mile or so of Stone Mountain. A hint that this non-existent battle is a form of the tall tale appears in the narrator's hyperbolic assertion that, using rocks and boulders, one side "won the fight and did more damage and more destruction to the other side than all the guns and cannon in the world could do."

The Confederates, according to the narrator, are atop the mountain with one howitzer pulled up with ropes while the Federals below them seek to take the mountain. Before a shot is fired with the howitzer, however, a shell from below hits it, splitting it exactly in two. "You couldn't have made a neater job of hit if you'd cut it down the middle with a saw." In the succeeding charges, the Federals are repelled by boulders rolled down on them.[16]

Col. W. C. P. Breckenridge, C.S.A., writing about the opening of the Atlanta Campaign, asserts that in a fight at "Dug Gap" his men rolled stones down upon their foes, "at first in a mere spirit of exuberant fun," later, under orders, "as part of our defense." Without the supplemental aid of boulders, he adds, "our ammunition would have given out."[17] Given this weaponry, what better name for the "battle" than that of Stone Mountain?

The insertion of this battle into the story seems to be part of the narrator's—or Wolfe's narrative skill. It forms part of a triad—a missed battle (Fort Donelson), an odd battle (Stone Mountain), and a real battle (Shiloh), which changes the narrator and his comrades from boys into men. Of the first two battles, Fort Donelson comes near the beginning of the war, and Stone Mountain allegedly comes near the end. Shiloh and Chickamauga come in between. Thus Fort Donelson and Stone Mountain serve as a frame for the two major battles.

A comparative listing of the actual movements of the 29th North Carolina Regiment with those of Wolfe's narrator reveals additional discrepancies with historical fact. About the only similarity between the two lists is that they begin with Asheville in 1861 and end at Chickamauga in 1863.

Historical Fact	**The Narrator's Account**
Regiment is organized at Camp Patton, Asheville, Sept. 24, 1861.	Joins at Clingman, NC, on his birthday, Aug. 7, 1861, age 19. There for two weeks.
Begins training at Camp Vance, near Sulphur Springs, in	To Altamont (Asheville) for two

Historical Fact	**The Narrator's Account**
Buncombe County (which contains Asheville).	months.
Oct. 28–Nov. 6, 1861–moving to Raleigh.	Late October, 1861–moves to Locust Gap, eighty miles away (three and one-half days).
Nov. 25–30, 1861–moving to Jonesboro, TN area.	To Richmond: arrives same day.
Early December 1861–Co. B is at Chattanooga.	Next day–sent "out west." Skirmishes and raids in Tennessee and Kentucky.
Feb. 20, 1862–Regiment is ordered to Cumberland Gap.	To the relief of Fort Donelson, TN [which surrendered to Grant on the *morning* of Feb. 16, 1862]. The narrator speaks of hearing the surrender cannonshot in the *evening*.
Aug. 5 or 6, 1862–Is moved to Baptist Gap, "about five miles south of Cumberland Gap."	At the Battle of Shiloh [April 6–7, 1862].
Sept. 18, 1862–Moves back to Cumberland Gap.	At Stones River, time unspecified.
Sept. 19, 1862–The First Division of the Dept. of East Tennessee, of which the NC 29th had been a part since July 3, 1862, moved to Kentucky.	At Shelbyville (late June, 1863).
Oct. 25, 1862–the Division is at Beans Station.	At Tullahoma (late June, 1863).
Late October, 1862–the 29th moves to Lenoir Station, TN, "twenty miles southeast of Knoxville."	At Chattanooga (early July to Sept. 8, 1863).
Nov. 15–18, 1862–Moving "to Normandy Station, ten miles east of Shelbyville."	Sept. 17, 1863–". . . . in position on the Chickamauga. . . ."
Nov. 28, 1862–Moves "ten miles east to Manchester."	Sept. 19–20, 1863–Participates in the Battle of Chickamauga.
Dec. 7–10, 1862–Moves "north to Readyville, near Murfreesboro."	–Data taken from Wolfe's story.
Dec. 18, 1862–Is "sent to McMinnville," detached from the brigade.	
Dec. 25, 1862–Is ordered to rejoin the brigade at Murfreesboro. The Battle of Stones River (Murfreesboro) follows.	
May 12, 1863–The Regiment is ordered to Mississippi, arriving in Jackson on May 18, moving on to Canton; by rail "to Vaughan's Station, forty miles north of Jackson."	

Historical Fact	The Narrator's Account
June 1, 1863—The Regiment moves to Yazoo City, remaining until the fall of Vicksburg in mid-July.	
July 23, 1863—Moves to Morton.	
July 27, 1863—Is ordered to Meridian, MS.	
Aug. 30, 1863—Reaches Chickamauga Station, south of Chattanooga.	
Sept. 19–20, 1863—Participates in the Battle of Chickamauga.	
—Data taken from Jordan (comp.).	

In narrating the actual battle, however (six and one-half pages of the story's thirty pages in the original edition), Wolfe's narrator is close to historical fact. The narrator emphasizes the wooded terrain where the battle was fought, saying, "The Battle of Chickamauga was fought in a cedar thicket. That cedar thicket, from what I knowed of hit, was about three miles long and one mile wide. We fought fer two days all up and down that thicket and to and fro across hit."[18] Other evidence bears this out. Glenn Tucker refers to "the deep trees at Chickamauga."[19] Capt. Isaac N. Dryden "would live until he entered the woods at Chickamauga" (p. 22). Col. Peyton H. Colquitt "had an appointment he would have to keep with death in the woods next day" (p. 100). "The armies were about to grapple in the deep woods. . . ." (p. 120). Moreover, the expanse of the forest was considerable: "The expanse of territory on which the armies were about to meet extends for six miles along the west bank of the Chickamauga *in the deeply wooded basin* [my emphasis] . . . between Pigeon and Lookout mountains. . . ." Other similar references occur, most strikingly in a detailed summary of the undergrowth and forestation:

> Much of the area over which the armies fought was in thickets, with a low growth of dogwood, scrub oak, cedar, and pine, matted with underbrush of blackberry briars, honeysuckle, poison oak and trumpet vine. . . . Here and there the underbrush gave way to more cathedral-like forests of great hardwoods: hickory, black gum, maple, white and Spanish oak; while all about were great cedars and short-leaf pine.[20]

The first day's battle, then, and part of the second were fought in the woods. Headquartered at the widow Glenn's, General Rosecrans, unable to see the action, had to be guided by the sound, the widow Glenn telling him, from her knowledge of the area, where sounds were coming from. The confusion and uncertainty must have been as intense for these within the forest as for those outside it. Wolfe's narrator suggests as much:

> The fight began upon our right at ten o'clock. We couldn't find out what was happenin': the woods thar was so close and thick we never knowed fer two days what had happened, and we didn't know fer certain then. . . . I've heared them say that even Old Rosey himself didn't know just what had happened when he rode back into town next day. . . . We fought back and forth across that cedar thicket fer two days, and thar was times when you would be right up on top of them before you even knowed that they was thar.[21]

Tucker quotes Capt. George W. Skinner of the 77th Pennsylvania as saying: "The artillery fire for the space of perhaps half an hour was simply terrible. Trees were mown down like grain, and the smoke of battle fell so thick among the foliage that it was difficult to pierce the gloom with the naked eye for any great distance."[22] This echoes the narrator's statements about enormous destruction of timber: "When the fight started that cedar thicket was so thick and dense you could a-took a butcher knife and drive hit in thar anywheres and hit would a-stuck. And when that fight was over that cedar thicket had been so destroyed by shot and shell you could a-looked in thar anywheres with your naked eye and seed a black snake run a hundred yards away."[23]

The narrator's remarks about the fluidity of movement also are echoed by Tucker, who comments, "The deadly fighting surged back and forth and all around," (p. 170), the battle lines being ill defined, unlike those at Gettysburg and Antietam. "At Chickamauga the fighting was almost continually over new ground and one army ended the battle roughly where the other began it" (p. 125). On the first day of the battle, "the action which began on the north end of the battlefield, nearest to Rossville and Chattanooga, moved southward as the day advanced. By late evening . . . the main conflict was being fought . . . at the far southern edge of the farm. . . ." (p.128). Wolfe's narrator says, "We fought fer two days all up and down that thicket and two and fro across hit. . . . We'd attack and then they'd throw us back, then they'd attack and we'd beat them off. And that was the way hit went from mornin' to night. . . . We busted through their right at two-thirty in the afternoon and got way over past the Widder Glenn's where Rosey had his quarters, and beat 'em back until we got the whole way cross the Lafayette Road [now Route 27, the main road through the battlefield park] and took possession of the road. And then they drove us out again. And we kept comin' on, and both sides were still at hit after darkness fell" (pp. 99–100).

Fighting on that first day continued into the night, although Ector's

Brigade, of which the 29th North Carolina Regiment was a part, seems officially not to have participated in this. In the Chickamauga Battlefield Park, the inscription on the marker (itself hidden in a thicket today) for Ector's Brigade says, "It halted in the vicinity of Jay's mill until near sundown and was not further engaged." Given the intense confusion of the day, there could well have been exceptions, with men becoming separated from their units. Wolfe's narrator says, "We kept fightin' fer an hour or more after hit had gotten dark, and you could see the rifles flashin' in the woods, but then hit all died down" (Wolfe, p. 101). Tucker speaks of the two armies "attacking each other guided by sound and powder flashes. For more than an hour the vicious fighting continued in darkness. . . ." (p. 183). Interestingly enough, Wolfe's narrator fails to mention the unseasonably freezing cold of this night and the next reported by survivors. Like Wolfe's narrator, Tucker speaks of "litter bearers working . . . on the night of the first day," and both describe the sound of hammering that kept many sleepless throughout the night as the Federals constructed barricades that the Confederates the next day were to find impregnable.

On the second day, fighting began around 10 a.m. as Breckenridge mounted his assault. At 10:55 a.m., Brig. Gen Wood received an ambiguously worded and contradictory order from Rosecrans to close a nonexistent gap in the Federal line. Wood promptly moved his men as ordered. The result was, as Wolfe's narrator reports, to leave a gap in the Union line through which Confederate forces rushed, precipitating the Northern rout that has already been noted. Tucker says that, accompanied by his staff, General Rosecrans "rode along voluntarily with the horde" (p. 307) rather than being swept along with them as Wolfe's narrator asserts. It seems extremely likely, however, that Rosecrans, as Wolfe's narrator suggests, would have been in a state of semi-shock at least as a result of this unexpected reversal resulting from his mistaken order to Wood. Upon reaching safety in Rossville, Rosecrans might well have had to be helped from his horse, as the narrator says he did (Wolfe, p. 103).

Now the fighting turned to Snodgrass Hill on Missionary Ridge, as Maj. Gen. George H. Thomas and his men repelled charge after charge by the Confederates. According to Tucker, the "process of attack and repulse was repeated again and again until the Minnesotans could scarcely see the ground in front of them because it was so covered with dead and wounded" (p. 333). Wolfe's narrator claims to have charged up this hill five times. "We'd charge up to the very muzzles of their guns, and they'd mow us down like grass, and we'd come stumblin' back—or what was left of us—and form again at the foot of the hill, and then come on again" (Wolfe, p. 105).

In later years, Longstreet is reported to have said that he "made twenty-five assaults in all on Snodgrass Hill" (Tucker, p. 357). Tucker calls these repeated attempts to storm the hill a fight that was "in its general aspects . . . the most determined and sanguinary fight of all this grisly meeting of the two armies along the Chickamauga" (p. 334), adding, "The fury of fighting of the two days had been only a prelude to the final test" here (*Ibid.*). Wolfe's narrator reflects this judgment: "Hit was like a river of red-hot lead had poured down on us: the line melted thar like snow" (Wolfe, p. 105).

According to Tucker, Thomas began his withdrawal from Snodgrass Hill "at sunset" (p. 359), and a caption beneath a drawing speaks of "Thomas' withdrawal, 5:30 p.m., into darkness." This last, seemingly an exaggeration or a miscalculation, can be defended, I think, in a literary sense as an approximation. The time would have been about sunset, as Tucker says. Completion of the withdrawal, however, would have been in darkness. Wolfe's narrator tells us simply that Thomas's troops withdrew during the night: in the morning, the Confederates discovered that the Federals had departed.

In presenting the Battle of Chickamauga as one of the most bloody and violent of the war, Wolfe's narrator is supported by "the general-historian Henry M. Cist," who wrote, "All things considered, the battle of Chickamauga for the forces engaged, was the hardest fought and bloodiest battle of the rebellion."[24] The 29th North Carolina Regiment is reported to have lost eighty dead or wounded and about thirty missing in this battle, according to a memo made Dec. 19, 1863, by B. S. Proffitt, commanding that regiment, to Maj. Gen. James A. Foote.[25] Overall losses in the two-day battle were heavy. According to Lieut. Col. Joseph B. Mitchell, "The Confederate Losses were about 18,000 from a total strength of some 66,000 while the Union suffered approximately 16,000 casualties from an army of about 60,000."[26]

4 SOME FINAL OBSERVATIONS

"Fiction is not fact," wrote Thomas Wolfe, "but fiction is fact selected and understood, fiction is fact arranged and charged with purpose."[27] Close examination of "Chickamauga" reveals that in it Wolfe followed his precept of arranging fact and charging it with purpose to produce a romantic tale with a narrative center—his great-uncle's account of the actual battle—and expanded upon it to supply background with minimal attention to historical accuracy apart from the battle itself. He added a love interest to sustain his reader's concern for the characters and to produce a story that would more likely sell.

Into this story Wolfe introduces not only the real-life figure of the narrator, based on his own great-uncle John Baird Westall, who died seven months after Wolfe's conversation with him, and the fictional Jim Weaver, but also "Bacchus Pentland," the visionary who was constantly predicting Armageddon. Bacchus (Noble Bacchus Westall), who is said by the narrator to have joined the 14th North Carolina Regiment, actually did that. A farmer from Buncombe County, Noble (the narrator refers to him as "Back") joined Company F of that regiment as a private in May of 1861 at the age of twenty-three. In 1864 he was wounded at Spottsylvania Court House, VA, and he was captured at Petersburg, VA, in April of 1865. Wolfe, then, has been accurate in giving us the regiment of both his narrator and of this minor character; he does not, however, give us Bacchus's company or that of his narrator. One assumes that he wanted to avoid over-explicitness in suggesting complete identification of a fictional character with a person in real life. His narrator is not literally John B. Westall anymore than Eugene Gant is literally Thomas Wolfe. After all, this is fiction, not history.

And yet history is involved here. Wolfe may have researched the battle for historical accuracy: we just do not know. One suspects that in the barely seven pages of battle narrative, old John Westall in the spring of 1937 was retelling a story he had told many times before.[28] The Battle of Chickamauga was perhaps the high point in his career as a soldier. Of the battles he was in during four years of war, is it not significant that he chose to describe this one to his great-grandnephew? It must have held a special significance for him.[29]

And so we come to the story's theme. The real theme of "Chickamauga" is not that war is hell. It has nothing to do with war as such. The real theme, one of Wolfe's favorites, is that life is unpredictable and strange—"stranger than a dream." Only about one-third of the story presents the Battle of Chickamauga; the rest of the story is romantic preliminary. Jim Weaver is introduced as a foil to Wolfe's narrator: Jim, newly in love, wants to live and get married, but he is killed. Wolfe postpones his death to the final charge up Snodgrass Hill—i.e., to the very end of the battle. Thus Wolfe prolongs our suspense as we wonder what will become of Jim. Because the narrator obviously has survived the war, he can not enlist our concern; Wolfe wanted a character whose fate was uncertain and would provide concern.

At the story's romantic conclusion, we learn that the narrator later married the girl that Jim had loved. Ending on the note of the unexpected and "strange" that serves as its major theme, the story shows Wolfe's skill as a craftsman of fiction, adding to Westall's battle narrative to produce not only a more salable work but one artistically more complex and satisfying. "Chickamauga" is far more than the almost literally transcribed account of an unsophisticated mountain man.

Notes

1. Elizabeth Nowell, *The Letters of Thomas Wolfe* (New York: Scribner's, 1956), pp. 624n, 625, 635, 646.

2. See "The Return of the Prodigal," Part 2, "The Real Thing," in *The Hills Beyond*, pp. 120–141, for an account of Wolfe's visit to "Zebulon," a county seat

(like Burnsville) to visit his mother's kin en route to Asheville in April of 1937. It was on this occasion that he witnessed a shooting about which he was later subpoened to testify as a witness. Wolfe relates the incident in this story. The shooting actually took place in Burnsville.

3. Nowell, p. 625.

4. *Ibid.*

5. Cf. "I was little, about the way you see me now, except that I've shrunk up a bit." In "Chickamauga," p. 78.

6. Wolfe himself hints that Jim Weaver may have been fictional. See his letter of July 22 (?), 1937, to his agent, Elizabeth Nowell, about her difficulties in placing "Chickamauga": "I think I may have put in a little too much Jim Weaver and his love affair in an effort to make it palatable to the big magazines." Nowell, p. 635.

7. Cf. "I never had no education. I never had a chance to git one before I went away. And when I came back I could a-had my schoolin' but I didn't take hit." In "Chickamauga," pp. 84–85.

8. See Wolfe's comment on the narrator's language quoted in the fourth paragraph of the present article.

9. According to W. T. Jordan, Jr., editor of the Civil War Roster of the Historical Publications Section, North Carolina Division of Archives and History, in Raleigh, the nearest rail heads to Asheville in 1861 would have been Morganton (54 miles away according to a modern highway map); Rutherfordton (perhaps a few miles closer); and Greenville and Jonesboro, TN (about the same distance). There are a number of sites in western North Carolina called Locust Gap, he says, but as that of a railroad terminus in 1861 the name seems to be fictional. "Clingman," the town from which the narrator sets out, also appears to be fictitious, although there is a modern town of that name in Wilkes County, NC, some seventy-five or eighty miles from the Toe River Valley area. Wolfe's narrator, however, gives the distance from his home to Clingman as twenty miles. And according to a comprehensive atlas of North Carolina, no town of "Big Hickory," from which Jim Weaver supposedly set out, seems ever to have existed in that state.

10. In a communication to the present author, Mr. Jordan comments that Chickamauga was not, even in 1937, "the bloodiest battle anyone has ever fought," as the narrator asserts. "Chickamauga," he says "is not to be compared with some of the battles of World War I, such as Verdun; and several other battles of the Civil War, such as Gettysburg and Sharpsburg (Antietam) were closely comparable."

11. John W. Moore (comp), *Roster of North Carolina Troops in the War Between the States* (Raleigh: Ashe Gatling, 1882), II, 480.

12. W. T. Jordan, Jr. (comp), *North Carolina Troops 1861–1865: A Roster*, Vol. VIII (Raleigh: State Division of Archives and History, 1981), seen in typescript. Another reason we can be sure that John B. Westall rather than John D. is the right man, according to Mr. Jordan, is that the Asheville *Citizen's* obituary for John B. says that he was wounded in the hand during the war. A North Carolina pension application shows that John B. Westall of Co. B was wounded in the left hand.

13. North Carolina Marriage Register, North Carolina State Library, Raleigh.

14. Jordan typescript.

15. Goldsboro: State of North Carolina, 1901, II, 485.

16. W. T. Jordan finds hyperbole in "the statement (perhaps implied) that the Confederates had nothing with which to defend themselves except one brass howitzer. "We can be sure," he writes (in a letter to this writer) "that if the Confederates were able to get a howitzer to the top of the mountain with ropes they were able to bring up their rifles the same way, if not on their backs. Nor is it likely that

they would have failed to do so." The splitting of the howitzer in two by a solid shot would indeed be possible, he adds, "if the howitzer was made by welding two halves together"; but he finds exaggeration in the narrator's "You couldn't have made a neater job of hit if you'd cut it down the middle with a saw." Bruce and Ivan Westall recall an alternative ending to the incident in which a fired shot enters the howitzer's mouth, destroying the weapon.

17. *Battles and Leaders of the Civil War* (New York: The Century Co., 1887), IV, 279.

18. Thomas Wolfe, "Chickamauga," *The Hills Beyond*, p. 97. Pages for most of the following references to the story will be shown parenthetically.

19. Glenn Tucker, *Chickamauga: Bloody Battle in the West* (Indianapolis: Bobbs Merrill, 1961), p. 21. Because Tucker's book affords an excellently detailed account of this engagement and the participants in it, this source is chiefly followed for a narrative of the battle it describes. Pages for subsequent references to this book will generally be made parenthetically.

20. *Ibid.*, p. 123.

21. Wolfe, pp. 99–100.

22. Tucker, p. 147.

23. Wolfe, pp. 97–98.

24. Tucker, p. 388.

25. Typed memorandum at the Division of Archives and History, North Carolina Division of Cultural Resources, in Raleigh.

26. "Battle of Chickamauga," *Battles of the Civil War* 1861–1865 (Birmingham: Oxmoor House, 1976, p. 53.

27. "To the Reader," *Look Homeward, Angel* (New York: Charles Scribner's Sons, 1929), p. vii.

28. For a discussion of mountaineer speech patterns, including those of Wolfe's narrator in this story, see Floyd C. Watkins, "Thomas Wolfe and the Southern Mountaineer," *South Atlantic Quarterly*, 50:1 (January 1951), 58–71.

29. Ignoring John Westall's other military activities during four years of war, the *Asheville Citizen-Times* in its obituary for him (Nov. 15, 1937, p. 2) said, "He took an active part in the Battle of Chic[k]amauga." On his death certificate, in the space reserved for his occupation, someone has written, "Confederate Soldier." Old John Westall would have liked that.

Weaving as Metaphor in Thomas Wolfe's *The Web of Earth*

Gloria Guzi*

In his introduction to Thomas Wolfe's *The Web of Earth*, C. Hugh Holman writes, "Nothing Wolfe wrote has been more highly praised than this short novel."[1] The character of Eliza is the unifying principle of the novel, and it is "revealed through a vast web of memories, stories, and recollections that crowd in on the narrator as she talks and that

*Reprinted from the *Thomas Wolfe Review*, 7, No. 2 (Fall 1983), 44–47. © 1983 by the University of Akron, Akron, Ohio.

stretch back seventy years."[2] While Holman is correct, something more than the character of Eliza unifies *The Web of Earth.* Wolfe's use of the weaving metaphor unifies the story, illuminates the character of Eliza, and gives rise to the theme of choice and responsibility in time. Though probably unfamiliar with the mechanics of weaving as a craft, Wolfe as an artist would have understood the principle underlying it: the interlocking of individual threads in a single web. This is not too different from the interlocking of individual people in a single, interdependent world. In Eliza, Wolfe finds a perfect weaver. He is able to make her both the weaver of her web and the central part of her woven fabric of time. This paper, then, attempts to trace the weaving metaphor in light of Eliza's character and the story's theme.

First, a glance at a weaver of a primitive culture—the Navajo, for example—shows us that her loom is not the four-harness floor model we are accustomed to seeing. Her designs are not predetermined by a specific threading pattern or treadling sequence, and she does not roll away from view on a cloth beam the already woven fabric. Essentially her loom is a vertical frame on which she lays in her own designs without preliminary drawings and can view her entire product from start to finish. She learns to weave not out of the frustration of time but in harmony with it and with faith in the product she will create. There is also a simplicity and directness in the craft that arises from the interaction between the weaver and her medium, a oneness grown from long hours of association over many years. It is therefore an organic craft: the tools are basic, the process rhythmic, and the weaver/loom relationship, a very natural one.

How, then, is Eliza Gant a weaver? Although it is Wolfe as artist who is conscious of narrative form, he assigns Eliza the task of weaving the story. Like the weaver, Eliza is a patient woman with an unshakable faith in her convictions. Having endured the vicissitudes of a life spanning over seventy years, she seems immune to the constraints of time that would encroach upon her narrative. Though not simple to read for one unfamiliar with the Gant saga, Eliza's web of recollection is direct enough through its conversational style. Not bound by a disciplined form of narration, the direction and substance of the story are dictated by the reach of her memory alone. Like the primitive weaver without a predetermined pattern, Eliza both creates her own design and keeps the entire narrative within focus by moving backward and forward in time. Like the weaver's, Eliza's "craft" is organic: the tools of speech are simple, the narrative rhythmic, and the connection between Eliza's memory and the experiences she relates, a close one. In fact, Eliza's association with her experiences is closer than the weaver/loom relationship. In contrast to the weaver's creative products, which come off the loom and are not a part of her, the thread of Eliza's life is actually a part of the web she weaves.

The weaving metaphor, of course, not only illuminates the character of Eliza, but also provides a structural framework for the story and allows its theme to surface. Eliza as part of the web she weaves shows us through the thread of her experience and those of people she has known that there are opportunities within the web of life to make choices that influence the course of our lives. It is imperative that we make those decisions responsibly. This is similar to the weaver who can and must make choices of design, color, and fiber if she is to weave at all, and who, if she desires her product to be admired, must further assume a creative responsibility to choose well. The weaver, with a considerable amount of control, can make responsible choices within a self-determined framework. Eliza, however, as both a weaver and part of the woven fabric, is different, for she can make choices only within the coincidence and chance of time. That is, time is external to her, an independent variable to which she can react only under given circumstances. For example, the story begins, "In the year the locusts came, . . . 'Two . . . Two,' says, 'Twenty . . . Twenty.' "[3] There is nothing inherently significant about this. The story might have begun, "In the year of the bad harvest," or "In the year of the flood," for it is coincidental. Yet, the year the locusts came, the year in which she heard the voices uttering the numbers "Two . . . Two, . . . Twenty . . . Twenty," is the given framework of time. Eliza begins the story with it. She ends the story with it. Intermittently throughout the narrative she uses it as a reference point to remind herself and the reader where she is. This is not unlike the weaver's number count, a count of threads to remind the weaver what thread to insert or how far to carry it across the warp.

Though Eliza has no control over events external to her, she chooses to react responsibly to them for the benefit of not only herself but her family. Once more, Eliza is like the weaver, who is responsible not merely for the individual threads she carries across the shed, but also of those threads in relation to others on the loom. To neglect this would invariably reduce the integrity and balance of the web, to leave it uneven in weight, appearance, and render it useless. And if Eliza's web is not exactly even, she at least fulfilled her responsibility and faced squarely the decisions she has had to make at various stages in her life and accepted the consequences. This is due to her ability to maintain the broader perspective about life. Just as the weaver who momentarily tires of the arduous task of beating down the yarn stands back to admire the progress of the whole design on her vertical frame, so does Eliza remain optimistic because she is able to keep her focus on the goodness of the whole of life rather than the frustrations and setbacks of the moment. Twice during her pregnancies she is faced with a choice regarding her relationship to her husband: to leave in self-interest or stay out of her responsibility to her family. The first time, after an argument about Eller Beals's letters to W.O., Eliza comments,

> Child! Child–I reckon I was young and proud, and it made me bitter to hear him talk that way. I got up and went out onto the porch and I wanted to go out and leave him then and there, but I was carrying my first baby around inside me, and it had rained and I could smell the flowers, the roses, and the lilies, and the honeysuckle vines, ... (p. 246)

The second time, in one of many arguments resulting from W.O.'s excessive drinking habits, she begins to have labor contractions and says,

> . . . I lay there in the dark listenin' to people comin' by, and I could hear music playin' somewheres and hear their voices laughin' and singin', and smell all of the blossoms–oh! the magnolias and the lilies and the roses, the poinsettias, and all the other flowers they had there and the orange trees and all, and the little childern sleepin' in the house, you know, and see the sky all full of stars and Lord God! I thought, what shall I do, what shall I do? (pp. 299–300)

Both instances show Eliza's ability to remove herself from life's bitter fragments to the total fabric of life through the earth's renewal of life, of the life within her womb, and her responsibility to it. Her optimism, then, is the inevitable result of her choice to live and judge the parts of life within the context of the whole. Even in her recollection of her husband, she forgives by dismissing the unpleasant moments to focus on the composite man.

> Oh! the good, the bad times, all of the happiness and bitter weepin', and there is something now that can't be said, I tried to hate him but now I have no words to say against him: he was a strange man but where he was no one was ever cold, no one was ever hungry, there was enough for all, . . . (p. 298)

In light of Eliza's decisions to remain with her husband, it might be argued that as a woman, she more or less has no choice: she must either live in an impossible situation or risk scandal because she refuses to endure it. But Eliza is more than the average woman of her time, for she can hold her own. She buys and sells real estate and has planter's hands that can make anything grow. As she puts it, "if the worst comes to the worst, I wouldn't starve, if I didn't have a penny I could live, I'd make the earth produce for me" (p. 300). Thus, it is with a relative amount of freedom that she makes her choices.

Just as important to Eliza as her own responsibility to act within the web she weaves and of which she is a part, are the threads of other peoples' lives that cross and overlap her own. Admonishing these folk for what she sees as their neglect of duty, Eliza carries her reminders on a personal crusade to members of her family, to members of the community, and even to a convicted murderer. She tells her son, for example, "Child, child, you mustn't be a wanderer all your days. . . ." (p. 214) Likewise, in a typical reminder to her husband, who longed for romantic adventures, Eliza says, "you have your family to consider, and you're not goin'." (p. 250) Eliza requests Ambrose Radiker, the saloon keeper, not to sell liquor to her husband, appeals to his sense of responsibility, and reminds him of his freedom to act accordingly. When Ambrose agrees that it is best for W.O. not to drink, Eliza tells him, "Now surely, you've got strength of mind enough not to be forced into a thing against your better judgment." (p. 269) Finally, even a convicted murderer, Ed Mears, is reminded that he too has choice and responsibility. At Eliza's urging, he gives up his gun and listens to her attentively as she tells him, "You've got a wife who's stuck by you through thick and thin and little childern, and now, . . . you must begin to think of them." (p. 289) Nowhere in the story is anyone able to ignore the responsibility of choice within the web of earth.

It is clear that the threads of individual lives do not exist independently of one another. They must invariably weave a web. Given the coincidence and circumstance of time, people have opportunities within the web to act responsibly if they choose. Weaving a web in which other lives are continually intersecting her own, Eliza finds it necessary to act in the common interests of her family rather than out of the romantic longings of her soul. Thus, she shows that the record of history belongs to those stabilizing forces and weavers of narratives like herself.

Notes

1. *The Short Novels of Thomas Wolfe* (New York: Charles Scribner's Sons, 1961, p. 75.
2. Holman, p. 76. See also Wolfe's own statement about the story in *The Letters of Thomas Wolfe to His Mother*, May 29, 1932.
3. *From Death to Morning* (New York: Charles Scribner's Sons, 1970), p. 212. (Subsequent citations will be made by page number within the context of the paper.)

The Ebb and Flow of Time and Place in "The Lost Boy"

Timothy Dow Adams*

Thomas Wolfe's famous phrase, "You can't go home again," was often repeated at his seventy-fifth birthday celebration in Asheville in October of 1975. Although this phrase was usually associated with Wolfe's difficulties with his home town after he published *Look Home-*

*Reprinted from *Southern Studies: An Interdisciplinary Journal of the South* (Winter 1980), pp. 400–08.

ward, Angel, it could have also applied to his other childhood home in St. Louis, Missouri, where he lived for six months in 1904 and where he returned in September 1935 to visit the actual house where he had lived during the World's Fair of 1904. Wolfe's return to St. Louis, like his first visit to Asheville following *Look Homeward, Angel*'s publication, became a literary work, "The Lost Boy," which used a strong and particular sense of time and place to show that "you can't go home again" applies to all childhood homes.

The use of the past, coupled with a pervasive fascination with time, has been characteristic of Southern writing almost since its beginning. As Allan W. Becker notes in an essay on Ellen Glasgow's place in the Southern literary tradition, "The sense of the past which we find in these writers (Roberts, Gordon, Tate, Warren, Faulkner, Wolfe, etc.) is almost a constant in Southern fiction. Kennedy, Simms, Cooke, Caruthers—all wrote of earlier times in the South: but their viewpoint differs from the new, in that regionalism contains an awareness of the presentness of the past."[1] The prevalence among Southern writers of this particular way of using the past—an awareness of its constant influence on the present—is discussed by Louis D. Rubin in an essay on Southern historical writing in which he says: "The present was focused into perspective by the image of the past lying behind it. Their own contemporary life was seen not only for its own sake but as formed and influenced by the life that had preceded it."[2] Rubin suggests that the first post-World War I generation of Southern writers was especially concerned with the past's encroachment on their present, and influence on their future, because of the time and place of their existence, because they were of the new South, but were able to understand the older South into which they had been born. Georges Poulet, in an extensive essay on time and literature, makes the point that this inner drive to isolate a moment in the present, in order to look backward and forward, is characteristic of a change in century:

> Begotten by feeling, imbued more and more with feeling, the thought of the century which is ending becomes more and more apt to discover in the depths of its vibrant actuality the interflowing images of reminiscence and premonition. Always isolated in the moment which gave it form, it sees this moment incessantly invaded, disorganized. Transfigured by states of mind from beyond, there comes to be superimposed upon actual existence the awareness of another existence, an existence which overlaps the frame of each moment. It is as if to exist meant to live two lives as the same time: the life lived day by day; and the life lived before and beyond the day or the moment; a life which lengthens into duration.[3]

These comments on time are particularly applicable to the works of Wolfe, as Rubin has shown in his essay, "Thomas Wolfe: Time and the South,"[4] and as H. Blair Rouse writes in his study of time and place in Southern fiction: "In the writing of Thomas Wolfe, time is a potent factor in the presentation of all the meaning of the lives of the characters; the past merges with the present and projects into the future."[5]

Wolfe's long story, "The Lost Boy," is a classic example of the Southern use of time which I have been discussing, because the story studies the past's interplay with the future and the present on so many levels. The story itself illustrates the effect of time on Wolfe, because he wrote it sometime in 1937 after having visited St. Louis.[6] The story reverts to an earlier time when Wolfe used Eugene Gant as his protagonist. Seeing the past come into the present by his visit to St. Louis, Wolfe wrote "The Lost Boy" which retells from another point of view and with many embellishments, the same scene in *Look Homeward, Angel*, described by Rubin as illustrative of Wolfe's use of the past and time.

"The Lost Boy" is organized into four sections: Grover, his mother, his sister, and his brother. The story begins with a picture of Grover, who is the lost boy, in the town square of Altamont. The second section, the mother's, is a monologue, addressed to Eugene—Grover's younger brother—in which the mother rambles about Grover and the trip to the World's Fair. In the third section, Helen—Grover's and Eugene's sister—recalls the events at St. Louis surrounding Grover's death. The last section details Eugene's visit to the house where Grover died, thirty years later. These four sections of the story are held together by several patterns of time.

For example, as the sections unfold, time moves in a straight chronological fashion, from the time when Grover was actually alive, through subsequent attempts to remember him, until the last section, which takes place after Eugene has tried, and failed, to get at the past by talking with his mother and sister. Each section has a different narrator but each narrator picks up the story where the previous teller has left it.

The sections of "The Lost Boy" are also held together by the concept of Eugene's growing awareness of how he had felt at the age of four about Grover. In the first section, Eugene is not mentioned. In the second, he is addressed by his mother, but he is only a small part of her recollection. In the third section, Eugene is also addressed and even questioned, but he is still a passive character, secondary to Grover. Eugene becomes progressively more a part of each section until the last, in which his point of view is presented as he tries to recapture the past as it relates to him. Eugene is interested both in reconstructing Grover from the past and in reconstructing himself. To Eugene, both Grover and himself are the lost boy. Thus the story moves from the past toward the present in an attempt to regain the past. As the sections progress, the continuing story of Grover is also being presented, so that we find out more and more information about him, in a manner similar to the revelation of the past in *Absalom! Absalom!* As in Faulkner's novel, each attempt to remember the real Grover is only an approximation, filtered through the memory of each speaker.

An important device which links all four parts and which appears in various forms throughout the story, is a repeated pattern of ebb and flow, coming and going and coming again. It is a pulsating pattern of stopping and starting which imparts a definite rhythm to the story. This pattern serves not only to bind the four parts to each other, but is also, in itself, a metaphor for the way memory works. The past comes and goes in the memories of each member of Grover's family. There is an elusive quality about the past that causes the memory of it to come and go, now becoming clear, now growing vague. This ebbing and flowing is seen in the universal phenomenon of a forgotten fact which is said to be on the tip of one's tongue, floating closer to conscious knowledge, and then retreating into the recesses of the mind, only to come back again, after it is no longer needed.

The pattern of coming and going is present from the first sentence of "The Lost Boy": "Light came and went and came again, the booming strokes of three o'clock beat out across the town in thronging bronze from the courthouse bell, light winds of April blew the fountain out in rainbow sheets, until the plume returned and pulsed, as Grover turned into the square."[7] There is a feeling in that sentence of ebb and flow—of pulsation. It is there in the light, which comes and goes, and in the throbbing peals of the bell, which vibrate in beats across the square. The fountain reflects this sense of pulsation, both as the spray is blown by gusts of wind and as the water spurts up from its base. In the next paragraph of the story, these images, with a little variation, are repeated. The courthouse square is a study of coming and going. Street cars come into the square from each compass point, pause briefly, and then move back out on their runs. Grover, ruminating in the midst of this flowing scene, realizes that the square remains the same, despite the changing rhythm of everything in it. Caught in the flux of life all around him, Grover is pensive. He thinks of the square as a permanent fixture. He fixes the year, month, and hour; and for a moment, he is caught on a point in time, just as old Gant and Eugene are in similar scenes in *Look Homeward, Angel.* After this brief moment of calmness, the story again begins to flow; Grover passes the shops, enters the candy store and encounters the proprietor. Then he is back out on the square. Wagons roll past but he does not see them. He stands in the square, again feeling that it is the center of the universe and that it represents Now. Grover enters his father's shop where the scene is quiet and restful. The stones are waiting. A stone angel, to be used as a grave-marker, is languid; there is a layer of stone dust on the chisels. The scene has a Keatsian quality of suspended action, especially when compared with the previous scenes of constant alternation of movement and calmness. Then Grover blurts out the story of the incident with the candy store owner and the father jumps into action. He comes and goes among his gravestones. He begins sentences and stops in mid-thought. With a sudden burst, he grabs Grover "and they went out flying. Down the aisle they went by all the gravestones, past the fly-specked angels waiting there, and down the wooden steps and across the Square. The fountain pulsed, the plume blew out in sheeted iridescence, and it swept across them" (p. 13). W. O. Gant atones for Crocker, the candystore owner, and his treatment of Grover by demanding his son's money back and hurling bitter words at the crippled Crocker. Suddenly Grover is alone and back out on the square again, as the light comes and goes. The switching from violent action to reflective peace continues throughout the first section. Grover knows that "something had gone out of the day and something had come in again" (p. 14). The pattern of coming and going is present in Grover's thoughts as well as in the physical action of the first section. After his father's help, Grover realizes that he has lost a measure of innocence but gained an equal amount of experience. "Out of the vision of those quiet eyes some brightness had gone, and into their vision had come some deeper color. He could not say, he did not know through what transforming shadows life had passed within that quarter hour. He only knew that something had been lost—something forever gained" (p. 14). As the first section ends, Grover sees a poster advertising the St. Louis World's Fair. The sense of ebb and flow in this section is pervasive. It can be felt in the square, in the boy's alternation between coming into others' lives, and going into the square for quiet thought before jumping back into the flow of life all around him. The pattern is seen in the movements of Crocker, who rocks as he walks, coming and going from the rear of his store, and in the boy's father, who alternates between the calmness of his work and the fury of his actions in defense of his son.

Section II is the mother's monologue. In describing Grover, she also holds to this pattern of coming and going, focusing and unfocusing. She talks about Grover and how he acted on the train to St. Louis, but she constantly interrupts her story to revert to the present. She says she can remember exactly how Grover looked on the trip, "with his black eyes, his black hair, and with the birthmark on his neck—so grave, so serious, so earnest-like—as he sat by the train window. . . . It was so long ago, but when I think of it, it all comes back, as if it happened yesterday" (p. 22). The pattern of coming and going is repeated in this section. Grover is calm in the midst of change, just as he was in the square. He quietly watches the changes in the countryside that he sees from the train window, while the other children are running up and down in the aisle, looking from side to side. As the mother talks, Grover comes and goes. She changes from the past to the present and then back to another time in the past.

Section III of "The Lost Boy" is Grover's sister Helen's monologue. At first Helen talks about the strangeness of looking at an old photograph and thinking of the present and "how everyone either dies or grows up and goes away" (p. 23). The past comes back to her while she thinks about the picture. She begins to talk about Grover and the time when the family lived in St. Louis. Helen reminds Eugene about his difficulty as a young child with the pronunciation of Grover's name. In her attempt to recall all of the events leading up to Grover's death, Helen repeats the pattern of ebb and flow that is so prevalent in the earlier sections. "My God, I wish I knew the answer to these things. I'd like to find out what is wrong—what has changed since then—and if we have the same queer look in our eyes, too. Does it happen to us all, to everyone? . . . Grover and Ben, Steve, Daisy, Luke and me—all standing there before that house on Woodson street in Altamont—there we are, and you see the way we were—and how it all gets lost. What is it, anyway, that people lost? . . . It seems that it must be something we heard somewhere—that it happened to someone else. And then it comes back again. . . . It all comes back as if it happened yesterday. And then it goes away again, and seems further off and stranger than if it happened in a dream" (p. 30).

Section IV, the last part of the story, is Eugene's portion. He is back in St. Louis looking for the house where Grover died, looking for the past, lost thirty years before. At first Eugene talks to a stranger to try to locate the house. He thinks of the street called King's Highway, which to himself as a four year old boy was "a kind of road that wound from magic out of some dim and haunted land, and that along the way it had got mixed in with Tom the Piper's son, with hot cross buns, with all the lights that came and went, and with coming down through Indiana in the morning, and the smell of engine smoke, the Union Station, and most of all with voices lost and far and long ago that said 'King's Highway' " (p. 31). Then Eugene is back in the present, still looking for the house. He sees that King's Highway is just a city street now. Eugene finds the house but feels "nothing but absence, absence, and the desolation of America" (p. 33). Again Eugene's thoughts slip back into the past. He is four years old sitting on the stairs feeling a vague sadness because everyone was gone, working at the Fair. He had waited until they would all return and spent the time wondering what the future would bring. Now in St. Louis thirty years later, knowing what the future brought, Eugene wants to return to the past by sitting on the actual stairs of his former house. He thinks that he could remember all that he had seen and been, recapture his own universe as a child.

> But as he thought it, he knew that even if he could sit here alone and get it back again, it would be gone as soon as seized, just as it had been then—first coming like the vast and drowsy rumor of the distant and enchanted Fair, then fading like cloud shadows on a hill, going like faces in a dream—coming, going, coming, possessed and held, but never captured, like lost voices in the mountains long ago—and like the dark eyes and quiet face of the dark, lost boy, his brother, who, in the mysterious rhythm of his life and work, used to come into this house, then go, and then return again. (p. 38)

When Eugene sees the same room where Grover died, "The years dropped off like fallen leaves: the face came back again . . ." (p. 41), and he remembers the same episode about his trying to pronounce Grover's name that his sister had told him in section III of the story. When Helen told him the story, he could not remember, but now, in the very house where it took place, he does remember—"It all came back, and faded, and was lost again" (p. 41). As Eugene leaves the house, he looks back and sees that it is only a house again. His ability to relive the past is gone now and Grover, the lost boy, is also gone, never to return. Through the constant use of the pattern I have been tracing in each section of the story, Wolfe emphasizes Eugene's attempts to escape from the distortions and blurrings of thirty years of elapsed time. He comes nearer and nearer to controlling his memories of Grover and then his ability begins to fade as he leaves the room where Grover died.

In his essay on Wolfe and time, Rubin continues his comments by saying that Wolfe "was a thoroughgoing romantic; his writing has the intensity of fiction written by an artist who is seeking furiously, through his literary craft, to impose on his recalcitrant experience his own highly personal valuations."[8] This view of Wolfe as a romantic trying to evaluate his past, is described by Poulet as typical of the romantic's use of time:

> Incarcerated in the instant, the romantic escapes into thought all the rest of his life. Or rather he tries to envelop his thought in the consciousness of the present moment. It is no longer a question, as it was in the preceding century, of extracting from the moment all its sensuous substance; it is a question of giving the moment all the profundity, all the infinity of duration of which man feels capable. To possess his life in the moment is the pretension or the fundamental desire of the romantic.[9]

"The Lost Boy" also illustrates by its use of place the pattern of coming and going and the difficulty of focusing on the past. St. Louis and the World's Fair serve as further metaphors for a looking backward and forward simultaneously. The Louisiana Purchase Universal Exposition, as the St. Louis Fair of 1904 was officially called, was designed for the dual purpose of celebrating the centennial of the Louisiana Purchase and demonstrating America's progress since 1804. Some of the major events and displays commemorated the past, but the major emphasis of the fair was on the future.[10] Thomas Wolfe, returning to St. Louis after thirty-one years, must have been as surprised as the Eugene of "The Lost Boy" was to see how the entire fairgrounds had vanished. What had seemed magical to a four year old boy, seemed magical still because it had vanished completely. Part of the planning for the fair included plans for the restoration of the park where the fairgrounds were located. David R. Francis, the president of the Louisiana Purchase Exposition Company, explains in his mammoth book on the fair that the "Board of Public Improvements" required the "removal of all buildings except the palace of Art and removal of the Intramural railway,"[11] as well as the following ordinance, "Within twelve months after the close of such Fair or Exposition fully restore the park selected as a site, or, in the case of Forest Park, that portion thereof above described, by doing all necessary grading, the restoration and repair, or the formation of all walks or roads, the planting of trees, the placing of sod and the planting of shrubs and plants, all in accordance with plans to be approved by the Board. . . ."[12] One of the buildings became a city museum; a few others became part of Washington University, but the majority were torn down immediately.

Eugene's attempt at reconstructing the past by visiting St. Louis and looking for his house is complicated by the fact that by 1935 hardly any traces of the fair remain. Street names had been changed, vegetation had grown, and the site of the largest and most famous World's Fair ever, had been transformed into an ordinary city park. The fantastic, magical fair—"A fair so comprehensive, so perfectly planned, that had some disaster wiped out every culture on the face of the earth, all could have been reconstructed from the materials on hand . . ."[13] —had come into his life and gone out of it as though a dream.

St. Louis is itself an example of the difficulty of focusing the past because it is a city whose identity has changed with time. The St. Louis celebrated by W. C. Handy in "St. Louis Blues," is in the same traditional Southern state as Mark Twain's Hannibal, but Missouri was a compromise state and by 1904 the city is thought of as only partly Southern. Eugene says of St. Louis, "He feels the way one feels when one comes back, and knows that he should not have come, and when he sees that, after all, King's Highway is—a street; and St. Louis—the enchanted name—a big, hot, common town upon the river, sweltering in wet, dreary heat, and not quite South . . ." (p. 33). Eugene's impression that St. Louis was not quite a Southern city anymore by 1904 is echoed in Henry James' *The Bostonians*, published only eighteen years before the St. Louis Fair, when Mrs. Farrinder declares that she has been warned not to lecture in Southern cities on the history of feminism. She is answered by Verena Tarrant, who replies, "*I* had a magnificent audience last spring in St. Louis."[14] She is answered by an anonymous voice, "Oh, well, St. Louis—that's scarcely the South."[15] St. Louis is partly Southern, partly Western and partly Mid-Western. Although the city calls itself "Gateway to the West," Wolfe thought of St. Louis as a Mid-Western city: "The loneliness and sadness of the high, hot skies, and evening coming on across the Middle West" (p. 33).

Wolfe's visit to St. Louis in 1935 and his subsequent literary use of that visit to describe the difficulty of recapturing the past by revisiting past locations, foreshadows his return to Asheville in 1937 and his well-known phrase, "you can't go home again," a phrase which Wolfe associated with "the old forms and systems of things which once seemed everlasting but which are changing all the time,"[16] and which he expressed in the pattern of ebb and flow in time and place that permeates "The Lost Boy."

Notes

1. Allan W. Becker, "Ellen Glasgow and the Southern Literary Tradition," *Modern Fiction Studies* 5 (1959–60), 301.
2. Louis D. Rubin, Jr., "The Historical Image of Modern Southern Writing," *Journal of Southern History* 22 (May 1956), 154.
3. Georges Poulet, "The Course of Human Time," trans. by Eliot Coleman, *The Hopkins Review* 6 (Spring-Summer, 1953), 27.
4. Louis D. Rubin, Jr., "Thomas Wolfe: Time and the South," *Writers of the Modern South: The Faraway Country* (Seattle, 1963), 72–104.
5. H. Blair Rouse, "Time and Place in Southern Fiction," in *Southern Renascence*, ed. Louis D. Rubin and Robert D. Jacobs (Baltimore, 1966), 132.
6. Elizabeth Nowell, *Thomas Wolfe, A Biography* (Garden City, N.Y., 1960), p. 379.
7. Thomas Wolfe, "The Lost Boy," in *The Hills Beyond* (New York, 1941), 1. Future citations are to this edition.
8. Rubin, "Thomas Wolfe, Time and the South," p. 103.
9. Poulet, p. 27.
10. Edward J. Coff, "St. Louis Celebrates," *Missouri Historical Society Bulletin* (October 1954), p. 54.
11. David R. Francis, *The Universal Exposition of 1904* (St. Louis, 1913), p. 667.
12. Francis, p. 668.
13. Coff, p. 67.
14. Henry James, *The Bostonians* (New York, 1956), p. 51.
15. James, p. 52.
16. Thomas Wolfe, *You Can't Go Home Again* (New York, 1940), p. 706.

Thomas Wolfe's Success as Short Novelist: Structure and Theme in *A Portrait of Bascom Hawke*

William Domnarski*

Maxwell Perkins said that Thomas Wolfe was a born writer if there ever was one.[1] Few critics have disagreed with that assessment of Wolfe's natural talent. Even Bernard DeVoto, who turned his heavy artillery on Wolfe in 1936, conceded that Wolfe had genius. But genius was not enough for DeVoto.[2] Others have felt the same way, thus making the vital issue in Wolfe's critical reputation not whether he had talent, but what he did with it.

The most frequent charges levelled against Wolfe have stressed his prolixity, structural formlessness, and excessive interest in autobiography.[3] These weaknesses can be seen in each of Wolfe's long novels. In contrast, however, they are not present in his short novels, which have received little attention despite their excellence.[4] In many ways these short novels present the best of Wolfe. Here he is under control, with the defined length of the short novel form imposing necessary restrictions on him.

An examination of structure and theme in *A Portrait of Bascom Hawke*, which Wolfe completed in 1932, illustrates his achievement as a short novelist. The novel is a brilliant portrait of the eccentric Bascom Hawke, who is modelled after Wolfe's uncle Henry Westall, but it is also a book about the narrator, David Hawke, who is Wolfe himself. The contrast between the elderly, despairing uncle and his young, hopeful nephew stands at the heart of the novel, with the ideas of life and death and growth and decay dominating. Wolfe summarized his hopes for *Bascom Hawke* in a note to Perkins. He wrote, "I've simply tried to give you a man—as for plot, there's not any, but there's this idea which I believe is pretty plain—I've always wanted to say something about *old men* and *young men*, and that's what I've tried to do here. I hope the man seems real and living to you and that it has the unity of this feeling I spoke about."[5]

Wolfe overstates *Bascom Hawke's* lack of plot. Scenes from Bascom's past, as well as what might pass as part of a day in his life, make up most of the novel. The only present tense narrative action centers on a conversation between Bascom and his nephew David late in the book. Wolfe's novel is not rooted in the present. Rather, the present is used as a complementary means of illuminating the past—both Bascom's past and the inexorable force of time—and the future. The concept of eternal time holds the novel and its two major characters together.

*Reprinted from the *Southern Literary Journal*, 13, No. 1 (Fall 1980), 32–41. © 1980 by the Dept. of English, University of North Carolina, Chapel Hill.

This continuum helps Wolfe achieve "the unity of this feeling" that he mentions to Perkins.

The plot of *Bascom Hawke* might be spare, but the novel is tightly structured. It opens with Bascom emerging from a Boston subway exit on his way to work as a real estate conveyancer. At this point we are part of the crowd reacting to the cadaverous, grimacing man as others on the street would. We cannot fail to notice this elderly man, whose "grimaces were made by squinting his small sharp eyes together, widening his mouth in a ghastly travesty of a grin, and convolving his chin and cheek in a rapid series of pursed lips and horrible squints as he swiftly pressed his rubbery underlip against a few enormous horse teeth that decorated his upper jaw."[6] More important, we see Bascom as he verbally assaults motorists who have nearly run him over because he has ignored the rules of safe pedestrian traffic. Bascom baits these unsuspecting motorists into arguments to show, in his distinctively imperious manner, his knowledge and their ignorance of automobile law.

Wolfe seems to pause following this opening scene. A clear transition sentence announces the physical description of Bascom that will follow. The description begins with his tall, tough, and angular body and proceeds to his worn and ill-fitting clothes that make him appear more like a beggar than the prosperous businessman he is. This discrepancy leads into an account of Bascom's history. All that our narrator tells us not only helps shade in Bascom's portrait, but also heightens the tension between youth and age and furthers our understanding of Bascom's bitter despair at the novel's conclusion. In a passage that takes on increased importance as we move through the novel, our narrator tells us that "Bascom's youth, following the war between the States, had been seared by a bitter poverty: at once enriched and warped by a life that clung to the earth with a root-like tenacity, that was manual, painful, spare and stricken, and rebuilt itself—fiercely, cruelly, and richly—from the earth"(13).

Poverty constricted Bascom's physical world and turned him to literature, where he found the joys of life otherwise denied him. He read voraciously and ended up at Harvard. There he lived monkishly and established a brilliant record as an undergraduate and graduate theology student. We read that "at thirty [Bascom] was a lean fanatic, a true Yankee madman, high-boned, with gray thirsty eyes and a thick flaring sheaf of oaken hair—six feet three inches of gangling and ludicrous height, gesticulating madly and obliviously before a grinning world. But he had a grand lean head: he looked somewhat like the great Ralph Waldo Emerson—with the brakes off" (14).

Like Emerson, Bascom first entered and then left the ministry. For twenty years he moved from town to town and from church to church hoping to find spiritual satisfaction. But it never came. After much soul-searching, and after investigating the Episcopal, Presbyterian, and

Unitarian churches, all with the hope of finding one that quelled his growing religious skepticism, Bascom turned his back on God and became an agnostic. Freed in a way, Bascom next sought to make as much money as possible as a real estate conveyancer in Boston, perhaps to avenge his youthful poverty. But he had lost more than just his faith during those twenty years. Beginning with his marriage to Louise, Bascom had also gained and lost a family. He and Louise are still together when we meet them in the novel, but Bascom sees his marriage as dead and his wife lost to him as a result of her insanity. His children, in a different way, are also lost because once they came of age they fled from home and never returned.

Having brought us up to date, Wolfe then continues the novel with scenes from a typical day at the office for Bascom. The description is again organized and meticulous. We are shown the outside and inside of the office building before meeting Bascom's office-mates. Their characters reflect the dullness of the office. There is the banal Miss Brill, the meager-looking Samuel Friedman, and the self-satisfied Stanley Ward. They do not understand Bascom and therefore make fun of his eccentricities. John T. Brill, the loud and dominating figure in the office, on the other hand, understands and respects Bascom, so much so that he brags of Bascom's intellect to visitors as though Bascom were his son. Bascom and Brill come from different backgrounds and have different sensibilities, yet there is much common ground between them; nephew David writes:

> Brill was a lewd and innocent man. Like my uncle, by comparison with these other people, he seemed to belong to some earlier, richer, and grander period of the earth, and perhaps this was why there was more actual kinship between them than between any of the other members of the office. These other people . . . belonged to the myriads of the earth, to the numberless swarms that with ceaseless pullulation fill the streets of life with their gray immemorable tides. But Brill and my uncle Bascom were men in a thousand, a million: if one had seen them in a crowd he would have looked after them, if one had talked with them, he could never have forgotten them. (30–31)

One reason we cannot forget Brill's conversation is that it is earthy and vulgar. We sense that Brill naturally incorporates obscenities into his language, but we also sense that he uses as many vulgarities as possible when Bascom is around. This is consistent with Brill's character and his relationship with Bascom, for Brill takes great delight in jokingly trying to offend him. The lengthy section discussing their relationship details many examples of Brill teasing Bascom. He teases Bascom, for instance, about his eccentric aversion to eating in restaurants. Bascom tries to explain that he finds the preparation of restaurant food unhealthy and that he will eat only raw health foods, but we know, as does Brill, that Bascom is simply reluctant to spend money. The same can be said about Bascom and overcoats. He claims that he never wears them because they carry cold-inducing germs; the truth is that Bascom is too cheap to part with the money needed for a warm overcoat.

But even though Bascom cringes at Brill's coarse language, and even though he finds himself the butt of many jokes, he admires and respects Brill. Brill is a man of character—of forceful and aggressive character. Brill lusts after life, and this is reflected in his language, his "invective" as Bascom terms it. In different ways, Bascom and Brill are remarkable men in that they understand life's possibilities and have been willing, in their different ways, to go after what they want. Bascom might bristle at his coarse language, but he also wishes that he had the peculiar kind of strength to use it. Brill's scathing invective thus links the section about the two men with the following section, a digression that focuses on an extramarital affair Bascom was once tempted to have while he vacationed in Florida.

The woman, a plump, sensuous widow, appears an odd match for Bascom. She is so dull-witted, for example, that she misunderstands his long and very obvious poem about his agnosticism. Ordinarily, Bascom would be offended by such stupidity in anyone. The widow may be stupid, but she is shrewd. She recognizes that he is the man she wants and she knows how to get him: by appealing to his vanity and by appearing willing to listen to his harangues. Bascom, who feels underloved and underappreciated by his wife, falls prey to the widow. Their relationship builds and moves to a climax when the widow offers herself sexually to Bascom, who has ambivalent feelings about the offer. On the one hand, he wants to fill the void created by his marriage to Louise. At the same time he cannot break free from social and marital conventions, nor can he overcome his repressed religious beliefs defining the appropriate expressions of love and sex. He wants to defy convention in the way that Brill defies convention when he unleashes his invective, but he does not have the necessary kind of daring. He feels frustrated by his inadequacy. Hence, Bascom declines the widow's offer and the romance ends.

With the conclusion of the aborted romance, the focus of the novel shifts to David, whom we hardly know, even though fifty pages of this short novel have passed. David is ostensibly detailing a conversation he had with Bascom, but their conversation fades into the background as David tells us about himself and his life in Boston. We soon realize that David's life has certain parallels to Bascom's. Both came to Harvard from North Carolina, and both possessed a nearly insatiable appetite for books and life. The following quotations reveal much about David. In addition, the quotations illustrate the sense of vitality that Wolfe infused into *Bascom Hawke*. In the first quotation, David demonstrates his love for life and learning when he discusses his burning ambition to know everything, an ambition Bascom had fifty years earlier. David says:

> My hunger and thirst had been immense: I was caught up for the first time in the midst of the Faustian web—there was no food that could feed me, no drink that could quench my thirst—like an insatiate and maddened animal I roamed the streets, trying to draw up mercy from the cobblestones, solace and wisdom from a million sights and faces, or prowled through the endless shelves of high-piled books tortured by everything I could not see and could not know, and growing blind, weary, and desperate from what I read and saw. I wanted to know all, have all, be all—to be one and many, to have the whole riddle of this vast and swarming earth as legible, as tangible in my hand as a coin of minted gold. (50)

The second quotation reflects David's sensitivity to life, to the earth, and to the products of the earth. He says:

> The air will have in it the wonderful odors of the market . . . the delicate and subtle air of spring touches all these odors with a new and delicate vitality; it draws the tar out of the pavements also, and it draws slowly, subtly, from ancient warehouses, the compacted perfumes of eighty years: the sweet thin piney scents of packing boxes, the glutinous composts of half a century, that have thickly stained old warehouse plankings, the smells of twine, tar, turpentine and hemp, and of thick molasses, ginseng, pungent vines and roots and old piled sacking; the clean ground strength of fresh coffee, brown, sultry, pungent, and exultantly fresh and clean; the smell of oats, baled hay and bran, of crated eggs and cheese and butter; and particularly the smell of meat, of frozen beeves, of slick porks and veals, of brains and livers and kidneys, of haunch, paunch, and jowl; of meat that is raw and of meat that is cooked. . . . (53)

This section outlining David's exuberant view of life sets the stage for the climactic concluding section. David is in Bascom's office to visit; but what transpires is not really a conversation between the two as Bascom does almost all the talking. Through his monologue, as well as through the further glimpses into Bascom's past that David gives us, we begin to understand the idea about *young men* and *old men* that Wolfe told Perkins he had.

Bascom's denigration of women occupies much of his harangue. The reason for this denigration stems from his unhappy marriage to Louise. Bascom had wanted to possess her totally when they married and when he realized after they were wed that he could not do so because Louise's beauty invariably brought complimentary looks from other men, a kind of madness overcame him. He raged with a black jealousy and felt that marriage and love had betrayed him. Because his life was self-centered and self-contained, Bascom could not cope with the idea that he shared his wife, even if sharing amounted only to having other men look at her. Unable to cope, and determined to maintain his fierce individuality and integrity, Bascom did what only he could: he forgot about Louise and treated her with indifference.

The results of this indifference were profound. The gap between Bascom and Louise widened to an unbreachable abyss. Because she could not understand the cause of Bascom's indifference, Louise slowly but inexorably lost her mind. Their children were also affected by his behavior. Bascom also treated them with indifference because he saw them as his wife's children, not his own. Moreover, he imposed his miserly ways on his children and denied them many of the pleasures he too had been denied as a child. As soon as they could, the children escaped from home, bearing bitter grudges that remained with them.

Bascom, then, sees his life as a series of frustrations and betrayals. His life at thirty, which had so much promise because he had been able to overcome the handicaps of youthful poverty with intelligence and perseverance, was attacked by the betrayals of his wife, his children, and his faith. These betrayals relate directly to the theme of the earth that Wolfe develops in *Bascom Hawke*. Wolfe describes Brill as a product of the earth, for example, because he possesses a challenging spirit and a lust for life. Similarly, Wolfe describes Bascom as a product of the earth because his tenacious desire to survive and prosper helped him escape from his bleak childhood. But at the same time, the theme of the earth also carried implications of organic unity, the sense that the individual is integrally bound with society, which represents the fruits of the earth. It is not surprising, therefore, that when Wolfe wants to show David as a product of the earth, he uses the above quotations that focus on David's relationship with the earth and its bounty. The sense of organic unity also extends to the concept of family, both in the particular terms of spouse and children and in the broader concept of the family of man. Believing he has been betrayed by a wife who is not really a wife to him, and by children who despise him, Bascom experiences frustration and bitter loneliness, a loneliness that is compounded by his loss of religious faith. Bascom communicates this genuine despair to David, who in turn tells us that by understanding Bascom we can understand the history of man's loneliness, his dignity, his grandeur, and his despair (39).

Bascom has lost and suffered much. Though some strength remains (his scolding of Boston motorists shows this), he is only a shell of the man he once was. David understands the life Bascom has lived and wants to graft Bascom's experiences onto his own to enrich the life he is to continue living. Sitting with Bascom in his office, David says:

> And now, as I looked at the old man, I had a sense of union with the past. It seemed if he would only speak, the living past, the voices of lost men, the pain, the pride, the madness and despair, the million scenes of the buried life—all that an old man ever knew—would be

> revealed to me, would be delivered to me like a priceless treasure, as an inheritance which old men owed to young, and which should be the end and effort of all living. My savage hunger was a kind of memory: I thought if he could speak it would be fed. (67)

But Bascom does not tell David what he wants to hear. Bascom only says, "It was so long ago . . . so long ago. I have lived so long. I have seen so much. I could tell you so many things" (67).

As the novel draws to its conclusion, David imagines a scene in which a group of old men and women are sitting at a dinner table. Like Bascom, they have suffered and lived on. David discovers in his vision, as he did with Bascom, that these people cannot speak of their pasts. He learns that the past cannot be transmitted. It must be lived again.

The enduring human condition is *Bascom Hawke*'s major theme. Bascom and David epitomize the continual cycle of hope, frustration, and despair, which is followed by renewed hope for the future. Wolfe's short novel is really about the birth and death of dreams. But the acknowledgement we see in old Bascom that dreams die does not stamp *Bascom Hawke* with pessimism. Rather, the novel affirms life. The affirmation of life at the novel's conclusion is to seek, to live. David says this with great beauty and force after he realizes that he cannot rekindle the flame of life in Bascom. He says:

> Then I got up and left him and went out into the streets where the singing and lyrical air, the man-swarm passing in its million-footed weft, the glorious women and the girls compacted into a single music of belly and breasts and thighs, the sea, the proud, potent, and clamorous city, all of the voices of time fused to a unity that was like a song, a token and a cry. Victoriously, I trod the neck of doubt as if it were a serpent: I was joined to the earth, a part of it, and I possessed it; I would be wasted and consumed, filled and renewed eternally; I would be emptied without weariness, replenished forever with strong joy. I had a tongue for agony, a food for hunger, a door for exile and a surfeit for insatiate desire: exultant certainty welled up in me, I thought I could possess it all, and I cried: 'Yes! It will be mine!' (71)

The juxtaposition between David and Bascom highlights what might be called the human cycle, which reflects nature's cycle of birth, growth, decay, and rebirth. Not surprisingly, the earth and what it represents play vital roles in *Bascom Hawke.* Wolfe structures his novel around the development of this theme. He begins with Bascom's youth and then amplifies this idea of the earth with comparisons and contrasts with John T. Brill, another product of the earth. David, the new Bascom, is next identified with the earth, thus providing the final contrast between youth and age. David's triumph stems from his willingness to risk life's disappointments, the disappointments of lost love and frustrated emotions that wearied the once hearty Bascom.

Wolfe knew what he was doing when he wrote *Bascom Hawke*. He carefully draws us into Bascom's world and then proceeds to make Bascom and his plight come alive for us in the subsequent sections. Every section has a purpose, and every character has a function. *Bascom Hawke* contains the great language, the great themes, and the great characterizations that Wolfe erratically achieved in novels such as *Look Homeward, Angel* and *Of Time and the River*. Significantly, *Bascom Hawke* is a tightly structured work—something his long novels are not—that contains all of these elements. It is a novel that should be read and remembered.

Notes

1. Maxwell Perkins, *Editor to Author: The Letters of Maxwell Perkins* (New York: Charles Scribner's Sons, 1950), p. 68.
2. See Bernard DeVoto, "Genius Is Not Enough," *Saturday Review* 13 (April 25, 1936), 3–4, 13–14.
3. See Robert Penn Warren, "A Note on the Hamlet of Thomas Wolfe," reprinted in *Selected Essays of Robert Penn Warren* (New York: Random House, 1958), p. 183.
4. Professor Hugh Holman was the first to point to Wolfe's talent as a short novelist. In his introduction to *The Short Novels of Thomas Wolfe* (New York: Charles Scribner's Sons, 1961), Holman writes: "In the short novel form Wolfe was a master of his craft . . . these successful products of his efforts should not be forgotten."
5. Quoted in Holman's introduction to *The Short Novels of Thomas Wolfe*, p. xx.
6. Thomas Wolfe, *A Portrait of Bascom Hawke*, collected in *The Short Novels of Thomas Wolfe*, pp. 4–5. All future references are in the text and are to this edition.

Thomas Wolfe's Search to Know Brooklyn

Webb Salmon*

Thomas Wolfe's "Only the Dead Know Brooklyn,"[1] though often anthologized, has received little critical attention.[2] The two best biographies of Wolfe, Nowell's and Turnbull's, do not acknowledge the story. There is no mention of "Only the Dead Know Brooklyn" in Wolfe's published letters and only two references by Wolfe in his notebooks—one that merely lists it under his stories written about New York and one, with the word *Exile* written after the title, that classifies the story as one of his works about "The Jungle Years."[3] Yet I should like to suggest that this brief story, only about 2000 words long, has an important role to play in our understanding of a basic theme in much of Wolfe's work—man's loneliness and lostness, and his search to find some relief from the resulting grief.

As we consider this basic idea, I shall try to show that both Thomas Wolfe and his fictional counterparts experienced the search to know Brooklyn; that the search was closely related in Wolfe's mind with his attempts to solve the artistic problems that plagued and almost destroyed him; and that the search, in addition to being viewed literally as an actual, physical search, should be interpreted figuratively to represent a search for calmness of spirit, for peace of mind.

"Only the Dead Know Brooklyn" is narrated by a Brooklyn native who tries to help a stranger—a very large man, who has been drinking but "talks good and is walkin' straight enough"—find his way by subway to a particular section of Brooklyn. En route, the guide becomes upset when he learns that the stranger, determined to learn all of Brooklyn with the help of a map, has wandered at night through an exceptionally dangerous section of the city. The narrator's concern becomes alarm when the big fellow persists in asking strange questions: how long would it take to learn all of Brooklyn, and what happens to people after they have drowned in Brooklyn? Fearing that the man is "some kind of nut," the guide leaves the train at the next stop as the stranger looks at his map and repeats "Drownin'," "Drownin'." Some time later the narrator still wonders about the "poor guy"—whether "someone knocked him on duh head" during his nighttime wandering and whether "he's found out by now dat he'll neveh live long enough to know deh whole of Brooklyn."

From March 1931 till March 1935, Wolfe lived and wrote in Brooklyn. These were the years when, after the generally favorable reception of *Look Homeward, Angel*, he struggled to find for his next novel the artistic pattern through which he could organize the hundreds of thousands of words that flowed from his creative and tortured mind.

He tells us in *The Story of a Novel*, a long essay about these four years of writing in Brooklyn, that he knew the central idea he wanted to express: "The deepest search in life, . . . the thing that in one way or another was central to all living was man's search to find a father, . . . not merely the lost father of his youth, but the image of a strength and wisdom . . . to which the belief and power of his own life could be united."[4] Of necessity, to keep from being destroyed by a thwarted obsession to write, he committed himself irrevocably to his work.

But, Wolfe says, ". . . a terrible doubt began to creep into my mind that I might not live long enough to get it out of me, that I had created a labor so large and so impossible that the energy of a dozen lifetimes would not suffice for its accomplishment."[5] Wolfe is certainly speaking of himself when he has George Webber, a Brooklyn resident for a time and the protagonist in *You Can't Go Home Again*, say, "I was more involved than I had ever been before with my inner struggle. Those were the years of the greatest doubt and desperation I had ever known."[6] Frustrated, Wolfe was tempted to change his residence, but he decided that leaving was no solution; he wrote his uncle, who had urged the move, that, though his "tendency [had] been to wander and roam in search of . . . peace and security," he must find these inside himself."[7] And so he stayed to search in Brooklyn and through his writing. Wolfe could have said, as did Webber, "For four years . . . I lived and explored the jungle depths of Brooklyn—jungle depths coincident with those of my own soul. . . ."[8]

This concept of the coincidence of an area and a search and one's soul takes us back to the closing of Wolfe's first novel, back to the imagined exchange between Eugene Gant and his dead brother Ben. Gene, believing in "harbors at the end," says he wants to find himself, "an end to hunger, and the happy land"; but Ben replies: "There is no happy land. There is no end to hunger." Gene insists on an answer with his question "Where, Ben? Where is the world?" "Nowhere. . . . *You* are your world."[9]

Thomas Wolfe and some of his characters learned that the outward search was truly representative of an inner search; and this search was for Wolfe related to his struggles to be a good writer, to find the map that would help him master his own Brooklyn, to avoid drowning in the flood of problems associated with his own creativity. Andrew Turnbull writes: "He knew that he would never again sleep the sweet sleep of childhood. . . . At last he knew the cost of being a writer; he saw what happens to a man who makes the writer's life his own."[10]

We do not have to wonder whether the nocturnal wanderings of Wolfe's characters are based on his own. In a letter written in late 1933 he says that he has lived in recent years in Brooklyn, in Manhattan, and in foreign countries—"and that the largest and most unknown continent of all is Brooklyn. . . . I have gone out into the wilderness five hundred times," he continues, "armed with a trusty map, now worn to tatters, and have prowled about, exploring the place in the dark hours of the night. . . ." In the same letter he says, "The Brooklyn people boast that you can live here a lifetime and never get to know their town, and they are right about it. . . ."[11] The evidence could hardly be more conclusive that in "Only the Dead Know Brooklyn," "duh big guy" (Wolfe was about 6' 7" tall and weighed 240 pounds), "wanderin' aroun' in duh subway in duh middle of duh night wit his little map" and concerned about what happens to people after they have drowned in Brooklyn, is based on Wolfe himself.

Prowling through the city streets was habitual with Wolfe. Maxwell Perkins, his loyal friend and editor, tells the now well-known story about Wolfe's walking through the rain in the early morning hours chanting "I wrote ten thousand words today—I wrote ten thousand words today."[12] Sometimes Wolfe would walk home with Perkins in Manhattan after an evening editorial session and a drink, and occasionally he would become so engrossed in talk that he would not leave until Perkins went out to get an early morning edition of the newspaper.[13] Then he might walk across the bridge and through the streets of Brooklyn. He particularly liked to walk along the waterfront and to go to the wholesale markets to watch the fresh produce unloaded at dawn. His friend and agent and biographer, Elizabeth Nowell, says that sometimes he would "roam around in the toughest sections" of Brooklyn. Like the large fellow in "Only the Dead Know Brooklyn," "he would stop in a bar and drink, or roam from bar to bar. . . ." Miss Nowell writes, "It was a wonder he never got held up or sandbagged: evidently his tremendous size and wild appearance intimidated even the Brooklyn thugs."[14] By dawn he would be so exhausted that he could finally fall asleep—though, according to his own account, the sleep was likely to be "an unceasing nightmare of blazing visions that swept across my fevered and unresting mind," a "nightmare pageantry to which my consciousness lay chained a spectator."[15]

But it would be erroneous to assume that Wolfe's night wandering served only to exhaust him and so make sleep possible. Turnbull explains that his ears were "tuned to the shouts of the drivers and grocery boys" and that he was sensitive to the language he heard on the docks and in the bars.[16] Conversations he heard were likely to appear in Wolfe's stories of the city at night. Robert Raynolds, a novelist and friend who occasionally walked in the city with Wolfe, explains that these walks were part of Wolfe's creative process. Raynolds writes, "Wolfe walked along the street as if his business were right there; his business was to hear, see, feel, taste and touch and smell the life on the street; he was working as he walked."[17]

We should remember that the years Wolfe lived in Brooklyn were years of the Depression. What he saw in his night wanderings contributed to the development of the social consciousness that is so obvious in his writings of this period. In *The Story of a Novel* Wolfe relates his own experience:

> I saw a man whose life had subsided into a mass of shapeless and filthy rags, devoured by vermin; wretches huddled together for a little warmth in freezing cold squatting in doorless closets upon the foul seat of a public latrine within the very shadow, the cold shelter of palatial and stupendous monuments of weath. I saw acts of sickening

> violence and cruelty, the menace of brute privilege, a cruel and corrupt authority trampling ruthlessly below its feet the lives of the poor, the weak, the wretched, and defenseless of the earth.
>
> And the staggering impact of this black picture of man's inhumanity to his fellow man . . . left a scar upon my life, a conviction in my soul which I shall never lose.[18]

George Webber, the protagonist in Wolfe's two posthumous novels, experienced, of course, the same New York that Thomas Wolfe explored. And Webber, like Wolfe, is a novelist. In *You Can't Go Home Again* Webber writes to his editor, Foxhall Edwards, of "the memory of my exploration of the jungle trails of night" and of unemployed boys and men who "had been cast loose by a society that had no need for them and left to shift in any way they could—to find their food in garbage cans, to seek for warmth and fellowship in foul latrines like the one near New York's City Hall, to sleep wrapped up in old newspapers on the concrete floors of subway corridors."[19] Like Wolfe, Webber was horrified by the "blind injustice" of the situation: "all around him in the cold moonlight, only a few blocks away from the abyss of human wretchedness and misery, blazed the pinnacles of power where a large portion of the entire world's wealth was locked in mighty vaults."[20] The similarity between Wolfe's and Webber's observations and reactions is, of course, inescapable.

Like Wolfe, Webber was cursed with sleeplessness. He would work "for hours at a stretch at his novel. Finally, he would stagger forth into the nightless streets, reeling like a drunkard with his weariness . . . because his mind was feverish and he knew he could not sleep, [Webber] would walk to the Brooklyn Bridge and cross it to Manhattan, and ferret out the secret heart of darkness in all the city's ways, and then at dawn come back across the Bridge once more, and so to bed in Brooklyn."[21]

In the earlier Webber novel, *The Web and the Rock*, we read of his prowling "a hundred streets" in the "darkness that stretched from light to light"; "he would come back in the morning, come back from death to morning, walking on the bridge."[22] And this restlessness plagued Webber (and Wolfe) whether he was writing in Brooklyn or agonizing abroad over the reception his first book would receive. In London after "prowling feverishly through the . . . streets until three or four in the morning, Webber would go to bed and fall into a diseased coma. . . ."[23] In Munich it was the same: "At night he walked the streets"; he "could find no end and seek no rest."[24]

George Webber began to understand that being lonely and being lost are inseparable and that loneliness is at the center of the "experience of every man."[25] He felt that men are lost; but he, like other Wolfe characters, was comforted by the thought of ships calling from the harbor. (The big fellow in "Only the Dead Know Brooklyn" was fascinated by the "ships oveh deh all lighted up.")

Other Wolfe characters in the Brooklyn period know about loneliness. The narrator of the short novel, *No Door,* who lives in "the huge and rusty jungle of the earth that is known as Brooklyn,"[26] says that he has been alone more than anyone he knows. He feels that he is a ghost walking among the city people; and he, like the big fellow trying to learn Brooklyn, has "the sensation of drowning in a sea of horror."[27] (He would have deplored the narrator of "Only the Dead Know Brooklyn," who does not even know that people can drown in the city.) The narrator in *No Door* is allowed to express only implicitly what the speaker in a second Brooklyn story, "Death the Proud Brother," says explicitly. The second narrator is relieved to come out into the open air from the presence of a man who has died alone—and for some time unnoticed—in a subway tunnel; the narrator says, "I knew I should not die and strangle like a mad dog in the tunnel's dark. I knew I should see light once more and know new coasts and come into strange harbors, and see again, as I had once, new lands and morning."[28]

As we move backwards into the earlier years of Wolfe's counterpart—this time Eugene Gant in *Of Time and the River*—we see another young man who, like Webber, believes in "harbors at the end."[29] He knows that men "walk the streets of life alone,"[30] unsuccessful in their search for the word or the stone or the door that will open the way to the knowledge they seek; but he cannot agree when an older youth, Francis Starwick, tries to tell him that his hunger will exhaust him, will break his heart, will drive him mad.[31] Starwick does not know of the compulsion that governs Eugene's search: he did not see him several years earlier in that memorable scene with the ghost of Ben on the porch of their father's marble shop. In that predawn scene Eugene vows that he will hunt "the ghost and haunter of [him]self," even though the search will lead to strange coasts and to "seas stranger than those haunted by the Albatross." A determined Eugene continues:

> ". . . no leaf hangs for me in the forest; I shall lift no stone upon the hills; I shall find no door in any city. But in the city of myself, upon the continent of my soul, I shall find the forgotten language, the lost world, a door where I may enter. . . ; I shall haunt you, ghost, along the labyrinthine ways until—until? O Ben, my ghost, an answer?"[32]

Ben, not so optimistic as Eugene, has no answer. Ben may understand, but cannot express, the cryptic thought that an older Eugene become the writer Thomas Wolfe can articulate:

> Naked and alone we came into exile. In her dark womb we did not know our mother's face; from the prison of her flesh have we come into the unspeakable and incommunicable prison of this earth.
> . . . Which of us is not forever a stranger and alone?

> . . . Remembering speechlessly we seek the great forgotten language, the lost lane-end into heaven, a stone, a leaf, an unfound door.[33]

The young Eugene is a kindred spirit to the big fellow who is convinced he can learn all of Brooklyn. "Lost? . . . No, I wouldn't get lost. I got a map." An older Eugene become George Webber become Thomas Wolfe might agree with the Brooklyn narrator when he says of the big stranger, "Maybe he's found out by now dat he'll neveh live long enough to know duh whole of Brooklyn. It'd take a guy a lifetime to know Brooklyn t'roo and t'roo. An' even den yuh wouldn't know it all."

* * *

Thomas Wolfe never learned in his lifetime the whole of Brooklyn, and he never was convinced that in his writing he had found the language that would release him from the "incommunicable prison." But, as Faulkner said, he failed more gloriously than other writers because he put more of himself into the attempt to develop his marvelous talent.[34]

For Wolfe the search was over a few days before his thirty-eighth birthday. His death came, ironically, at a time when he was optimistic about his work. In May of 1938 he wrote Miss Nowell that he thought he had "come through a kind of transition period in [his] life . . . and [had] now found a kind of belief and hope and faith [he] never had before."[35] Four months later he was dead.

When Maxwell Perkins heard that his friend would die, he kept thinking over and over of Kent's lines about the dying King Lear:

> He hates him
> That would upon the rack of this tough world
> Stretch him out longer.

"For," Perkins would write later, "he was on the rack almost always, and almost always would have been. . . ."[36]

Thomas Wolfe was dead. Perhaps, at last, he could know Brooklyn.

Notes

1. In Thomas Wolfe, *From Death to Morning* (New York: Charles Scribner's Sons, 1935), pp. 91–97.

2. The merit of the story was recognized early. It was included in Edward J. O'Brien's collection, *The Best Short Stories, 1936*.

Bruce R. McElderberry [*Thomas Wolfe* (New York: Twayne Publishers, 1964), pp. 116–17] thinks the story is "much more successful" and "less pretentious" than "Death the Proud Brother." He believes "the ugly idiom and monotonous rhythm of the dialect" are appropriate for expressing a "callousness of feeling." Herbert Muller [*Thomas Wolfe* (Norfolk: New Directions Books, 1947), p. 77], on the other hand, says the dialect is "a tiresome exercise in Brooklynese." Muller thinks the story is merely one of several "exercises from a writer's notebook" that appear in *From Death to Morning*. Richard Walser [*Thomas Wolfe: An Introduction and*

Interpretation (New York: Holt, Rinehart, & Winston, 1961), p. 124] speaks of the theme of loneliness in the Brooklyn stories and says that "the vast area [of Brooklyn] is undiscovered even by the 'pavement ciphers' who people it." None of these three critics devotes as much as a paragraph to "Only the Dead Know Brooklyn."

The most extensive discussion of the story that I know is Edward A. Bloom's [*The Order of Fiction: An Introduction* (New York: Odyssey Press, 1964), pp. 143–46; reprinted as "Critical Commentary on 'Only the Dead Know Brooklyn,'" ed. Leslie Field, *Three Decades of Criticism* (New York: New York Univ. Press, 1968), pp. 269–72]. Bloom thinks the story is an allegorical portrayal of the conflict between "the restless individual search for the bluebird and the passivity of acceptance," a struggle "between a broad idea of absorptive materialism and threatened ideals."

3. Thomas Wolfe, *The Notebooks of Thomas Wolfe*, ed. Richard S. Kennedy and Paschal Reeves (Chapel Hill: Univ. of North Carolina Press, 1970), Vol. II, pp. 879, 956.

4. Thomas Wolfe, *The Story of a Novel* (New York: Charles Scribner's Sons, 1936), p. 39.

5. *The Story of a Novel*, p. 55.

6. Thomas Wolfe, *You Can't Go Home Again* (New York: Harper & Bros, 1940), p. 725.

7. Thomas Wolfe, *The Letters of Thomas Wolfe*, ed. Elizabeth Nowell (New York: Charles Scribner's Sons, 1956), pp. 316–17.

8. *You Can't Go Home Again*, p. 739.

9. Thomas Wolfe, *Look Homeward, Angel* (New York: Charles Scribner's Sons, 1929), p. 624.

10. Andrew Turnbull, *Thomas Wolfe* (New York: Charles Scribner's Sons, 1967), p. 177.

11. *The Letters of Thomas Wolfe*, p. 390.

12. Maxwell Perkins, Introduction to *Look Homeward, Angel* (New York: Charles Scribner's Sons, 1957), p. xiv. [Reprinted from the *Harvard Library Bulletin*, I, No. 3 (Autumn 1947.)] Perkins attributes this story to Nancy Hale, who lived near the Perkinses at the time.

13. Turnbull, p. 192.

14. Elizabeth Nowell, *Thomas Wolfe: A Biography* (Garden City, N.Y.: Doubleday & Co., 1960), p. 200.

15. *The Story of a Novel*, pp. 61–62.

16. Turnbull, p. 175.

17. Robert Raynolds, *Thomas Wolfe: Memoir of a Friendship* (Austin: Univ. of Texas Press, 1965), p. 23.

18. *The Story of a Novel*, pp. 59–60.

19. *You Can't Go Home Again*, p. 729.

20. *You Can't Go Home Again*, p. 414.

21. *You Can't Go Home Again*, p. 398.

22. Thomas Wolfe, *The Web and the Rock* (New York: Harper & Bros, 1939), p. 555.

23. *The Web and the Rock*, p. 623.

24. *The Web and the Rock*, p. 661.

25. *You Can't Go Home Again*, p. 499.

26. Thomas Wolfe, "No Door," in *From Death to Morning*, p. 12.

27. "No Door," p. 4.

28. Thomas Wolfe, "Death the Proud Brother," in *From Death to Morning*, p. 67.

29. *The Web and the Rock*, p. 299.

30. Thomas Wolfe, *Of Time and the River* (New York: Charles Scribner's Sons, 1935), p. 74.

31. *Of Time and the River*, pp. 708–09.

32. *Look Homeward, Angel*, p. 625.

33. *Look Homeward, Angel*, p. 2.

34. Frederick L. Gwynn and Joseph L. Blotner, *Faulkner in the University* (Charlottesville: Univ. of Virginia Press, 1939), pp. 144, 206.

35. Nowell, p. 16. Also, *The Letters of Thomas Wolfe*, p. 763.

36. Nowell, p. 16.

The City in the Short Fiction of Thomas Wolfe

James D. Boyer*

In the summer of 1937 Thomas Wolfe returned to Asheville. He had not been back since the great outcry against him after the publication in 1929 of *Look Homeward, Angel,* that nakedly autobiographical novel that had exposed and enraged many people in his home town. The Asheville reception in 1937 was a warm one. Wolfe had become famous in the intervening years and people had forgiven him. Family and friends flocked around him, and for a while the attention was pleasant and flattering. But by fall the joys of the old home town had worn thin, and Wolfe went hurrying back to New York City. He had found that he couldn't go home again, or more accurately, that fourteen years of living in New York City had made it his real home.

When he had come to the city in 1925, Wolfe was, of course, as much the provincial as his fictional protagonists, Eugene Gant and George Webber. He had grown up in the mountain country of Asheville, had gone to a rural university in Chapel Hill, and had spent three years cloistered at Harvard. After that, from 1925 until his death in 1938, he made New York his home. He had brought to the city more than the usual number of fears and prejudices. Those fourteen years show a significant change in his feelings toward the city, a growth in understanding and sympathy for its people that is clearly reflected in his writing.

Wolfe's earliest fiction dealing with New York is "The Train and the City," a story published in *Scribner's Magazine* in May 1933, but written in 1930 or earlier. The story reflects deep division in the feelings

*Reprinted from the *Thomas Wolfe Review*, 7, No. 2 (Fall 1983), 36–40. © 1983 by the University of Akron, Akron, Ohio.

of his protagonist between what he had anticipated of the city and what he found it to be. In a passage early in the story he pictures the city as he experienced it on a glorious first day of spring when everything came to life:

> Over the immense and furious encampment of the city there trembled the mightly pulsations of a unity of hope and joy, a music of triumph and enchantment that suddenly wove all life into the fabric of its exultant harmonies. It quelled the blind and brutal stupefactions of the street, it pierced into a million cells, and fell upon ten thousand acts and moments of man's life and business, it hovered above him in the air, it gleamed and sparkled in the flashing tides that girdled round the city, and with a wizard's hand it drew forth from the tombs of winter the gray flesh of the living dead.

The wonders of that day rekindle in the speaker his childhood vision of the city:

> It was a vision simple, golden, unperplexed, carved from deep substances of light and shade, and exultant with its prophecy of glory, love and triumph.
>
> I heard, far-off, the deep and bee-like murmur of its million-footed life, and all the mystery of the earth and time was in that sound. I saw its thousand streets peopled with a flashing, beautiful, infinitely varied life. The city flashed before me like a glorious jewel, blazing with the thousand rich and brilliant facets of a life so good, so bountiful, so strangely and constantly beautiful and interesting that it seemed intolerable that I should miss a moment of it. I saw the streets swarming with the figures of great men and glorious women, and I walked among them like a conqueror, winning fiercely and exultantly by my talent, courage, and merit, the greatest tributes that the city had to offer, the highest prize of power, wealth, and fame, and the great emolument of love.[1]

The feelings are, of course, those generalized anticipations of the rural-bred youth heading for the city, a vision more powerful perhaps in the 1920's than now, but still close enough to our own experience to rekindle strong feelings, if only nostalgia.

But a few phrases in those passages—"the blind and brutal stupefaction of the streets" and "the gray flesh of the living dead"—reveal a contrasting response that surfaces in the narrator even as he tries to recapture the childhood vision. This response, a feeling of mistrust and repulsion, deepens as he moves from description of place to description of people: "I saw again," he says, "the million faces—the faces dark, dingy, driven, harried, and corrupt, the faces stamped with all the familiar markings of suspicion and mistrust, cunning, contriving, and a hard and stupid cynicism. There were the faces thin and febrile, of the taxi drivers, the faces cunning, sly and furtive, the hard twisted mouths and rasping voices, . . . the faces cruel and arrogant and knowing of the beak-nosed Jews, the brutal heavy figures of the Irish cops." The reader feels embarrassment for the antagonism and prejudice of the narrator as he goes on: "Hard mouthed, hard-eyed, and strident tongued, with their million hard gray faces, they streamed past upon the streets forever, like a single animal, with the sinuous and baleful convolutions of an enormous reptile." Though the narrator tries to tie these people in with his vision of wonder over the city, the reader remains unconvinced. Clearly the real city is, for the narrator, filled with strange, frightening, unfriendly people.

In another early story, "Death, the Proud Brother," (*Scribner's Magazine*, June 1933) Wolfe gives us further insight into what was wrong with city life; here the city is impersonal, isolating, mechanical, violent. The story is a graphic account of four unrelated city deaths: a street vendor is crushed by a truck, a worker fall to his death from a steel beam high above a construction site, a skidrow bum crushes his head in a drunken fall, and an Irishman dies peacefully on a subway bench. What pervades each of these incidents is the impersonality of the city: the truck driver who has killed the street vendor continues on, unaware of the death his truck has caused; the death fall of the riveter causes a traffic jam that angers the inconvenienced people; the dead drunk is the butt of jokes by two callous sophisticates. And although the narrator describes the fourth death differently, telling how death came quietly and bestowed dignity and awe on the man in the subway, the reader is still aware of a disturbing detachment on the part of those present—the crowd makes jokes and a young black prostitute lures away a vulpine-faced Italian. The city, judged by these four episodes, is uncaring. In it man appears to lose the capacity for compassion and brotherhood. The narrator's anger is so intense at one point that the action of these city people made him "want to smash them in the face." The tone of the story changes dramatically in the long lyric apostrophe to death, loneliness and sleep that ends it, but that beautiful lyric fails to erase the narrator's angry feelings toward man alive.

This sense of city man as "man swarm"—abrasive, strident, reptilian, vulpine and uncaring—reflects Wolfe's early response to the city. Characteristic of his writing done before 1932, the response tells us more about his own isolation and defensiveness during that period than about the city, for as he lives in the city over a period of years, especially after his move from Manhattan to Brooklyn in 1931, his angry tone is softened considerably. "No Door," written after that move, shows some beginning steps in that change of feelings. In its opening section, where the narrator is conversing with a pleasant, aesthetic-looking millionaire, it is clearly the wealthy host who is naive about city life and the narrator who understands the real richness of life there. And the city people, as the narrator describes them now, contribute to the richness. Of his landlady in Brooklyn, he explains "what a good and liberal-hearted woman she is; how rough and ready, full of life and energy, how she likes drinking and the fellowship of drinking men, and knows all the rough and seamy sides of life. . . ."[2] And other neighbors are favorably presented too. Even as he describes the neighbors who fight and brawl, or the prostitute in the street at 2:00 a.m. who screams at her escort, "Yah gotta pay me, yuh big bum," and the escort who counters, "I won't pay yuh until you start acting like a lady," he presents them with the pride and affection of an insider. And ironically, though the overall theme of "No Door" has to do with man's inescapable isolation, the narrator appears to be experiencing acceptance and feeling community with these people. "No Door" is clearly a turning point.

This changing attitude toward the city and its people is further illustrated in one of Wolfe's simplest and most impressive short stories, "Only the Dead Know Brooklyn," published two years later in 1935.[3] Here one of the city people, a Brooklynite, narrates the story. Like earlier city people he is pugnacious, brash, and uneducated. But he is curious and kind, too. While waiting for a subway one evening, he encounters a tall, half-drunk, half-crazed stranger. (The reader at once recognizes this stranger as the familiar Wolfe protagonist.) The stranger is exploring Brooklyn with a map and wants to find "Benson-hoist," and the Brooklynite is anxious to help. But as the stranger talks of wandering through the Red Hook section at night, clearly not a sensible thing to do, and questions what the Brooklynite would do if he ever found someone drowning in Brooklyn, the native explains that people don't drown in Brooklyn, then begins to realize just how drunk or crazy the stranger is, and gets off the subway early to escape, repeating that it would take a whole lifetime to know Brooklyn,—that in fact, only the dead really know Brooklyn.

The reader, of course, has more understanding of the whole situation than does the narrator. The reader sees that the stranger with the map is trying to absorb the city, to experience everything; he understands that drowning, while not a literal but a metaphorical danger, is a serious danger nonetheless for the stranger. (It is Wolfe's greatest struggle with the protean city.) But the final wisdom in the story is given to the city man, even though he doesn't fully understand the implications of his own words: "It'd take a guy a lifetime to know Brooklyn t'roo and t'roo. An even den, yuh wouldn't know it all." Though the tall stranger in the story hasn't learned yet, Wolfe is clearly learning to curb the insatiable appetite for experience.

The extent to which Wolfe came to identify with the lower classes in the city—in his fiction and in his life—is spelled out in one of the final stories he worked on before his final trip west in 1938 and his death. "The Party at Jack's" concerns the other side of the society of the city, the very rich. Wolfe had, of course, come to know personally the ways of the rich through his relationship with Aline Bernstein. She worked as a designer in the theater, but her husband had amassed a fortune as a stockbroker, and through their parties Wolfe came to know a significant circle of the rich and powerful of the city. And for a time he had viewed that life as a glorious goal to reach out for. But through his years of living in Brooklyn, by observing first hand the poverty and deprivation of the poor, he had begun to recognize the injustice and evil of the system that supported Aline's family and others of that privileged class. Having moved from his romantic period to one of great social concern, Wolfe wrote "The Party at Jack's" to make clear where he stood.

The story covers a single day in 1929, just before the great stock market crash, and is set in the fashionable apartment of Esther Jack, mistress of Wolfe's final protagonist, George Webber. The central event of the story is a party George attends, at which the fashionable people gather. At the party, aspiring writer George meets other writers, critics, stage stars and aging dilettantes. Chief entertainment for the evening is Piggy Logan and his circus of wire dolls. The party is a rather dismal affair, at least for George. As it draws to a close, fire breaks out in the building, causing those still present to flee to the streets. Though the fire is soon extinguished and things returned to normal, the experiences of the evening, the luxury and pointlessness of the whole affair, convince George that he must break with Esther Jack and her world of sterile luxury.

Wolfe calls "The Party at Jack's" the most densely woven piece of writing that he had ever attempted. In the story, a sweeping attack on the capitalistic system, virtually everything is symbolic. Richard Kennedy, in *The Window of Memory*, has given a careful analysis of the social criticism.[4] The apartment building, complete with elevator operators and serving girls, represents a whole world of wealth and privilege. Beneath runs the subway, whose rumblings, scarcely felt above, suggest the shakiness of this system of privilege resting on the working classes who pass beneath. The fire in the building, suggestive, perhaps, of the depression itself, causes much concern but only temporary dislocation for these privileged souls. But the uncertainty remains. Characters in the story represent important types: old John Enborg is the willing servant who works for and defends the Jacks and their class; Amy Van Leer, the aging socialite whose inability to articulate ideas—and whose bored resignation represent the "lost generation," those who had experienced too much too soon; and the Jacks themselves, the liberals of the world, basically good people who are yet caught up in and responsible for the evils of the system. And images are used to reinforce narrative: Piggy Logan's grotesque mechanical circus serves as a striking image of the tastelessness of the cult and the reduction of art among the wealthy class. Characters, events, images—all function in the story to condemn the privileges of the wealthy, the greed and the essential sterility of the upper classes. Wolfe's final statement on the city, it aims its criticism not at the city at such, but at its privileged class. It demonstrates Wolfe's real allegiance to and love for the city people he had been living with.

Though he pictured city man as poor, often the victim, often alienated, he showed a growing compassion for and identification with these people throughout his career. As a result, he was able to write of Brooklyn in summer, "There are so many million doors tonight. There's a door for everyone tonight, all's open to the air, all's interfused tonight . . . and there is something over all tonight, something fused, remote and trembling . . . upon the huge and weaving ocean of the night in Brooklyn."[5] And before that fatal Western trip, he had carefully reinstalled himself in a Manhattan apartment. After his reconciliation with the South, he did come home again, to New York City.

Notes

1. "The Train and the City," *Scribner's Magazine*, 93 (May, 1933), 285–286.
2. "No Door," *Scribner's Magazine*, 94 (July 1933), 47.
3. "Only the Dead Know Brooklyn," *The New Yorker*, 11 (June 15, 1935, 13–14.
4. (Chapel Hill: Univ. of North Carolina Press, 1962), pp. 347–354. "The Party at Jack's" is Chap. 15 of *You Can't Go Home Again*.
5. *You Can't Go Home Again* (New York: Harper and Brothers, 1940), p. 430.

General

Thomas Wolfe: Halting the Flow of Time

Larry Rubin*

One of the first things that every careful reader of Thomas Wolfe's work notices is the author's deep concern with time. Wolfe's novels,[1] says Margaret Church, "echo the voice of time."[2] Like most of his recurrent themes, the desire to recapture the past and bring it into the present is introduced in the prose poem which prefaces *Look Homeward, Angel*, in which the author exclaims: "*O lost, and by the wind grieved, ghost, come back again*" (*LH*, 2). The "ghost" here probably refers to Eugene's dead brother Ben; but on another level it is possible to interpret the word as connoting the ghost of the past. Yet before Wolfe's many recurrent images of time can be examined in an attempt to trace the motif in his contrapuntal design, some general discussion of the novelist's view of time is essential.

Actually, the time problem in these books can be viewed as a natural outgrowth of Wolfe's idea of the lost paradise. This heaven was lost to the hero at the time of birth, and, as in Wordsworth's "Ode," its last vestiges recede and disappear as one grows older and, in a temporal sense, moves further and further away from the enchanted period of pre-existence. Consequently, any means by which the hero can recapture the past—in however fragmentary a fashion—will be seized upon as a sign that the loss of paradise is not completely irreparable. Indeed, extravagant as it may sound, one feels that Wolfe would like somehow to halt the flow of time, to become master of the fourth dimension, as it were, and so prove to himself that paradise, which he feels still exists somewhere in the past, has not been lost to him forever.[3]

Such an approach to time, of course, involves a certain amount of reworking of what we normally consider conventional chronology, or "clock time." Take, for example, Wolfe's recurrent motif of the relativity of time.[4] This idea is directly opposed to our customary notions about

*Reprinted from *Americana-Austriaca*, 4 (1978), 105–18.

the possibility of measuring time in an absolute way; for although we ordinarily think of each and every hour as being equal in length, *subjectively* speaking, at least, such is not necessarily the case. Nor is this idea entirely new in our literature. For instance, consider Rosalind's remarks in *As You Like It* about "who time gallops withal" and "who time trots withal" (III, ii, 326–351). Far from being mere idle chatter, her comments constitute essentially a lighthearted treatment of the same problem. In Wolfe's case, it should be kept in mind that basically we are dealing with a romantic lyricist—an extreme subjectivist. As far as he is concerned, it seems, nothing has any reality except as he himself experiences the thing in question. For Wolfe, the nature of time at any given moment is determined by the state of his own consciousness at that moment. It is in this sense that his view of the passage of time may be termed a psychological one—as contrasted to the conventional one.

The main purpose of this article, however, is to discuss images of "time immutable." This is a concept which offers an even more radical departure from our orthodox views of time than does the idea of time's relativity. "Time immutable" is perhaps best explained by the author's own statement in *The Story of a Novel*: it is "the time of rivers, mountains, oceans, and the earth; a kind of eternal and unchanging universe of time against which would be projected the transience of man's life, the bitter briefness of his day."[5] This "timeless time," as it were, appears at first to present a paradox; but again, subjectively considered, the concept acquires real meaning. Above and beyond the observable mutability of our daily, workaday existence, Wolfe seems to sense a realm of timelessness—typified here by "rivers, mountains, oceans, and the earth"—which defies change. Now, since change is, in the phenomenal world, the unescapable mark of time's passage, anything that defies change *ipso facto* defies time and is, so to speak, "timeless." Such things, then, can be said to belong to the realm of "time immutable."

In such a realm, of course, there can be no temporal distinctions between the events of yesterday and those of today, or between the events of today and those of tomorrow. Thus, carried to its logical (or, perhaps, illogical) conclusion, the idea of time immutable gives rise to that of the unity of time—a focal concept in Wolfe's work. According to this idea, past, present, and future are merely illusory phenomena; essentially, all time exists at once, so to speak; or, as a deeply religious man might put it, "All time exists in the mind of God." The simple and familiar analogy of the man in the boat and the man in the airplane may have clarifying value here. If one is in a boat on a winding river, everything that he has already passed and can no longer see behind the bend is in the past. Everything ahead of him around the next bend is in the future; that, too, is hidden from him. He can see only what is alongside him now—the present. But if he is in an airplane high above the same river, he can take in all these areas with one glance. "Past," "present," and "future" in this sense no longer exist: he has in a way annihilated these illusory and artificial divisions of time.

To the practical man accustomed to limiting his knowledge of reality to what he can apprehend directly by means of his five physical senses, all such notions may appear to be sheer nonsense; but to an essentially mystical, romantic temperament—one, like Wolfe's, which relies largely upon an intuitive apprehension of reality—these ideas are vital, for they help orient his entire view of life. Wolfe himself seems to adhere to these highly metaphysical ideas more or less instinctively, without trying to formulate them into any neat, logical system. As Margaret Church observes, "Wolfe, unlike Proust, was no philosopher and would without question have been confused by an array of Bergsonian metaphysics."[6] At any rate, as with his idea of the lost paradise, it is Wolfe's mystical insight and subjective approach that complicate matters and make it necessary to explain at length the various themes relating to time in his novels before the images which embody and convey these concepts can be meaningfully discussed.

The author himself, however, can be quite concise and explicit in his statement of these concepts of time. The idea that all time exists at once, for example, is established at the very outset of the tetralogy when, in *Look Homeward, Angel*, Wolfe notes that "every moment is a window on all time" (*LH*, 3). Another explicit statement of this concept appears in *The Web and the Rock*, when the protagonist George Webber is said to feel that "there was no temporal past or present, no *now* more living than any reality of *then*; the fiction of temporal continuity was destroyed, and his whole life became one piece with the indestructible unity of time and destiny" (*WR*, 541).

With the time barriers between *now* and *then* thus destroyed, the past becomes part of the living present. Because of this fact, history can be viewed, not as something recorded and done with, but as something which is part of man's present life; for the events of history are also included in the all-embracing unity of time. Under certain conditions these events may be more appropriately classified under "the relativity of time." The main point here, however, is that Wolfe has a strong sense of the *presentness* of the past. Now, to convey in concrete and hence meaningful terms this highly abstract concept, the author relies heavily upon the use of images—images which appear throughout his work and so give the theme unifying value for his mass of material. Appropriately enough, the recurrent images he uses for this purpose all contain an historical content. At times, indeed, he will dig deep into history and insist upon the blazing vividness of scenes and images caught up out of time. So intense is his feeling for the presentness of the past that occasionally he finds it difficult not to believe that people alive today existed in previous incarnations, as it were, down through the centuries. For example, when Stephen Hook, a friend of Esther Jack (George

Webber's mistress), thinks how timeless she seems, he meditates: "Had he not been beside her at the launching of the ship? Had they not been captives together among Thracian faces? Had he not lighted tapers to the tent when she had come to charm remission from the lord of Macedon?" (*YC*, 253). When, in Marseilles, Eugene Gant, Wolfe's protagonist in *Look Homeward, Angel*, has the dream which foreshadows his all-important meeting with Esther on the French coast, the setting is a beach of antiquity—"a scene out of the classic period of the earth" (*TR*, 892). And Esther later tells the hero of a vision she had as a young girl—a vision in which she saw a beautiful woman race an ancient Greek chariot along the beach (*WR*, 426–427).

Indissolubly linked with this basic concept of the unity of time, as we have seen, is Wolfe's "sense of time immutable"—in his own phrase, "the time of rivers, mountains, oceans, and the earth." The main images of time immutable in the novels are thus geological: the earth, the mountains, the river, and the rock. To the poet, if not to the geologist, these things are permanent; hence images making use of them are well fitted to serve as embodiments of that realm of experience, previously discussed, which Wolfe feels to exist eternally, beyond the domain of time. To the boy Eugene, for instance, the mountains surounding his home town seem suspended in infinity—beyond the limits of time and space: "They were his absolute unity in the midst of eternal change" (*LH*, 190).[7] Several times Wolfe refers to "the haunting eternity of these mountains" (*LH*, 7) and of "the hills" (*LH*, 412). "Only the earth endured," he writes, "the gigantic American earth . . ." (*LH*, 423). Esther, too, realizes that "only the earth endured, and that the earth would endure forever" (*WR*, 681). Indeed, the very expression "the everlasting earth" becomes a frequent one in the novels following *Look Homeward, Angel*.[8] As is true of most of Wolfe's thematically relevant images, this image of the enduring earth is thus one that runs through the tetralogy, providing a continuous thread of meaning and serving as a unifying factor for the author's diverse materials.

Reinforcing this thematically dominant image is a cluster of other images alluding directly or indirectly to the enduring earth and thus helping to translate the idea of time immutable into concrete terms. For example, the hero's maternal kinsfolk from the mountains—the Pentlands in the Gant cycle, and the Joyners in the Webber volumes—are almost invariably described as a clan which has somehow transcended time and death.[9] Its members are always present at funerals, for they "banqueted on death" (*LH*, 15). They are "more enduring than life, more strong than death" (*LH*, 574). Characteristic epithets are "death-devouring" (*WR*, 82), "time-devouring" (*WR*, 83), and "time-triumphant" (*TR*, 80). Perhaps most significant, however, is the fact that they have sprung from "the everlasting earth" (*WR*, 262), which virtually clinches their claim to being partakers of the quality of time immutable.

Of this group George Webber's Aunt Maw, "a rusty crone of fate," is the most eloquent spokesman; through her stories Georgia hears "the quiet, drawling voices of the Joyners who could never die and who attended the death of others like certain doom and prophecy" (*WR*, 8). Again, she "fed on all the loneliness and death of the huge, dark past with a kind of ruminant and invincible relish, which said that all men must die save only these triumphant censors of man's destiny, these never-dying, all-consuming Joyner witnesses of sorrow, who lived, and lived forever" (*WR*, 69). And when, to the hero's near-amazement, Aunt Maw herself dies, the author gives a capsule review of the whole concept of the Joyners as "death-triumphant" (*YC*, 46–47).

Trains in particular evoke the idea of the enduring earth, as when the hero watches a train hurtle "across the immense and lonely visage of the everlasting earth" (*TR*, 410). The sensation of swift movement, combined with the stillness of the earth, moves Wolfe to dwell on the picture of the speeding train as another image of time immutable.[10] When Eugene is en route to Boston, for example, the sound of the train is "the rhythm of suspended time, the sound of silence and forever" (*TR*, 63). To Eugene "it almost seemed that they were poised there in that image of eternity forever—in moveless movement, unsilent silence, spaceless flight" (*TR*, 77). The series of oxymorons in the passage just quoted emphasizes the fundamental paradox involved in the concept of "time immutable" as an eternal backdrop or substratum to the constant flow of time superficially apprehended by the finite human intellect. Thus we are told that "the great trains would hurtle on forever over the silent and eternal earth—fixed in that design of everlasting stillness and unceasing change" (*TR*, 42). It should be noted, however, that it is the *movement* of the train across the enduring earth, and not the train per se, that arouses this psychological response; for Eugene feels the same way during a trip by automobile through the foggy night. Riding back to Paris from Rheims with some friends, he feels as though they are moving "through a spaceless vacancy without progression . . . as if they were hung there in the horrible ethers of some planetary emptiness where their wheels spun futilely and forever in moveless movement, unsilent silence, changeless change" (*TR*, 738).

Wolfe's well-known symbol of Manhattan Island as a "rock"[11] also takes on added significance as an image of the enduring earth and hence becomes another geological image of time immutable when, referring to that borough, he uses such expressions as the "eternal rock" (*TR*, 508).[12] This timeless quality of the city, however, pertains only to the foundation rock and perhaps to the rock-like buildings in which the citizens "swarm"; for the variegated life that frets the surface of the metropolis is forever in flux.[13] Above ground, save for the buildings themselves, the city is Proteus (Book IV of *Of Time and the River* is entitled "Proteus:

The City")—"a place where the one permanent thing is change itself" (*WR*, 230). Elsewhere, the author apostrophizes the city as "everchanging and ephemeral city," "mutable city, mercurial city," and "eternal rock, in which the forms of life came, passed and changed intolerably before us" (*TR*, 508). It is "a protean and phantasmal shape of time" (*TR*, 509). Like the speeding train, the city offers "changeless change" (*YC*, 586) and thus presents an "eternal unity of fixity and variousness" (*WR*, 449). The image of the rock, therefore, again suggests the paradox inherent in Wolfe's vision of things highly mutable as seen against the backdrop of eternity.

But the most familiar image of time immutable in Wolfe's novels, of course, is that of the river—still another geological phenomenon. "The essence of Time," the novelist affirms, "is Flow, not Fix" (*YC*, 731). Albrecht gives what is probably the most lucid statement of this Heraclitian concept: "In *Of Time and the River* and *The Web and the Rock*," he states, "time immutable is symbolized by the river. The river of time suggests both transience and permanence. Time passes, and with it man's life. But time is also eternal in its flow, so that it becomes the immutable background for mutable life."[14] Since in the works mentioned references to the river of time are legion, I shall simply cite a few which are fairly typical.

At one point, developing the idea that our days feed this river, Wolfe writes: ". . . darkened by our dumpings . . . the river, the dark immortal river, full of strange tragic time is flowing by us—by us—by us—to the sea" (*TR*, 333). The peculiar effectiveness of the river image may be profitably studied from this example. The phrase "flowing by us—by us—by us— to the sea" is frequently included in the expression of this image and so, like "a stone, a leaf, a door," becomes another refrain. Since the image appears quite often in *Of Time and the River* and *The Web and the Rock*, much of the effect of this refrain is cumulative. The key phrase is "by us—by us—by us," for the sheer hypnotic repetition of the words begins to suggest a hopeless kind of yearning, as the author helplessly watches his life flow by in the river of time.

Again, like the other thematically relevant images in Wolfe's novels, this image serves to tie together the hero's turbulent thoughts and feelings at widely separated stages of his peregrinations. This fact can be illustrated on a purely geographical level by an enumeration of the different rivers which evoke the image. It is the Hudson which usually inspires the author to use the river as an image of time. Visiting his friend Joel Pierce at the latter's family estate on the Hudson, for example, Eugene feels that the earth there is "forever haunted by a drowsy spell of time, and the unfathomed mystery of an elfin enchantment, the huge dream-sorcery of the mysterious and immortal river" (*TR*, 568–569). The East River, which bounds Manhattan on the east, is sometimes included by implication, however, when New York City is part of the image, as here: "For this will always be one of the immortal and living things about the land, this will be an eternal and unchanging fact about that city whose only permanence is change: there will always be the great rivers flowing around it in the darkness . . ." (*TR*, 859). At least two rivers in Europe are also utilized to this end. The Thames at Oxford Wolfe calls a "full, flowing little river of dark time and treasured history" (*TR*, 654). And Paris, he says, is "forever threaded by the eternity of its silent, silent river" (*TR*, 748).

A variety of persons, locales, themes and ideas scattered through the novels are thus linked by the recurrence of this image at different stages of the hero's progress. For example, Wolfe states that the Joyners of Old Catawba "lived forever as a river lives" (*WR*, 83). In New York, Esther, reminiscing about her childhood, stops to think for a moment; and the author declares: "She paused by the river of life and time" (*WR*, 367). ". . . dark time was flowing by her like a river" (*WR*, 368). And in Boulogne the hero is "conscious of time, dark time, secret time, forever flowing like a river" (*WR*, 631). The image is taken up once more in *You Can't Go Home Again*, in which Wolfe states that "the years flow by like water" (*YC*, 89). Finally, after describing the land, "more large than earth," which the hero believes will be his after death, the celebrated prose-poem which closes the tetralogy ends with the words, "a wind is rising, and the rivers flow" (*YC*, 743). It is likely that no single image in Wolfe's novels has more thematic relevance than this one of time and the river.[15]

It is not only through geological images of the enduring earth and of rivers, however, that Wolfe conveys his concept of time immutable. High above the noisy streets of large cities, the hero seems to hear the sound presumably made by this kind of time. Boston is the first city in which the author notes this phenomenon. There, in his Uncle Bascom Pentland's office, Eugene hears "the immense and murmurous sound of time, which rose above the city, which caught up in the upper air all of the city's million noises, and yet seemed remote, essential, imperturbable and everlasting—fixed and unchanging, no matter what men lived or died" (*TR*, 136). The sound that hovers above Paris is described in virtually the same terms; from St. Germaine, Eugene and his friends seem to hear "the huge, seductive, drowsy murmur of that magic and eternal city. . . . And though all life was mixed and intermingled in that distant, drowsy sound, it was itself detached, remote, eternal and undying as the voice of time. And it hovered there forever in the timeless skies of that elfin city, and was eternally the same, no matter what men lived or died" (*TR*, 748–749).[16] Similarly, at the Oktoberfest in Munich, George notices "far away, like time, like the ceaseless and essential murmur of eternity, the distant, drowsy, wavelike hum of the great Fair" (*WR*, 671). New York, of course, provides the dominant source of the image; there, "high above the fabulous walls and towers of the city, the sound of time, murmurous and everlasting, brooded forever in the upper air" (*WR*, 486).[17]

This sound is also to be heard, appropriately enough, in the upper reaches of great, high-vaulted railroad terminals; for the hero is aware of "the immortal sound of time that murmured constantly above the walls of mighty stations" (*WR*, 608). In Boston this sound is heard "in the vaulting arches" of the Boston train station (*TR*, 245). It is New York's Pennsylvania Station, however, which moves Wolfe to develop the image fully; the interior of the building, he writes, is "murmurous with the immense and distant sound of time. . . . the calm voice of time hovered along the walls and ceiling of that mighty room, distilled out of the voices and movements of the people who swarmed beneath. It had the murmur of a distant sea. . . . It was elemental, detached, indifferent to the lives of men. . . . the voice of time remained aloof and unperturbed, a drowsy and eternal murmur below the immense and distant roof" (*YC*, 48). It is significant to note that just as time immutable is symbolized by the ever-flowing, ever-changing river, the sound of eternal time is composed of various ephemeral sounds. Wolke likes this kind of paradox and uses it often, apparently to show that the eternal and unchanging subsumes the ephemeral; that is, what seems to be temporary is, in a larger sense, actually assimilated into the all-inclusive unity of time. Moreover, the fact that time immutable is imaged forth by one kind of sound and that the lost paradise is imaged forth by another (music) is not without significance; for it helps confirm an important idea already advanced in this article. This idea is that these two themes are directly related—that prenatal existence itself actually belongs to a timeless realm and therefore has not really been "lost." Such relationships among Wolfe's themes establish the contrapuntal harmony which pervades the various motifs as a group.

Sometimes a certain quality in the light of the atmosphere (and in the mood of the hero) will arouse thoughts of time immutable, as when George has a rendezvous with Esther to celebrate his twenty-fifth birthday. It is a sparkling day in October; and as the youth gazes at the woman, "the immortal light of time and of the universe fell upon her" (*WR*, 349). And in Paris, after a moment of recollection in which he sees himself as he was three years earlier, George looks up "to the timeless skies, which shed their unperturbable light upon the street and all its fashions . . ." (*WR*, 649). The appropriateness of these images becomes evident when it is remembered that to one possessed of a mystical, subjective turn of mind, like Wolfe's, such apparently eternal physical phenomena as light and sound might very well carry suggestions of that transcendental realm beyond time whose existence he feels so strongly. And by thus conveying the theme of time immutable at various points in the tetralogy, these recurrent images of light and sound help weave this motif into the overall contrapuntal design.

One important use that Wolfe makes of the concept of time immutable is to employ it as a background for the depiction of the tragedy of man's mortality. Thus, with time immutable and the everlasting earth, Wolfe frequently contrasts the "bitter brevity" of man's lifetime upon that earth.[18] This recurrent theme is often expressed in terms of images of the transient and ephemeral—particularly in terms of a brief flame or its smoke. "We are passing away in smoke," he declares in *Look Homeward, Angel* (*LH*, 295). In his vision at the end of the book, Eugene sees whole ancient races and cultures rise and fall—"the little rocket-flare of centuries" (*LH*, 623). Again, in *Of Time and the River*, Wolfe writes: "For what are we, my brother? We are a phantom flare of grieved desire, the ghostling and phosphoric flicker of immortal time, a brevity of days haunted by the eternity of the earth" (*TR*, 869). The "brief candle" image is maintained in *The Web and the Rock*, in which George compares man's life to "a tiny spurt of flame that blazed out briefly in an illimitable and terrifying darkness" (*WR*, 585). This simile Wolfe liked so well that he used it again verbatim in the prefatory quotation to *You Can't Go Home Again*. Occasionally man's bitter brevity is linked with the river of time; the effect of this, of course, is to emphasize the contrast between man's mortal plight and the eternity of time immutable. "... we know that we are dying as the river flows!" the novelist exclaims (*WR*, 59). And when the hero, lying in a hospital bed in Munich, hears the clock strike, "The news it bore to him was that all men living now were just that one hour closer to their death ... [and] suddenly it seemed to him that all man's life was like one small tongue of earth that juts into the waters of time, and that incessantly, steadily, in the darkness, in the night, this tongue of earth was crumbling in the tide, was melting evenly in dark waters" (*WR*, 674). Another image of transience appears when man is termed "this moth of time, this dupe of brevity and numbered hours" (*YC*, 435). Such images, much like most of the others discussed in this chapter, run all the way through the four novels, conveying a recurrent theme and providing a unifying thread for Wolfe's sprawling content.

In *The Web and the Rock*, it is spring, especially, which evokes the hero's feeling of man's "temporal brevity against the eternity of the earth" (*WR*, 456).[19] George, now living in New York, watches the shifting play of lights on the April green of the tree growing in his backyard; as he does so, the tree becomes "coherent with his destiny, and his life was one with all its brevity from birth to death" (*WR*, 540). Again, watching everyone in the city streets rushing about his petty business, Esther thinks how futile all this activity is: "... April would come as sweetly and as fairly and with as sharp a cry when all their strident tongues were stopped with dust" (*WR*, 572).

But it is as a symbol of regeneration that spring finds its principal function in Wolfe's work. So conceived, spring—together with its associated images of burgeoning life and fertility—serves to reconcile the contrasting ideas of earth's permanence and man's bitter brevity. Speaking of *Look Homeward, Angel,* Albrecht declares: "Earth's cycle of growth preserves for Eugene something of past time, for after Ben's death Eugene knows that Ben will 'come again . . . in flower and leaf. . . .' "[20] The indicated passage, in which Eugene meditates alone at his brother's grave, is highly characteristic: "What things will come again? O Spring, the cruellest and fairest of the seasons, will come again. And the strange and buried men will come again, for death and the dust will die. And Ben will come again, he will not die again, in flower and leaf, in wind and music far, he will come back again" (*LH*, 582–583). In his vision at the end of the book, Eugene perceives the cycle of rebirth: ". . . amid the fumbling march of races to extinction, the giant rhythms of the earth remained. The seasons passed in their majestic processionals, and germinal Spring returned forever on the land—new crops, new men, new harvests, and new gods" (*LH*, 623). On a less Olympian scale it is spring's youth and fertility, respectively, which are emphasized when the author describes Eugene's girl friend, Laura James, as having "the firm young line of Spring, budding, slender, virginal" (*LH*, 428), and when he describes the June day on which his hero is graduated from college: "The air was charged with the fresh sensual heat, the deep green shimmer of heavy leafage, a thousand spermy earth and flower-scents" (*LH*, 599).

Spring in New York is no less evocative of the imagery of rebirth than it is in Old Catawba, as George revels in "the spermy fragrance of the earth that seemed to burst in waves of rich fecundity through all the steel and stone" and in "the pageantry of glorious women who seemed themselves to have burst out of the earth overnight and to be blooming in the streets one day like splendid flowers" (*WR*, 609). In another place Wolfe begins what is virtually a prose-poem to spring with the line, "Spring came that year like magic and like music and like song," with everything bursting into bloom (*WR*, 441). "The streets were bursting into life again, they foamed and glittered with new life and color, and women more beautiful than flowers, more full of juice and succulence than fruit, appeared upon them in a living tide of love and beauty" (*WR*, 447). In *You Can't Go Home Again* Wolfe tells how one waits for spring in the city through the bleak month of March and through much of April; then, near the end of April, "spring comes—explodes out of the earth in a green radiance—comes up overnight!" (*YC*, 466). Finally, in this last volume of the tetralogy, the author comes full circle by stressing once more, as he did in *Look Homeward, Angel,* the promise of spring as representing a denial of death's dominion: beneath change and beyond death, a voice tells George, "'there will be something growing like a flower, something bursting from the earth again, forever deathless, faithful, coming into life again like April'" (*YC*, 44).

Wolfe's concept of the unity of time, then, helps account for his intense feeling for history and for the images of historical events and periods that recur in his works. More important, considered in its immutable aspects, the time idea provides Wolfe with an opportunity to convey an important theme by means of the recurrent geological images of the enduring earth—including those of the mountains, the rock and the river—together with the associated images of the Pentland-Joyner clan, the train rushing across the enduring earth, and the sound and light of time. Images of man's "bitter brevity," again, are centered about images of the transient and ephemeral and are associated with those of the enduring earth by contrast, with spring, the symbol of regeneration, serving to reconcile the two. Now, since all these images run through the tetralogy, conveying the theme of time's immutability, as opposed to man's brevity, what we have here is another recurrent motif in the development of Wolfe's polyphonic form—a motif which, like that of the lost paradise, links scattered parts of the novels and thus helps to unify the whole.

Notes

1. Wolfe's tetralogy consists of *Look Homeward, Angel* (New York, 1929), *Of Time and the River* (New York, 1935), *The Web and the Rock* (New York, 1939), and *You Can't Go Home Again* (New York, 1940)—hereafter cited as *LH, TR, WR,* and *YC* respectively. The reader will recall that the hero of *LH* and *TR* is Eugene Gant, and that the hero of *WR* and *YC* is George Webber.

2. Margaret Church, "Dark Time," in Richard Walser (ed.), *The Enigma of Thomas Wolfe: Biographical and Critical Selections* (Cambridge, Mass., 1953), p. 261—hereafter cited as *Enigma.*

3. Cf. the excellent discussion of time in Wolfe by Louis D. Rubin, Jr., in his book, *Thomas Wolfe: The Weather of His Youth* (Baton Rouge, 1955), pp. 28–53. Rubin notes that by temporarily recapturing the past through memory, Wolfe temporarily halts the flow of time. See also George Snell, *The Shapers of American Fiction:* 1798–1947 (New York, 1947), p. 180.

4. Cf. Larry Rubin, "Thomas Wolfe and the Telescoping of Time," *Interculture: A Collection of Essays and Creative Writing Commemorating the Twentieth Anniversary of the Fulbright Program at the Institute of Translation and Interpretation,* University of Vienna (1955–1974) (Vienna, 1975), pp. 284–295. For a fuller discussion of the theme of the lost paradise, cf. Larry Rubin, "Thomas Wolfe and the Lost Paradise," *Modern Fiction Studies* 11 (Autumn, 1965), 250–258; reprinted in Paschal Reeves (ed.), *The Merrill Studies in Look Homeward, Angel* (Columbus, O., 1970), pp. 107–116.

5. Thomas Wolfe, *The Story of a Novel* (New York, 1936), p. 52.

6. *Enigma*, pp. 249, 250. But cf. Louis D. Rubin, Jr., "Thomas Wolfe in Time and Place," *Southern Renascence: The Literature of the Modern South*, eds. Louis D. Rubin, Jr., and Robert D. Jacobs (Baltimore, 1953), pp. 294–95. A more complex metaphysical approach than the one presented in my study is provided by W. P. Albrecht in his discussion of linear and cyclical concepts of time in "Time as Unity in Thomas Wolfe," *Enigma*, pp. 239–48.

7. Cf. Louis D. Rubin, Jr., *Weather*, pp. 31–32.

8. Examples appear in *TR*, 42, 68, 246, 410, 413; *WR*, 262; *YC*, 88.

9. Louis D. Rubin, Jr., also points out the recurring image of timelessness which is associated with the Joyners and Pentlands (*Weather*, pp. 120–21, 132–33).

10. Cf. Albrecht, *Enigma*, p. 245, and Louis D. Rubin, Jr., *Weather*, pp. 39–40.

11. See, for example, Blanche Heusman Gelfant, *The American City Novel* (Norman, Okla., 1954), p. 129.

12. Other references to Manhattan as a "rock" occur in *TR*, 907; *WR*, 204, 219, 316, 448, 471, 574; *YC*, 4.

13. Cf. Gelfant, pp. 122–23.

14. *Enigma*, p. 242. See also Church, *Enigma*, p. 257.

15. Other time-river images appear in *TR*, 245, 474, 509–10, 551, 598, 909; *WR*, 59, 263, 428, 601, 682, 688.

16. The repeated phrase "no matter what men lived or died" emphasizes the indifference of the eternal universe to the problems of individual mortal men. The powerful strain of naturalism in Wolfe suggested by this idea doubtless merits study.

17. Virtually the same image appears in *WR*, 444.

18. Cf. Albrecht, *Enigma*, p. 245, and Louis D. Rubin, Jr., *Weather*, pp. 35–36.

19. Cf. again Louis D. Rubin, Jr., *Weather*, pp. 35–36.

20. *Enigma*, p. 245.

Thomas Wolfe: The Presbyterian Connection

John Boone Trotti*

Thomas Wolfe's *Look Homeward, Angel* rose like a meteor on the national literary horizon, but burst like a bombshell in Asheville, NC in 1929. It provided an exciting distraction, perhaps, from the economic crash of that year and set in motion a flood of discussion about Wolfe which continues unabated until this day. Wolfe has been analyzed literarily, socially, psychologically, historically, and to some degree philosophically. Little notice has been paid to his religious upbringing and to the theological implications of his work.

Despite his negative evaluation of Wolfe's writings on religion in his second novel, *Of Time and the River*, John Donald Wade exclaimed near the end of a review of the book "None the less Eugene [Wolfe] is

*Reprinted from the *Journal of Presbyterian History*, 59, No. 4 (Winter 1981), 525–42.

a Catawba, mama-and-papa saying, Presbyterian Southerner; or he is nothing. And he is emphatically not nothing."[1] As a later son of Asheville and of the First Presbyterian Church there, it has been my interest to investigate Tom's Presbyterian connections, believing them to be of considerably more moment than is usually assumed. We cannot here assay all of the Wolfe corpus for religious and theological themes, but we can examine his relationship to, attitude about, and the influences of his church experiences. What is the Presbyterian connection?

I

The Wolfe family held membership in the First Presbyterian Church in Asheville, N.C., throughout Tom's lifetime. Tom's father, W. O. Wolfe, raised in the United Brethren Church in Pennsylvania, became a Baptist with his second wife when living in Raleigh, NC.[2] During the early years of his third marriage, to Tom's mother, both W. O. and Julia Wolfe attended the First Baptist Church of Asheville.[3] On 3 April 1897, W. O. and Julia Wolfe joined the First Presbyterian Church by "making statement of their faith in Christ."[4] By this action they joined the church tradition of Julia's family, the Westalls.

Tom's mother, Julia Westall Wolfe, came from western North Carolina Scots Presbyterian stock for generations back. Richard S. Kennedy notes that Tom's maternal grandfather, Thomas Casey Westall, raised his large family "in Scotch Presbyterian orthodoxy," noting that Julia was brought up in a tradition of regular churchgoing.[5] Julia told Hayden Norwood that Tom's story of Uncle Bacchus was largely based on Grandfather Westall, adding that "father was brought up right when he was a child. His mother was a good woman, a good Presbyterian, and Sunday mornings they all had to go to Sunday school."[6] At least to this extent Julia herself was "a good woman, a good Presbyterian" in that her children were raised on churchgoing and Sunday school in the First Presbyterian Church. Some writers feel that it was W. O. who exercised the most significant spiritual influences, who was the churchman who insisted that the children go to Sunday school and that they say their prayers.[7]

It was the Westall, Scots and Presbyterian, side of the family that Tom found most interesting and about which he wrote most copiously. There the Presbyterian connection is longest and strongest; however there were some notable defectors from that tradition. Julia recounted how her father was a good Presbyterian, but when teaching young converts the *Confession of Faith* broke with the church over its views on predestination in what became a public doctrinal debate in the church press.[8] Another notable Westall defector was Tom's Uncle Henry Westall (the famous literary figure Uncle Bascom). Uncle Henry was an ordained Presbyterian minister who made a pilgrimage through Universalist and then Unitarian churches before leaving the ministry to become a lawyer in Boston.[9] Elaine Westall Gould explored her family heritage and notes that Henry Westall's Unitarian congregation was composed of a small cream of intellectuals, "a cold, if not a frozen cream, Tom may have thought it, for the service lacked the sensuousness he ascribed to the Presbyterian, in spite of its far colder Calvinist doctrines."[10] Tom wrote in *Look Homeward, Angel* that the Presbyterian worship instilled in him an appreciation for "the sensuous beauty of religion."[11]

It is difficult to ascertain with what regularity the Wolfes attended church, although it is clear that this was not a dominant influence in their lives. Tom wrote, somewhat cynically, that "my family could not be termed a religious family . . . attendance at church was advocated mainly because it gave one business and social 'standing' in a small community."[12] This sentiment is expressed forcefully in the light-hearted religious banter between George Graves and Eugene Gant sauntering up Church Street in *Look Homeward, Angel.* There Graves notes: "The best people in this town are church members . . . It's a fine thing." When Eugene asks why, Graves replies "You get to know all the people who are worth a damn. . . . It helps you in a business way. They come to know you and respect you. You won't get far in this town, Gene, without them. It pays . . . to be a Christian."[13] It would be logical to deduce that W. O. and Julia, a couple new to the middle class and on the rise, would be equally sensitive to this and be somewhat regular in attendance even if the motivation were rather secular. To be conspicuously absent in that small town environment would have worked at cross purposes with their business interests and desire for community standing.

Tom wrote of Sunday and the pattern of Sunday dinner as though it were their typical pattern, as it was for other Asheville churchgoers—the little boys anxiously waiting for the preparation of the Sunday dinner "for two hours since their return from church."[14] The whole family had gone to church, not just the children, thus they all had to wait while dinner was prepared.

There is a record of the Wolfes' giving $100 to the building fund in the 1890s, but no other records in First Presbyterian Church to indicate their level of participation either personally or financially. This is not surprising, as few churches kept written records as to the participation of their members. It is clear that the Wolfe family regarded the First Presbyterian Church as their church home. They had warm regard for the old family pastor, Dr. Robert F. Campbell, throughout his ministry and his retirement years. They also welcomed and became quite attached to their new pastor, Dr. C. Grier Davis, who served the church from 1938 throughout the later years of the Wolfe family.

One note in Julia's reflections on her life gives a glimpse of Presbyterian pastoral care at a crucial time. In 1904 Mrs. Wolfe was in the depths of despair over the death of her son Grover and "tried to get interested in Tom." She was unable to participate in decisions about redecorating the house and apparently had lost interest in making money and dealing with real estate—a sure sign of the depth of her depression. An unnamed "Northern" Presbyterian minister approached her about the sale of the Owenby place to the Presbyterian Church, U.S.A., mission board. Seeing her sad estate, the minister gave her counsel, sharing his own story of grief at the death of his wife, and told her that he did not know why "God has required it of me. I live only to work, to do church work. That is the only way you can do—keep busy and work." She notes that he was right. She resumed in earnest the work in real estate and never faltered again from tending to such matters. She did sell the thirteen acres to the Presbyterians "at a pretty good price."[15]

There is ample documentation that the major events of weddings and funerals were in the Presbyterian context. Dr. Campbell performed the weddings of Thomas Wolfe's sisters: Effie (1909) and Mabel (1916).[16] It was Dr. Campbell, assisted by a Dr. Lunsford, who officiated at Grover's funeral (1904) and who was the "Scotch minister" of *Look Homeward, Angel* at Ben's funeral (1918).[17] "Beloved Dr. Campbell" officiated at W. O.'s funeral (1922).[18] With Dr. Davis, Dr. Campbell as Emeritus Pastor conducted Tom's funeral (1938) and Julia's funeral (1945).[19] Tom's sister Effie (Mrs. Fred Gambrell) was buried in Anderson, SC, with services conducted by the Reverend Samuel S. Wiley of the First Presbyterian Church there where she had continued her Presbyterian membership. Sister Mabel Wolfe Wheaton's funeral was conducted by Dr. Davis (1958).[20] Like his sister Effie, Fred Wolfe transferred his membership to another Presbyterian church when he left Asheville, continuing in the Presbyterian Church of Spartanburg, S.C., until his death (1980).[21]

It was not the family pattern, probably because of W. O.'s Baptist background, for the children to receive infant baptism. On 22 May 1902, Effie Nelson Wolfe was examined by the Session and received into the communion of the church and, presumably, baptized at that time.[22] Fred Wolfe made an adult profession of faith at the North Avenue Presbyterian Church in Atlanta while a student at Georgia Tech and subsequently transferred his church letter to Asheville's First Presbyterian Church (25 March 1923).[23] Mabel Wolfe Wheaton and her husband Ralph made adult profession of faith and received baptism (2 February 1922) in First Presbyterian Church in Asheville.[24] Over the years Mabel was the most active church member of the family, serving in the choir and in women's work both in the local church and in the presbytery.[25]

There is no record of Tom's baptism nor of his making a profession of faith. He was enrolled on the cradle roll of the First Presbyterian Church straightaway (1900).[26] A wide variety of sources, including Tom's own writings, indicate that he attended Sunday school until well into his teen years. A document in the Historical Foundation in

Montreat lists descendants of Robert and Rebecca Patton "who are or were members of the First Presbyterian Church, Asheville, N. C." This list includes not only Mrs. Julia Wolfe and Mrs. Mabel Wheaton, but also "Mr. Thomas Wolfe."[27] This paper no doubt reflects the common belief that Wolfe was a member, but in the technical sense of baptism and profession of faith he was not. In the family sense, as a child of the covenant, Tom was treated as a non-communing member as are all children of Presbyterian parents.

There can be little question that Tom remembered his early Sunday school days vividly and fondly. The Pack Memorial Library in Asheville possesses a certificate given Tom announcing his successful completion of third-grade work in the Sunday school of the First Presbyterian Church dated 2 October 1910, one day before his tenth birthday.[28] Betty Lynch Williams discussed Tom with Mr. James Coleman in Asheville. She writes:

> He knew the Wolfe boys well and was a good judge of youthful character. The Coleman boys and the Wolfe boys went to the same Presbyterian Sunday School. His memories of this first reaction to the book (*Look Homeward, Angel*) are these:
>
> I soon learned that I was in the book. I'm Zeno Cochran . . . one of the few people Tom seemed to like in the book . . . me and our minister, Dr. Campbell. . . . The vulgarity was as much a shock to Asheville as anything else. I could hardly believe the parts about his escapades in the bad districts. Tom was a clean living sort of boy.[29]

One of Tom's Sunday school teachers, Mr. James S. Howell, fondly recalled his attendance and participation in the classes. He noted that Tom got along well with the other children and always enjoyed the Sunday school picnics. They would take a wagonload of kids to Malvern Hills Park.[30] Fred Wolfe filled out the picture a bit, describing the picnics at Riverside Park or Sulphur Springs where Mr. Cobb, a jeweler, provided great red and white tubs of lemonade, iced down by chips from a 100-pound block of ice, from which they drank with tin cups feeling the icy coolness. There were long tables filled with food which both he and Tom enjoyed.[31]

At age eight, Tom wrote a letter to his mother in which he mentions "We had our Sunday school picnic up at Overlook Park this year and I ate so much that I could hardly eat my supper."[32] Tom intended to write up this aspect of church life as his *Notebooks* indicate: "An outline on the back flyleaf of the October Fair London Ledger indicates that an early chapter was to be 'The Sunday School Picnic.' "[33]

At another point of reverie, Wolfe simply notes "Sunday (going to church—the little boys trotting to bring up the rear)."[34] Those who attended church, and especially Sunday school, in the old First Presbyterian Church before it was remodeled (completed in August, 1951) can easily identify persons, the physical layout, and the pedagogical pattern Wolfe fictionalizes in this thinly disguised autobiographical pattern in *Look Homeward, Angel.*[35] Even when Tom changes his character from Eugene Gant of the first two novels to George Webber in *The Web and the Rock* and supposedly moves to a non-autobiographical style, he cannot describe church relationships without recourse to his upbringing at First Presbyterian. Young Webber is reared by strict Baptist Aunt Maw, but when Wolfe describes the walk to church, Asheville natives know that it is the walk to the Presbyterian Church.[36] Similarly, when he describes the typical Sunday morning worship, the description of decency and order, the preacher's collar, and the decor reflect Dr. Campbell and First Presbyterian, not a Baptist service.[37]

In his "Autobiographical Outline" Wolfe refers back to 1914 and indicates that at that time he "began to slip away from Sunday school," a typical adolescent pattern.[38] Tom was attracted to the church, yet he felt somewhat out of place there. He wrote of Eugene:

> This starched and well brushed world of Sunday morning Presbyterianism, with its sober decency, its sense of restraint, its suggestion of quiet wealth, solid position, ordered ritual, seclusive establishment, moved him deeply with its tranquility. He felt concretely his isolation from it, he entered it from the jangled disorder of his own life once a week, looking at it, and departing from it, for years, with the sad heart of a stranger. And from the mellow gloom of the church, the rich distant organ, the quiet nasal voice of the Scotch minister, the interminable prayers, and the rich little pictures of Christian mythology which he had collected as a child under the instruction of the spinsters, he gathered something of the pain, the mystery, the sensuous beauty of religion, something deeper and greater than this austere decency.[39]

As Dr. Campbell would mention in Tom's funeral service, Wolfe had a fierce sectarian snobbishness about the Presbyterian denomination as a lad. The First Presbyterian Church is located at 40 Church Street, facing the Central Methodist Church and one block up the hill from the Trinity Episcopal Church. In Eugene Gant's famous stroll up Church Street Wolfe described First Presbyterian Church as follows:

> The old church, with its sharp steeple, rotted slowly, decently, prosperously, like a good man's life, down into its wet lichened brick. Eugene looked gratefully, with a second's pride, at its dark decorum, its solid Scotch breeding. "I'm a Presbyterian," he said. "What are you?"
>
> "An Episcopalian, when I go," said George Graves with irreverent laughter.
>
> "To hell with these Methodists!" Eugene said with an elegant, disdainful face. "They're too damn common for us."[40]

This passage is but one of many in which Wolfe described the social sources of denominationalism, noting that the Episcopalians were at the top of the heap with the Presbyterians close behind, reserving his put-downs and derisive jibes for the Baptists and especially the Methodists.[41] While one and all are chided for pretentiousness and cant, the sharpest attack comes on their straightlaced or puritanical views on sex and alcohol—the latter making the Methodists particularly odious to Wolfe. Wolfe describes a "Negro Calvary Baptist Church" in Altamont (Asheville). However Floyd C. Watkins correctly observed: "There is, however no Negro Calvary Baptist Church in Asheville, but in West Asheville there is a white Calvary Baptist Church, and there is a Negro Calvary Presbyterian Church. Did Wolfe forget the denomination and thus satirize accidentally, or was he, as a Presbyterian, bantering the Baptists?"[42] Wolfe did not forget denominations. One suspects that he knew full well what he was doing and that he wished to spare the Presbyterians and to "banter" the Baptists in that episode.

It is generally reported that in his college years Wolfe abandoned religion altogether—some saying he was freed from its restraints, others simply noting that he became an atheist, or at least an agnostic. Andrew Turnbull furthered this notion in his biography of Wolfe saying that "Tom stopped believing in the God of his fathers at fourteen or thereabouts."[43] Fred Wolfe, when asked about this in a personal interview, noted that this was but one of many errors in Turnbull's book which he had asked to be corrected, but which were not changed before publication. Waxing hot on the subject, Fred said that the charge that Tom was an agnostic was "the biggest lie ever!" recalling that on his last visit home in 1937 Tom went to church and people "by the dozens came to shake his hand after the service."[44] There is, of course, a difference in church attendance and actual belief. However it would appear that there was no such sharp break with the church at an early age. In fact, Don Bishop reports that Wolfe still knelt by his bedside for prayer at night when a senior at the University of North Carolina—a pattern predictable enough for them to expect Tom to do it and thus to play a prank on him.[45]

During those college years Wolfe engaged in lengthy discussions of morality and theology with fellow students, often in the context of visits by the local Presbyterian pastor[46] or with the YMCA secretary.[47] We should take seriously the fact that Tom was on the YMCA cabinet, a post not given nor taken lightly in those days.[48] As a senior and Editor of the *Tar Heel*, Tom wrote two editorials in glowing praise of "Parson" Moss, the pastor of the Chapel Hill Presbyterian Church.[49] Wolfe could scarcely have written as he did without firsthand knowledge of the man both in the pulpit and in the dorms. Agatha Boyd Adams noted that Moss "was a favorite of Tom's"[50] and Richard Walser notes that Tom had to attend compulsory chapel, and that "on Sundays Wolfe went to the Presbyterian Church to hear 'Parson' Moss, who drew in a large congregation of student worshippers with sermons comparing Christianity to athletics."[51] Wolfe and Moss both spoke on YMCA College Night once.[52] Moss was a Scot and a Presbyterian and Tom liked him. During those college years Tom regularly kept in touch with Dr. Campbell in his home church,[53] received Campbell's praise for a poem "The Challenge" published in the *Asheville Citizen*,[54] and attended the Presbyterian Church in Chapel Hill.

There is little to be said for the influence of the church during Tom's Harvard years. He did frequently visit his uncle, the Reverend Henry M. Westall, who had once been a Presbyterian minister. Westall's pilgrimage through Presbyterian, Episcopal, Congregational, Universalist, and Unitarian churches before becoming a Boston attorney intrigued Tom.[55] Tom felt that the idealism and fire of Westall's youth had left him and somehow he condemned his uncle for leaving the ministry, perhaps even more for leaving the Presbyterians. After his wife died, Westall "returned to the church" Tom noted in a letter to his mother.[56] At his death, nine years after Tom's, Henry Westall was buried in the family plot in Riverside Cemetery in Asheville with graveside rites performed by Dr. C. Grier Davis, Presbyterian.[57]

In his official Harvard files Wolfe listed himself "Presbyterian." Oscar Cargill speculates that this note may have commended Wolfe for a teaching post at Washington Square College of N.Y.U. Wolfe's application was read by Dean Andrew Watt, whom Cargill described as "a religious man in the very formal sense, occupying important posts in suburban Presbyterian and Congregational churches in the different towns in New Jersey in which he resided."[58]

Cargill notes that "if Dr. Watt was not impressed by Wolfe's endorsers and what they said about him, he surely was by the fact that Wolfe avowed himself to be a 'Presbyterian.' "[59] Despite this avowal of Presbyterianism we have no record pro or con on church attendance in Cambridge or Boston. We do have, however, a solemn covenant with God vowing clean and honest living recorded in his *Notebooks*.[60] In letters to his mother in the Harvard years Tom affirms that an inclination to faith "in spite of the church and the ministers"[61] and that "the God of my Grandmother—the nice old gentleman with the long whiskers—has so far been good to me."[62]

During Tom's brief life as an author in New York and in his world travels, there is little documentation of the Presbyterian connection. The dominant influence in his life by far was the relationship with his editor, Maxwell E. Perkins, an Episcopalian who was not active in the institutional church.[63] Chard Powers Smith discusses the way in which Max was like a god to his authors and had a strong sense of predestination, or "election," with regard to their talent and future. He writes "Lacking any visible religion, he was yet a Puritan divine accredited to administer the sacrament to the Elect, to assist them in their worship, and to cherish them generally . . . with all the power of predestination behind him, he knew that he could not err in his perceptions and selections."[64]

All of this is to say that Perkins, who was a father-figure, friend, and editorial "god" to Wolfe, gave little impetus toward church attendance or institutional Presbyterianism, however he reinforced much of Tom's belief in election, destiny, puritanical personal ethics, and rejection of cant and hypocrisy. During this time Wolfe affirmed that he was on good terms with God[65] in 1925. He writes of his "dark faith" and affirms the beauty of "divine falsehood" or "superstition" of religion as opposed to ugliness of lacking belief.[66] His *Notebooks* frequently reflect grappling with faith and belief.[67]

Dr. Robert F. Campbell asserted in Wolfe's funeral that "Year after year as he returned from the university he would come to the church, usually on a Sunday morning after the service to pay his respects to his old friend and pastor."[68] Many interpreters take Campbell's words to mean that Tom did not come for worship, but only afterwards for visits. Fred Wolfe said that Tom went to the First Presbyterian Church to worship, not just for a visit, whenever he was in Asheville.[69] Mabel Wolfe Wheaton supported this contention, saying Tom "attended from his cradle-roll days until his last visit home the year before (he died)."[70]

There is no mistaking the Presbyterian connection in Wolfe's death and funeral. Wolfe was given Christian burial from the First Presbyterian Church in Asheville with great crowds attending and front page write-ups in the *Asheville Citizen*, the *Asheville Times*, and newspapers across the country. The officiating ministers were Dr. C. Grier Davis, the new pastor of the church, and Dr. Robert F. Campbell, the pastor emeritus. Dr. Davis relates that Dr. Campbell varied from his usual funeral pattern which was to include no sermon or eulogy, and in the case of Tom Wolfe gave some comments as well as readings from Tom's writings. Dr. Campbell made very cautious and guarded statements about Wolfe's religious beliefs, recognizing the philosophical questioning and anguished searching he had had, but also holding to a fond hope that Tom had found his peace with God. In addition to an emotion-charged reading of Psalm 23, Campbell quoted with great affection the very moving preface to *Of Time and the River*.[71] Dr. Davis added that he himself used portions of Wolfe's writings in funerals from time to time in his ministry in Asheville.[72]

Jonathan Daniels described the funeral somewhat cynically, saying "the old preacher (Campbell) . . . knew Tom was saved because he had always come to call on him when he was in Asheville."[73] Daniels wished for Tom to be there to describe the proceedings and all those who came and "who helped make it the funeral of a small city's son, son accepted, son forgiven, son somehow saved for the Presbyterian Church."[74] Despite the fact that this was her church home and that she had been the most active member of the family, Mabel Wolfe Wheaton was too emotionally worn out to attend the funeral. Elizabeth Nowell writes "However, Mabel had reached the limit of her endurance; she didn't even attend the funeral held at the Presbyterian Church where he had gone to Sunday school as a small boy, but, as she described it, 'went out with a bang.' "[75]

The Presbyterian connection? Wolfe lived in and around the Presbyterian Church, presented himself as a "mama-and-papa saying Presbyterian southerner," and took some pride in that connection. We turn now to his attitudes toward that church and the church's attitudes toward Wolfe.

II

Paschal Reeves expounds upon the admiration Wolfe had for Scotch-Americans, noting "He felt this influence and portrays it in his region, his neighborhood, his church, and in his own family."[76] Wolfe admired the Scotch who "believe in prayer and argument . . . reverence, authority, tradition, and leadership. . . ."[77] Wolfe appreciated his Scots neighbors, his being guided to "the true kirk, the Presbyterian Church," and the stabilizing influence of Dr. Robert F. Campbell (the Scotch Dr. H. H. McRae of *Look Homeward, Angel*).[78] To this picture must be added his affection for the Scot "Parson" Moss of his Chapel Hill days.

Hugh Holman describes the Scotch-Irish and Scottish folk moving into the backcountry of the Carolinas and notes that the South which Wolfe described was "grimly Calvinistic in its religious orientation."[79] Wolfe noted this grim quality in his *Notebooks*, sketching a grandfather character with "thin, sinister, and yet somehow jolly face, lit by a kind of diabolic humor that somehow, when I think of it, always suggests the Presbyterian Church. . . ."[80] There, again, he described a "Presbyterian face, to fleshpots hostile, to wine, women, belly-warmth, exuberance, and life's fluidity, unskilled, opposed, and all unknowledgeable, but face of cold high Passion, too, fire-glacial face . . . of purpose, faith, and fortitude."[81]

Wolfe had a love/hate relationship to Presbyterianism and to his Scots heritage, with by far a preponderance of affection. He struggled against its pietistical, puritanical Calvinism all his life, yet he declared himself to be "a puritan."[82] He was critical of the hypocrisy of all pietistic church people, attacking with special relish the conservative and evangelical Baptists and the teetotaling Methodists, but criticizing Presbyterians as well for lack of conformity of life with creed. Even his good friend and beloved pastor, Dr. Campbell, falls under this criticism as Wolfe notes that Campbell preached against the innocent amusement of Sunday baseball as a violation of the sabbath, yet at the same time Campbell had two black cooks sweating in his kitchen to prepare Sunday dinner.[83] In this sharp critique in a letter to Maxwell Perkins, Wolfe revealed not only his sharp eye for hypocrisy, but also his social conscience with regard to blacks that was well in advance of his day.

That same letter to Perkins contains documentation of the disappointment Wolfe felt when he discovered that the churchgoers and Sunday school teachers who had drilled him in Presbyterian dogma and the ten commandments broke the commandments themselves. These facts had come out, of course, in *Look Homeward, Angel*, where Wolfe laid them bare for all to see. This hypocritical behavior, long the solace and main argument of those who become disaffected with the institutional church, was Wolfe's chief complaint with his church.

In that first novel, Wolfe not only boasts of the value of Presbyterian connections for social status, but also speaks of the lasting impact of his Sunday school days on him: "He had all the passionate fidelity of a child to the laws of the community: all the filtered deposit of Sunday morning Presbyterianism had its effect."[84] Wolfe appreciated the ritual and form of Presbyterianism, but was not above sniggering at the teachers of Presbyterian dogma and the "oppressively Christ-like" church school teachers.[85] In his *Notebooks* he indicated that he would give further treatment to the Presbyterian Church, noting:

> Saturday Night and Sunday Morning
>
> The Presbyterian Church: Because that decayed and dying system of institutions comprised by the Protestant Church in North Armerica is not yet utterly extinct, it may be useful here to enquire into some of the causes of its dissolution, its loss of function, its waning power. Twenty-five years ago—even in the most backward provinces of the Church-bound South—the disintegration of the Protestant Church had begun, and was well under way.[86]

Wolfe did not rejoice in that dissolution, although it is clear that he, like his mentor Max Perkins, found little power and meaning in participation in the regular worship and activities of a local congregation.

On the other hand, to discover what the attitudes of the Presbyterian Church were towards Thomas Wolfe is more difficult. No doubt *Look Homeward, Angel* scandalized many members who participated in the general community turmoil and attack on Wolfe so well documented and well known. In many places the assertion has been made that the ministers of all the leading churches denounced Tom in private and even from the pulpit.[87] A deduction has been made that Dr. Robert F. Campbell joined those who denounced Tom. Andrew Turnbull, in his biography of Wolfe, wrote that Campbell had a particularly difficult time with the Wolfe funeral because he regarded Tom as a heretic and had been one of those reacting strongly against *Look Homeward, Angel*.[88] This is another of the several points which Fred Wolfe said

Turnbull had gotten wrong, indicating that Dr. Campbell never attacked Tom nor rejected him.[89]

A close investigation of Dr. Campbell's papers uncovered no sermons which make reference to Wolfe, no letters, no clippings, indeed no trace of Wolfe in all of Campbell's files save one reference in a letter to Campbell from Tom's Uncle Henry Westall.[90] This gap is problematic in light of the extensive collection of materials preserving notes of Campbell's activities no matter how small or inconsequential. Even the major front-page newspaper spread with extensive quotes from Campbell's funeral oration is lacking.

Observing the danger in an argument from silence, we refrain from using this gap in the files either as evidence of Campbell's dislike of Wolfe, or as evidence that he so valued Tom that he developed a special file on him. Possibly someone wishing these matters to be disassociated from Campbell purged the files, or some Wolfe collector took them.[91] Robert F. Campbell, Jr., the staff of First Presbyterian Church, and the staff of the Historical Foundation are in agreement that all of Dr. Campbell's papers were deposited in the Foundation intact.

The testimony of Fred Wolfe and Mabel Wolfe Wheaton that Dr. Campbell remained their "beloved pastor" and Tom's friend argues against any such attack. Mr. James S. Howell, Asheville attorney and one-time Sunday school teacher of Tom's, clearly stated that Dr. Campbell never took a public stand against Wolfe.[92] Similarly, Mrs. Ralph Lee asserts that "Dr. Campbell was quiet about Tom."[93] Miss Ida Bates wrote "I do not recall ever having heard Dr. Campbell make any reference to Thomas Wolfe."

Miss Ora Blackmun, longtime member of the church and its historian, indicates that Dr. Campbell was rigid in his beliefs and might well have talked plainly to Tom in private, but would not have attacked him from the pulpit. Miss Blackmun believes that Campbell treated Tom as one among many in the church family and "would not have given Tom that distinction" when asked if Campbell might have created a separate file on Wolfe. She further comments that Dr. Campbell did not have much to do with young people in his later years, that he could not bend or change much with the times, and that he likely objected strenuously to *Look Homeward, Angel.* "He probably never saw the bigness in Tom," she said.[94]

Dr. C. Grier Davis testified that Dr. Campbell never attacked Wolfe from the pulpit to his knowledge. In fact, Davis noted, Campbell was cordial to Wolfe and appreciated him as a writer for some years before Wolfe's death and the famous funeral. Davis added an interesting footnote here indicating that some years after Wolfe's funeral a very prominent Methodist minister from Baltimore, Dr. William L. Stidger, was delivering a series of sermons at First Presbyterian Church in Asheville. Just before moving from the corridor into the sanctuary, Stidger stopped on the steps and turned to Davis and asked in a hushed voice, "Is this the church from which Tom Wolfe was buried?" Davis indicated that it was. They entered the sanctuary and when Stidger stood at the pulpit to deliver the sermon he stopped for a long pause, then said in his hushed and reverent voice, "I feel as though I am standing upon holy ground, for it was from this church that Thomas Wolfe was buried." Dr. Davis confessed to mixed emotions about this as he heard it, for he well knew that a number of people in the congregation would not feel that way about Tom Wolfe, but also quite a number would heartily agree.[95]

Wolfe's bombshell of a book caused much division in the church in the early years after 1929. In the 1951 history of First Presbyterian Church there is no reference to Thomas Wolfe whatsoever.[96] Over the years the climate of opinion in Asheville and in First Presbyterian Church changed and Tom was honored in a variety of ways. In the 1970 expanded history of the church Miss Ora Blackmun gave a full and cordial paragraph to Wolfe, expressing something of the pride of the church in that connection.[97] In the end we can say that for both Tom and the church there existed more of an affectionate connection than an abrasive rejection.

III

At a most stimulating symposium on Wolfe at the University of Georgia, Richard Walser provoked some theological discussion with his address "The Angel and the Ghost." In that paper Walser discussed Eugene's musings in *Look Homeward, Angel*, where Eugene asked "How may we save ourselves?"[98] In the discussion that followed Walser suggested that Ben (Eugene's brother) *may* be seen as the sacrificial victim, saying "It seems like the Christlike-cross business to me." To this Mr. Paschal Reeves added:

> Well, it is bound to be Christ-like cross business, because Wolfe was reared in the Presbyterian church, and he was heir to the Christian heritage . . . I think it is characteristic of all great writers that they put more into their work than they realize they are doing.[99]

One clear influence from Wolfe's early Sunday school training and from his family upbringing is his lasting affection for the Bible. Dr. Campbell was a highly educated man and an able expositor of Scripture. The Sunday school was noted not only for teaching the catechisms, but for teaching the Bible and stressing Bible memory work. Throughout his life Wolfe read and reread the Bible. This memory work and reading influenced his style and became so much a part of him that he scattered Biblical quotes and allusions throughout his public and private writings.

A theme that figures prominently in Wolfe's writings and which characterizes his style of life is that of the old Protestant work ethic.

No one can say that the Presbyterians have a peculiar corner on that teaching. Tom, however, viewed this as a manifestation of his "Presbyterian conscience." It is clear from the novels that the Presbyterian Sunday school teachers drilled into their pupils the virtues of hard and diligent work and the fruitfulness that comes from such work. Wolfe later wailed to his mother "They tell us in Sunday school to be industrious and saving, and steady; . . . we will be rich. It is not true."[100] Wolfe overtaxed himself in this pattern of furious work and said "Hereafter, I believe, I shall be able to do my work more quickly—I yet strain my Presbyterian conscience; and I believe I do too much."[101] Two weeks later he was still hard at it and wrote again "Now back to the grind. It's useless to say 'don't work too hard.' I've got a great deal of my Presbyterian conscience left, and I can't shirk the job."[102]

Whatever questions may be raised about Wolfe's life-style, few men lived with fewer frills and softness or worked with more intensity and drive than he. Perhaps critic Terence Dewsnap put his finger on it when he saw in the name of "Monk" Webber (Wolfe) in *The Web and the Rock* a suggestion of "his participation in the quest of a bookish medieval *monk* for meaningful existence" rather than simply an animal image related to his physical shape.[103] If he worked in Spartan quarters not unlike some monastic cell, Wolfe was not calm and composed in his labors. This Presbyterian "monk" worked at a fever pitch, sensing the pressure of time, his own election to this task, and the restraints of his Presbyterian conscience so long ago instilled at 40 Church Street.

Another theme regularly associated with Presbyterians, though it is widely shared by others, is predestination. This difficult theological teaching is easily confused with fatalism—a confusion clearly evident in the Wolfe family thinking. Julia Wolfe combined mysticism, an interest in the occult and the supernatural generally, fatalism, and a deep heritage of belief in the sovereignty of God and the doctrine of predestination in a marvelous way. Contemporary John Skally Terry writes "Mrs. Wolfe evolved a very personal religion, a strange beautiful mixture of Presbyterianism and spiritualism—though she would refute either name."[104] We can see no basis for thinking she denied the name Presbyterian, although there was surely a considerable admixture of other beliefs in her theology.

So, also, W. O. Wolfe decried the heavy hand of God on the affairs of men. With this family emphasis upon, and distortion of, the Presbyterian doctrine in which Tom was drilled in Sunday school, it is no wonder that Tom had a strong sense of destiny. In this regard it is important to note again the Chard Powers Smith article which indicated that Maxwell Perkins had a keen sense of the "election" of his writers.[105] Perkins played upon and reinforced the notion that Tom was predestined to be a great writer. Wolfe later described Perkins' commitment to the notion of predestination and his acceptance of the status quo as fatalism akin to Ecclesiastes. Wolfe rejected this fatalism in the break with Perkins and Scribners. To Tom a special calling or destiny was one thing, but a static acceptance of things as they are predetermined to be was anathema to him.

In his writings, Tom describes his parents wrestling with the problem of the sovereignty of God and predestination again and again. For example, W. O. shouts out against the accidents of life with one breath[106] and affirms that God is in control of all, even the most minute affairs, and is punishing him in another.[107] So also Eliza (Julia) speaks of the weaving of the Dark Sisters[108] and of the fulfillment of her own divine destiny.[109] Uncle Bascom is depicted as a fated man and one who speaks of God's will in the affairs of his life.[110] Again and again Wolfe muses, either through Eugene or through his own omniscient narrator role, on chance and God,[111] "dark chance and destiny,"[112] design and ordered destiny,[113] and gives an extended poetic passage on human destiny.[114]

No consistent and "Presbyterian" view of God appears. Many contend that the dominant theme of the search for the father is really the search for God, the Father. Elizabeth Nowell in her biography of Tom notes that this is "not merely an attempt to find a paternal substitute but to find the God-the-Father of a religion which he, intellectually, could not accept but for which he still felt a need."[115] This notion is given support in Wolfe's own words when he said

> the deepest search in life, it seemed to me, the thing that in one way or another was central to all living was man's search to find a father, not merely the father of his flesh, not merely the lost father of his youth, but the image of a strength and wisdom external to his need and superior to his hunger, to which the belief and power of his own life could be united.[116]

It is strange that those given to psychoanalyzing Wolfe see in this quest for the father only an adolescent parental hangup, and overlook Wolfe's own interpretation. Biographer Fritz Ryssel sees this as a religious quest and bluntly asserts that Wolfe did not understand himself, that Wolfe was by his own testimony "a deeply religious man, who made no secret of his doubt," and that "he sought God and eternity but never called them by name."[117]

Similarly, Wolfe's views of the person and work of Jesus Christ fall far short of the Presbyterian confessional standards, yet he deeply appreciated Christ, wrote appreciatively of his earthy teachings and common touch, and espoused the way of Christ to be far better than his own.[118] But Wolfe felt he could not follow that way of Christ.[119] He could not bring himself to wrap this powerfully alive Jesus in dogma and creed. He rejects what he views as superstitions involved in the creeds, especially in the affirmation of the Virgin Birth.[120] At many points Wolfe chides the church for holding to outdated beliefs in the conflict of science and religion.[121]

Perhaps the greatest legacy from Wolfe's Presbyterian background comes in the area of his awareness of the force and power of evil.[122] Richard S. Kennedy noted "Hence, a very real sense of evil, Wolfe's Presbyterian heritage, keeps cropping up in his writings . . ."[123] In memorizing the *Larger* and *Shorter Catechisms*, Tom had learned of "original sin" and of the evil in mankind. It is surprising that Thomas Lyle Collins writes that "Wolfe believes, in a non-Christian sense, in Original Sin."[124] It would appear more logical to say that this Christian, and specifically Presbyterian, teaching stayed with him, influenced his thinking.

Frank F. Finney, Jr., in a major essay documented Wolfe's move from a more psychological vision of evil in his first novel to an increasingly Christian awareness of evil in his last, and posthumous, novel.[125] Wolfe had sought psychological answers to the meaning of life in a changing world and a world of spiritual confusion. Tom's father, although a rebel against it, was at heart a Victorian puritan. Tom's mother knew no such dualistic battle in her life—she was a thoroughly integrated puritan with "a fatalistic sense of her moral perfection as well, supported by her indestructible determination and will."[126] Finney argues persuasively that Julia's self-righteousness, seeing the world through rosecolored glasses, did not allow her to see or to accept others' needs or the ambiguities of evil in her own life. Tom described her as "above and beyond moral judgment and as guiltless as a child."[127]

Tom was torn by his father's vitalism and attractive passions set over against W. O.'s strict moralizing. He depicts his father as a "comic-opera mixture of the drunken lecher and Victorian puritan father."[128] Julia he described as "an infuriating combination of the martyr and morally immaculate mother of a large family . . . with smug, self-righteous respectability."[129] The ensuing struggle between their parents pushed and pulled Tom and the other children to their emotional and spiritual harm. W. O. taunted and baited Tom, made him feel unworthy, and laid on him a heavy load of the old Protestant work ethic. Julia used Tom to goad his father, drilled him in her unrelenting self-righteousness in opposition to the base male urges seen in his father, and, in the long run, convinced Tom that the Fall existed for others, that sex was nasty, and the use of alcohol forbidden. Tom "lost the capacity to recognize the spiritual dualism in man," Finney notes.[130] In this process the drilling of the Sunday school teachers about sin was at least distorted. Others struggled with sin and found in the faith a way of dealing with it, but not Julia—nor young Tom. Women became either pristine mother figures or degraded whores. Men became either strict commandment-teaching and strict commandment-observing models of Presbyterian piety, or God-cursed hypocritical liars and hell-deserving sinners. The restless and sensual energies were to be denied. The virtues of stability, hard work, and clean living were to be affirmed.

Wolfe grew and matured, moving to a rediscovery of the Presbyterian teachings about original sin and the pervasiveness of evil. Unfortunately he perceived little at the level of feeling and experience of the Presbyterian, and more broadly Christian, concepts of forgiveness, grace, and the conquest of that evil that is ever present at the door. Wolfe described that social and cosmic evil vividly as we see in his Credo in *You Can't Go Home Again.*[131] Finney discusses that book and notes "Judge Bland's almost Calvinistic awareness of evil,"[132] Why, we ask, "almost" Calvinistic? Is this not in fact Wolfe's Calvinistic heritage cropping out?

C. Hugh Holman discusses Southern writers generally and notes their proclivity to expressions of guilt saying "This sense of guilt may be the product of the pervasive Calvinism of the region."[133] This "may be" surely may be altered to "is" in the case of Wolfe and his training. It is painful to hear that the last reported words of Wolfe as he went into a coma before death were "Mama, I've been a bad boy, I've been a bad boy all my life."[134] He had written earlier

> And *beyond, beyond*—forever *above, around, behind* the vast and tranquil consciousness of my spirit that now held the earth and all her elements in the huge clasp of its effortless subjection—there dwelt forever the fatal knowledge of my own inexplicable *guilt.*[135]

If Tom's personal lifestyle troubled him (especially his hedonistic excesses with food, alcohol, or sex), his social conscience and convictions did not. He felt himself to be a "righteous man," above the pettiness of conservative pietistical morality, and fell into the role of the prophet of God in denouncing social sin. There may be nothing particularly "Presbyterian" in his perceptions. They do reflect his bibilical training and he did react to issues raised in his home church. It is remarkable how closely his views paralleled those of Dr. Campbell. It is a moot point as to how much those regular visits to see Dr. Campbell did influence Tom—or Tom influence Dr. Campbell.

Despite the "albatross" of racial prejudice so common to Tom's heritage and unflinchingly depicted in his writings, Wolfe did rise above this to a remarkable degree for his day. We noted above that Tom was even ahead of Dr. Campbell in the episode of the black women cooking for Campbell on Sunday. Dr. Campbell, in turn, was well in advance of his time in working for the rights of black people, inviting blacks to speak in First Presbyterian Church, serving for twenty-five years as chairman of the Asheville Inter-Racial Committee, and preaching powerfully on "Some Aspects of the Race Problem of the South."[136] Perhaps Wolfe's more enlightened views in his later years were due in part to seeing Jesse Owens best the Nordics in the "Hitler Olympics" as

Richard Kennedy suggests.[137] But equally possible is the thesis that Dr. Campbell and First Presbyterian Church exercised great influence on Tom, as it would on others to follow him.

Tom boldly criticized the greed and materialistic opportunism which abounded in Asheville and in society at large. He sympathized with Dr. Campbell whose blast from the pulpit on materialism and the spiritual blindness leading to the crash in "Our Civic Crash" was printed in the local paper the next day and widely discussed throughout the state. Just as Tom had criticized improper political influences during his college days, so Campbell exposed and attacked "the ring" in Asheville. Maxwell Perkins was dismayed at some of the writings of Wolfe which smacked of communism, or at least Marxism, but Wolfe never avowed communism. Rather his caustic criticism of greed and the excesses of capitalism reflected the more Presbyterian position of Dr. Campbell.

Another major theme in Wolfe's life and work is his concern with death and dying. One might argue that there was little distinctively Presbyterian in his views about death other than the frequent laments about determinism and destiny, but his reflections on these matters do take place largely in the context of Presbyterian funerals. Wolfe worried about his own death which his "Scotch clairvoyant soul" perceived as coming at an early age.[138] Tom was deeply affected by the death of his brother Grover when Tom was but a lad of four,[139] but by far the most moving reflection on death comes in the painful presentation of the death of his beloved brother Ben during Tom's college years.[140] Facing the death of Ben, Tom finds his philosophical convictions of no help, and in a paroxysm of ritual, mysticism, and "foxhole" religious impulses cries out to the unknown God "Whoever you are, be good to Ben tonight," repeating his prayer in a singsong ritual.[141] In this passage Wolfe is clearly aware of dark forces, but unsure of angelic ones. He notes that there may be nothing to this faith business, but there surely is something to Ben. He asserts that Ben simply cannot cease to be and, despite his sophisticated philosophy or sophomoric denials of faith, affirms life beyond the grave.

Wolfe reacted negatively to the "American way of death" in that marvelous passage where the undertaker, Horse Hines, shows off his artistic work in preparing Ben's body for burial.[142] Luke and Eugene are less than impressed with the cosmetic art done on their brother. Finally the attempted artistic gloss over death, the unreality of it all, gets to Eugene who breaks up in hysterical laughter. "It's the strain," Hines remarks. No doubt it was, but it was also Wolfe's nervous and angry reaction to the pagan avoidance of death common to the funeral practices he knew.

Dr. Campbell performed the service for Ben and received high marks, being described thus: "his decent soul lay above all the loud posturings of grief like a bolt of hard clean wool."[143] Once again the Scots Presbyterian presence injects decency and order into a scene which as a whole is judged to be "the glazed corruption of Christian burial."[144] In his next novel Wolfe would lodge a similar protest to his father's funeral. He had his Presbyterian theology in order at this point: death is a part of life and should not be glossed over nor denied, but faced decently, cleanly, simply. He and Campbell agreed on this point.

In his own life Wolfe moved from a fear of death to a belief in an immortal destiny. In "Death the Proud Brother" as well as portions of *From Death to Morning*, Wolfe affirmed that death is man's final dignity. Death, as dark as it may be, opens doors for those who found no door and leads to new light, new coasts, and seeing "again, as I had once, new lands and morning."[145] The last thing Tom wrote, a letter from his hospital bed to Maxwell Perkins, reflects Tom's attitude toward death and his own existential encounter with the possibility of death:

> I've made a long voyage and been to a strange country, and I've seen the dark man very close; and I don't think I was too much afraid of him, but so much of mortality still clings to me— . . . and I know now that I'm just a grain of dust, and I feel as if a great window has been opened on life I did not know about before—and if I come through this, I hope to God I am a better man, and in some strange way I can't explain, I know I am a deeper and a wiser one.[146]

At Wolfe's funeral, Dr. Campbell quoted the preface to *Of Time and the River:* "Where shall the weary find rest? . . . What doors are open for the wanderer?"[147] Campbell added "As Tom's friend and pastor, I shall always cherish the hope and the belief that in the yearning desire of his restless heart to find his rest, his home, his peace in the heavenly Father's presence, there was the pith and substance of the Christian faith."[148]

Whether he had that "pith and substance" of faith, we cannot say. We must agree with Louis Rubin that Tom's style would allow him to embrace no system nor subscribe to the narrowness of any church's dogma.[149] In his "Credo' which forms the last chapter of *You Can't Go Home Again*, Wolfe had written

> I have never before made a statement of belief . . . although I have believed in many things and said that I believed in them. But I have never stated my belief in concrete terms because almost every element of my nature has been opposed to the hard framework, the finality, of formulation.[150]

Tom was forever changing, growing, flowing. The fragile and changing web or the ever flowing river were images for his thinking, not the rock.

He had written somewhat fondly, and yet as an outsider, of the Presbyterian Sunday school teacher who droned on and on about Presbyterian dogma.[151] His own lifelong posture toward institutional Christianity was that of the inquirer, the listener, the critic, mildly amused, not fully committed, and yet in a wistful way attracted to the Christian faith and, in personal ways, to Presbyterianism.

While at Harvard, Tom wrote a paper on Coleridge in which he reflects on Coleridge's prodigal journey of revolt, in part against religion, and how Coleridge finally made his peace with the institution despite its foibles. Wolfe indicated that his life, too, was patterned on that biblical account of the prodigal son when he wrote his mother asking for money and set himself to go to a "far country" saying, "But when I leave here this year, it will be to make my prodigal journey of experience, which all must make, into the world, and I will try to return home some day justified in the eyes of all."[152]

When T. S. Eliot made his move from the secular and cynical (or was it prophetic?) stage of "The Waste Land" and "The Hollow Men" back into the bosom of his church, there were attacks on him from many quarters for hypocrisy, failing mental powers, loss of nerve, and the like. Eliot was alive to speak and write from his Christian stance. Wolfe is no longer with us. To make exaggerated statements about Wolfe's return to the Father which Dr. Campbell hoped and believed in, or to overstate the possibility that Tom would go full circuit in his prodigal journey and seek Presbyterian baptism and membership, would be to venture too much. There were signs, however, that this prodigal was glimpsing the Father on the road of return. At least, he said he had glimpsed the "dark man" without fear and seen new horizons beyond death's door. What we can and do affirm insistently is that on his way "all the filtered deposit of Sunday morning Presbyterianism had its effect."[153]

Notes

1. "Prodigal" in *Southern Review*, 1 July 1935), pp. 192–8 reprinted in *Thomas Wolfe: The Critical Reception* edited by Paschal Reeves (New York 1974), p. 74.

2. Letter to Hiram H. Shenk, 3 April 1933, in *The Letters of Thomas Wolfe* edited by Elizabeth Nowell (New York 1956), p. 367.

3. Mabel Wolfe Wheaton, *Thomas Wolfe and His Family* (Garden City, NY 1961), p. 70.

4. First Presbyterian Church, Asheville, NC, Session Records 1896–1904, on deposit in the Historical Foundation, Montreat, NC.

5. Richard S. Kennedy, *The Window of Memory: The Literary Career of Thomas Wolfe* (Chapel Hill 1962), p. 25.

6. Hayden Norwood, *The Marble Man's Wife: Thomas Wolfe's Mother* (New York 1947), p. 98.

7. Andrew Turnbull, *Thomas Wolfe* (New York 1969), p. 14.

8. Norwood, pp. 45*f*.

9. *Ibid.*, p. 126.

10. *Look Behind You, Thomas Wolfe: Ghosts of a Common Tribal Heritage* (Hicksville, NY 1976), p. 34.

11. Thomas Wolfe, *Look Homeward, Angel* (New York 1929), p. 140. Hereafter cited as *LHA*.

12. MSS at Harvard, "Reflections on Religion," n.d.

13. *LHA*, pp. 329*f*.

14. *Ibid.*, p. 40.

15. Norwood, pp. 185*f*.

16. Wheaton, pp. 139, 144. See also First Presbyterian Church Session Records.

17. *LHA*, p. 574.

18. Wheaton, p. 203.

19. *Ibid.*, pp. 307*f*, 321.

20. *The Asheville Citizen*, 30 September 1958.

21. Fred Wolfe said he paid his "dues and tithes for 15 or 20 years" to Asheville First Presbyterian Church before moving to Spartanburg. Interview, 7 August 1975.

22. First Presbyterian Church Session Records.

23. *Ibid.*

24. *Ibid.*

25. *Ibid.*

26. *Ibid.*

27. Typescript in the Historical Foundation.

28. Reported in *The Thomas Wolfe Newsletter*, II, 2 (Fall 1978), p. 35.

29. Betty Lynch Williams, "Asheville and Thomas Wolfe: A Study in Changing Attitudes," *Appalachian Heritage*, III, 2 (Spring 1975), p. 44.

30. Interview in Asheville, NC, 15 October 1975.

31. Interview with Fred Wolfe in Spartanburg, SC, 7 August 1975.

32. John Skally Terry, ed., *Thomas Wolfe's Letters to His Mother, Julia Elizabeth Wolfe* (New York 1943), p. 1.

33. Richard S. Kennedy, and Paschal Reeves, eds., *The Notebooks of Thomas Wolfe*, 2 vols. (Chapel Hill, 1970), 517. Wolfe made other notes for future writing to include Sunday school episodes in *The Notebooks*, pp. 375, 860.

34. *Ibid.*, p. 518.

35. See especially pp. 137–40; also pp. 253*f*., 329*f*.

36. *The Web and the Rock* (New York 1939), p. 11. Hereafter cited as W&R.

37. *Ibid.*, p. 103. In *LHA*, p. 375, Tom characterized the denominations by their favorite hymns, assigning the "River" one to the Methodists, here assigned to the Baptists, the two denominations being quite similar in their orientation to Tom. However, when describing his own Presbyterian Sunday school singing in *LHA*, Tom quoted this very hymn and verse—he clearly thinks of the Presbyterians, p. 138.

38. MSS at Harvard University.

39. *LHA*, pp. 139*f*.

40. *Ibid.*, p. 329.

41. *Ibid.*, pp. 329, 375; see also *Of Time and the River* (New York 1935), p. 670. Hereafter cited as *OT&R*.

42. *Thomas Wolfe's Characters: Portraits From Life* (Norman, OK 1957), p. 12.

43. Turnbull, p. 14.

44. Interview in Spartanburg, SC, 7 August 1975.

45. *The Enigma of Thomas Wolfe: Biographical and Critical Selections*, edited by Richard Walser (Cambridge 1953), p. 8.

46. Richard Walser, *Thomas Wolfe Undergraduate* (Durham 1977), p. 21.

47. Walser, *Enigma*, p. 14.

48. Agatha Boyd Adams, *Thomas Wolfe: Carolina Student: A Brief Biography* (Chapel Hill 1950), p. 43.

49. In the *Tar Heel*, 8 May 1920. Also cited by Walser, *Undergraduate*, p. 113. Note that "Preacher" Reed, supposedly an Episcopalian, in *W&R* is based upon the Presbyterian "Parson" Moss, pp. 197*ff*. Once again Tom could not move into another religious setting without describing it in terms of his Presbyterian background and experience. The editorials in the *Tar Heel* are unsigned, but those of the 1919–1920 era belonged to its editor, Thomas Clayton Wolfe.

50. Adams, p. 50.

51. Walser, *Undergraduate*, p. 10. Readers desiring to get some brief biographical data on Moss and/or to read his sermons should see: William Dygnum Moss, *Sermons and Prayers* (Chapel Hill 1940).

52. *Ibid.*, p. 100.

53. *The Asheville Citizen*, 19 September 1938. Also supported by Fred Wolfe in the 7 August 1975 interview.

54. Walser, *Undergraduate*, p. 45.

55. *Ibid.*, p. 107.

56. Terry, *Letters to Mother*, p. 126.

57. *The Asheville Times*, 19 August 1947.

58. Thomas Clark Pollock, and Oscar Cargill, *Thomas Wolfe at Washington Square* (New York 1954), p. 10.

59. *Ibid.*, p. 17.

60. *Notebooks*, pp. 10*f*.

61. Terry, *Letters to Mother*, p. 42.

62. *Ibid.*, p. 47.

63. Turnbull, pp. 122, 124, 229*f*.

64. Chard Powers Smith, "Perkins and the Elect" in *The Antioch Review*, XXII (Spring 1962), p. 96.

65. Terry, *Letters to Mother*, p. 87.

66. *Notebooks*, p. 104.

67. *Ibid.*, pp. 49–52, 57, 350.

68. See Campbell's funeral address quoted in *The Asheville Citizen*; also, Wheaton, p. 307.

69. Interview in Spartanburg, SC, 7 August 1975.

70. Wheaton, p. 307.

71. *The Asheville Citizen*, 19 September 1938.

72. Interview in Asheville, NC, 16 October 1975.

73. Jonathan Daniels, *Tar Heels: A Portrait of North Carolina* (New York 1941), p. 233.

74. *Ibid.*, p. 234.

75. *Thomas Wolfe: A Biography* (Garden City, NY 1960), p. 439.

76. Paschal Reeves, *Thomas Wolfe's Albatross: Race and Nationality in America* (Athens, GA 1968), p. 93.

77. *Ibid.*, p. 91. (Noted from Wolfe's "Men of Old Catawba" in *From Death to Morning*, p. 201. Hereafter cited as FDTM.)

78. *Southern Folklore Quarterly*, XXVII (June 1964), pp. 138*f*.

79. C. Hugh Holman, *The Loneliness at the Core: Studies in Thomas Wolfe* (Baton Rouge 1975), p. 128.

80. *Notebooks*, p. 517.

81. *Ibid.*, pp. 803*f*.

82. Nowell, *Letters*, p. 587.

83. *Ibid.*, p. 582.

84. *LHA*, p. 104.

85. *Ibid.*, pp. 138–40, 253.

86. *Notebooks*, p. 795.

87. *Milwaukee Journal*, 29 December 1948, "Asheville Forgives Thomas Wolfe."

88. Turnbull, p. 307.

89. Interview in Spartanburg, SC, 7 August 1975.

90. Nine archival boxes of Dr. Campbell's papers are deposited at the Historical Foundation.

91. A similar problem exists at Johns Hopkins where Wolfe's x-rays have "disappeared" from his medical records.

92. Interview in Asheville, NC, 15 October 1975.

93. Interview in Asheville, NC, 16 October 1975.

94. Interview in Asheville, NC, 15 October 1975.

95. Interview in Asheville, NC, 15 October 1975.

96. George W. McCoy, *The First Presbyterian Church, Asheville, N. C. 1794–1951* (Asheville 1951), 67 pp.

97. Ora Blackmun, *A Spire in the Mountains: The Story of 176 Years of a Church and a Town Growing Together 1794–1969* (Asheville 1970), p. 185.

98. Paschal Reeves, ed., *Thomas Wolfe and the Glass of Time* (Athens, GA 1971), pp. 45–67.

99. *Ibid.*, p. 76.

100. Terry, *Letters to Mother*, p. 75.

101. *Ibid.*

102. *Ibid.*, p. 77.

103. *Thomas Wolfe's You Can't Go Home Again & The Web and The Rock*, Monarch Notes and Study Guides (New York 1965), p. 18. See also pp. 26, 50.

104. Terry, *Letters to Mother*, XV. See Tom's description in *LHA* of her superstition (21), belief in the Dark Sisters of fate (43), her clairvoyant Scotch soul (59), and "that Pentland spooky stuff" (378).

105. Smith, pp. 85–102.

106. *LHA*, p. 22.

107. *Ibid.*, p. 27.

108. *Ibid.*, p. 43.

109. *OT&R*, p. 352.

110. *Ibid.*, p. 180.

111. *LHA*, pp. 191*f*.

112. *OT&R*, pp. 821, 833.
113. *Ibid.*, p. 893.
114. *Ibid.*, p. 909.
115. Nowell, *Thomas Wolfe*, p. 28.
116. *The Story of a Novel* (New York 1936), p. 39. Hereafter cited as *SOAN*.
117. *Thomas Wolfe* (New York 1972), pp. 3, 5.
118. *The Hills Beyond* (New York 1941), p. 196.
119. *Ibid.*
120. *Notebooks*, p. 11.
121. *Ibid.*, pp. 43, 56 for example.
122. See my article "On Divers Spirits: Theological Themes in Thomas Wolfe," *Journal for Preachers* (Pentecost 1980), pp. 18–24.
123. Kennedy, *Window*, p. 11.
124. Walser, *Enigma*, p. 171.
125. "A Critical Examination of the Transition from a Psychological Vision of Life to an Increasingly Christian Awareness of Evil in the Fiction of Thomas Wolfe," Ph.D. dissertation (Norman, OK 1961).
126. *Ibid.*, p. 368.
127. *OT&R*, p. 4.
128. Finney, p. 113.
129. *Ibid.*, p. 184.
130. *Ibid.*
131. Pp. 739–43.
132. Finney, p. 498.
133. *Ibid.*, p. 436.
134. *Life*, 24 September 1956. p. 183.
135. *SOAN*, p. 64.
136. Blackmun, p. 116.
137. Kennedy, *Window*, p. 316.
138. Terry, *Letters to Mother*, pp. 7, 55.
139. Norwood, p. 185.
140. *LHA*, p. 557.
141. *Ibid.*, p. 556.
142. *Ibid.*, pp. 565–72.
143. *Ibid.*, pp. 574–5.
144. *Ibid.*, p. 575.
145. *FDTM*, p. 67.
146. Nowell, *Letters*, p. 777.
147. *The Asheville Citizen*, 19 September 1938. Quotation from the preface to *OT&R*.
148. *Ibid.*
149. *Ibid.*
150. *YC*, p. 739.
151. *LHA*, pp. 253–4.
152. Terry, *Letters to Mother*, p. 22. Letter dated 21 February 1921.
153. *LHA*, p. 104.

Thomas Wolfe in Miniature

Kenneth Seib*

The conventional opinion of Thomas Wolfe over the years has been that he was, as Sinclair Lewis stated in his Nobel Prize address of 1930, a "Gargantuan creature with great gusto for life,"[1] a genius *in extremis* whose own intemperance and excesses were translated into fictional monstrosities and great globs of yawping verbiage. Pamela Hansford Johnson, whose book on Wolfe, *Hungry Gulliver*, has a title that suggests her critical view, writes that Wolfe was a "man of gigantic stature (his height was six-foot-six), [whose] sensitivity was extreme. He wrote to match his height, he roared to match it, he ate and drank to match it. . . ."[2] Gerald Johnson, in a 1935 article in the *Virginia Quarterly Review*, claimed that Wolfe "roars against the immortal gods. He girds at Fate, he grapples and goes to the mat with Destiny."[3] Alfred Kazin, in *On Native Grounds*, found Wolfe "a gargantuan boy,"[4] while Stephen Vincent Benét felt that Wolfe "committed the errors of a giant. . . ."[5] Bernard De Voto, who published his notorious essay on Wolfe, "Genius is not Enough," in the *Saturday Review* along with a photograph of himself brandishing a six-gun, claimed that Wolfe's novels were "long whirling discharges of words, unabsorbed in the novel, unrelated to the proper business of fiction, badly if not altogether unacceptably written, raw gobs of emotion, aimless and quite meaningless, jabber, claptrap, belches, grunts and Tarzan-like screams."[6] The list could go on and on.

Wolfe was not unaware of this view of himself as a literary King Kong engaged in hand-to-hand combat with the Godzilla of Destiny. "For God's sake, try to kill false rumors when you hear them," he wrote to Maxwell Perkins in 1935. "Before I left [New York], I saw that they were beginning to make another rubber stamp under the name of 'criticism.' Apparently they had discovered that I was six and a half feet tall, and very large: therefore it follows that all my characters are seven feet tall—bellow and roar when they talk—that I can create nothing but a race of gigantic monsters. Max, for Christ's sake, I beg and plead with you, don't let this horrible god-damned lie go unanswered."[7] Later, in correspondence with Scott Fitzgerald, Wolfe took a more detached and humorous view of such criticism:

> The little fellows who don't know may picture a man as a great "exuberant" six-foot-six clod-hopper straight out of nature who bites off half a plug of apple tobacco, tilts the corn liquor jug and lets half of it gurgle down his throat, wipes his mouth with the back of one hairy paw, jumps three feet in the air and clacks his heels together four times before he hits the floor and yells our "'Whoopee, boys, I'm a rootin, tootin, shootin son of a gun from Buncombe County—out of

*Reprinted from the *Thomas Wolfe Newsletter*, 2, No. 2 (Fall 1978), 10–15.

> my way now, here I come!"—and then wads up three-hundred thousand words or so, hurls it at a blank page, puts covers on it and says "Here's my book!"
>
> Now, Scott, the boys who write book-reviews in New York may think it's done that way; but the man who wrote "Tender is the Night" knows better.[8]

Although the view of Thomas Wolfe as an exponent of gigantism and gargantuan overkill has been somewhat modified in recent years, it is still not unusual to find essays with such titles as "Thomas Wolfe's GarGANTuan Family" among the latest writings about him. Critical cliches, widely repeated, die hard. In addition, such imbalanced emphasis has severely damaged Wolfe's reputation, preventing his receiving the careful scrutiny that others of his generation—Faulkner and Hemingway, for instance—have enthusiastically been given.

As I intend to show in this paper, moreover, it is not magnification at all that is central to Wolfe's writing; it is exactly the opposite. Wolfe's method is most often that of the miniaturist, and his depiction of character and scene is dependent upon extracting minute details from a larger whole, focusing upon the specific against a more generalized background, and rendering into concrete images abstract qualities of man and nature. His method is that of the cinema director who, in order to centralize our dramatic focus, begins with a long shot, pans in to the specific scene, and finally gives us a close-up of the essential images within the larger framework.

The opening paragraphs of *Look Homeward, Angel*, for example, move from a panoramic view of human existence directed by time, destiny, and chance—not unlike Thomas Hardy's opening of *The Dynasts*—through forty thousand years of "minute-winning days" from primeval beginnings, through Crete, London, and Texas, and finally to a particular "moment" of time: a movement from the immense to the minute. In the same way, the history of the Gant family is condensed and miniaturized from its earliest American ancestry—an Englishman named Gilbert Gaunt who came to Baltimore from Bristol in 1837—to Oliver Gant of Altamont. Finally, the imagery of the writing itself moves from the nonsentient toward the living—from mineral, through vegetable and animal, to the human:

> The seed of our destruction will blossom in the desert, the alexin of our cure grows by a mountain rock, and our lives are haunted by a Georgia slattern, because a London cutpurse went unhung. Each moment is the fruit of forty thousand years. The minute-winning days, like flies, buzz home to death, and every moment is a window on all time.[9]

From desert and mountain rock, to the tiny and insignificant fly, we come to the "window" through which we will witness the drama of the Gants, whose moment has developed in the same way that a seed becomes blossom and finally fruit; each living object—fruit, fly, and human being—is particularized in time, the aggregate of its entire past in one momentary embodiment. Just as desert and mountain suggest insensate nature and immensity beyond human comprehension, fly, fruit, and window suggest the trivial and fragile existence of each human life (Shakespeare's "As flies to wanton boys are we to the gods"), the richness of human sensate experience (fruit), and isolation of the individual (window as barrier between outside and inside worlds). The movement of the entire paragraph is from abstract nature and incomprehensible linear time ("forty thousand years") to human particularity and the brief moment—from the large to the small.

In the same way, Wolfe miniaturizes his individual fictional characters by placing them against an immense and abstract background. Consider, for instance, this description of Bascom Pentland from *Of Time and the River:*

> Shortly before nine o'clock of every working-day he would emerge from a subway exit near the head of the street and pause vaguely for a moment, making a craggy eddy in the tide of issuing workers that foamed swiftly about him while he stood with his enormous bony hands clutched comically before him at the waist, as if holding himself in, at the same time making the most horrible grimaces with his lean and amazingly flexible features. These grimaces were made by squinting his small sharp eyes together, widening his mouth in a ghastly travesty of a grin, and convolving his chin and cheek in a rapid series of pursed lips and horrible squints as he swiftly pressed his rubbery underlip against a few enormous horse teeth that decorated his upper jaw. Having completed these facial evolutions, he glanced quickly and, it must be supposed, blindly, in every direction; for then he plunged heedlessly across the street, sometimes choosing the moment when traffic had been halted, and pedestrians were hurrying across, sometimes diving into the midst of a roaring chaos of motor cars, trucks, and wagons, through which he sometimes made his way in safety, accompanied only by a scream of brake bands, a startled barking of horns, and the hearty curses of frightened drivers, or from which, howling with terror in the centre of a web of traffic which he had snarled hopelessly and brought to a complete standstill, he was sometimes rescued by a red-faced and cursing young Irishman who was on point duty at that corner.[10]

Again there is miniaturization in the portrayal of the comical figure of Bascom Pentland swimming against the "tide of issuing workers that foamed swiftly about him" and the "roaring chaos of motor cars, trucks, and wagons" in the center of which he flounders. The essential imagery of the paragraph is aquatic, suggesting an immense ocean of city life in which small and helpless Bascom daily drowns. At best, Bascom makes only a "craggy eddy" in the vast ocean foaming about him; he plunges and dives into the traffic, howling with terror as he sinks "in the midst of roaring chaos"; and he is finally rescued by the only available lifeguard, "a red-faced and cursing young Irishman." Passages such as this one are used throughout Wolfe's novels to reinforce the principal theme that in the face of time and the river of events, man is a small creature indeed.

In the main, character in Wolfe's fiction is reduced by a style that employs few words, phrases, or descriptive passages—or that simply uses the same words over and over again. In his most vivid fictional portraits, Wolfe uses the rhetorical device of the "frame reference"—small details singled out and repeatedly emphasized—in order to convey essential qualities of personality. In the case of Bascom Pentland, it is his voice, with its "Ow! Ow! Ow!" terrified howl, and his "big horsey upper teeth." With Eugene Gant's brother Ben, it is the knifeblade flicker of his smile by which we best remember him; with his brother Luke, it is his stutter; with Eliza Gant, it is the repeated gesture of rubbing her finger alongside her nose. Details are singled out and repeated like Wagnerian leitmotifs, brief words, phrases, and descriptions that allow Wolfe to identify and typify his numerous characters for the reader with a surprising economy.

Similarly, Wolfe's seeming verbosity comes from the stylistic device of repeating certain words and phrases for incantatory effect—stone, leaf, and unfound door in *Look Homeward, Angel,* for instance. It is not so much that Wolfe uses too many words; he instead uses the same ones too many times, often conveying merely wearisome repetition rather than poetic power. His failure is often in that he has condensed too much into too few words, that words such as *stone, leaf*; and *door* are unable to carry the heavy metaphysical baggage that they are clearly meant to bear. If Eliot's term "objective correlative" were useful here, I would invoke it; but I fear it would only cloud matters. Let it suffice to say that what are most often taken as Wolfe's stylistic excesses are more accurately large metaphysical concepts miniaturized into insufficient tropes.

A final form of miniaturization comes from the structural methods that Wolfe employs in his best fiction. While novels like *Look Homeward, Angel,* and *The Web and the Rock* have the tone and texture of myth without achieving corresponding identity to any recognizable mythic pattern, some of Wolfe's fiction is consciously patterned on the framework of past mythic plots. *Of Time and the River,* with its subtitle claiming the status of "legend" for Eugene Gant's wanderings and with its division into eight "books," each named for a legendary figure, is the clearest illustration of Wolfe's myth-based fiction, particularly the chapter entitled "Orestes: Flight Before Fury." The obvious link between the title and the plot of this chapter is impossible to miss. Eugene Gant is fleeing the mountains of Old Catawba and is being driven, like Orestes, by his personal Furies.

But there is a much more subtle parallel between this chapter and

Aeschylus's *Eumenides.* In the play by Aeschylus, Orestes is at the shrine of Apollo in Delphi. Heeding the advice of the oracle, Orestes heads for Athens to seek justice from Pallas Athene. But the ghost of Clytemnestra stirs up the Furies, who have been sleeping around the shrine, and the legendary pursuit begins. The first chapter of Wolfe's novel bears striking affinity to the details of this myth. *Of Time and the River* begins "on the platform of the railway station of a town in the hills of western Catawba,"[11] a site with many attributes of the Delphic shrine. Like Delphi, the station is "the popular point of arrival and departure for travellers to and from the cities of the east" (3). Just as the Delphic shrine was located a few miles southwest of Mt. Parnassus, so the station is described as being a few miles southwest of Wolfe's analogous mountain—Altamont.

The oracle of the Altamont station is Eliza Gant, who, along with Eugene's sister Helen, is "surveying the other people on the platform and the new arrivals with a ravenous and absorptive interest, bestowing on each a wealth of information, comment, and speculation which suggested an encyclopaedic knowledge of the history of every one in the community" (5). To Eugene, who is waiting along with Eliza and Helen for the arrival of the train, Eliza's comments are "mysteries," "damned gloomy hints and revelations," and "Pentland spooky stuff", uttered with an "I-could-if-I-wanted-to-tell-you air of mystery, horror, and damnation" (7). With true oracular wisdom, in fact, she reveals to an almost complete stranger on the platform that he was "born . . . on September 2nd, 1898" and is "just two years and one month and one day older" than Eugene (18).

Playing the symbolic role of Clytemnestra (in spite of her name), Helen stirs up the personal Furies that will haunt Eugene throughout the novel. Her constant repetition of the word *time* becomes one of Eugene's—and the novel's—constant obsessions:

> . . . *You're* the lucky one! *You* got away! You're smart enough to go way off somewhere to college—to Boston—Harvard—anywhere—but *you're* away from it. You get it for a short time when you come home. How do you think I stand it?" she said challengingly. "I have to hear it *all* the time. . . . Oh, *all* the time, and *all* the time, and *all* the time!" she said with a kind of weary desperation. "If they'd only leave me *alone* for five minutes some time I think I'd be able to pull myself together, but it's this way *all* the time and *all* the time and *all* the time. You see, don't you?" (8)

The word *time* is repeated nine times in this short section, and the three words that are italicized by Wolfe in the passage and reiterated by Helen are "You're all alone," a statement that stirs a major Fury in Eugene's haunted life. It is also Helen who reminds Eugene of his second chief obsession—the river, the flow of life, time, and events that he so desperately tries to capture. "There's no place for the weary,"

Helen tells him. "It's like that river that goes on forever" (8). And finally it is Helen who predicts to Eugene that "Papa's a dead man now!" (14) and sends Eugene on his search for the lost father.

Wolfe's method here again involves miniaturization, the reduction of Olympian legend to human proportion, and of tragic passion to melodramatic self-pity. Wolfe, who is too often presented as an author unaware of what he is about, clearly intends a subtle parallel between past and present, legend and reality, Greek and modern culture. Delphi has been reduced to a small-town railroad station, the depot its temple; Mt. Olympus to an insignificant mountain range; and the tragic coming of the Furies to the arrival of a steam locomotive, "an event which has always been of first interest in the lives of all Americans" (1). Genuine oracular mysteries of the Delphic priestess have become "Pentland spooky stuff" muttered by a wearisome old lady; the tragic utterances of Clytemnestra have become the whining complaints of a jealous sibling; the flight of Orestes has become the frenzied escape of a confused youth.

Mistaken for a realist, Wolfe is overlooked as a satirist, writing in what Northrop Frye in *Anatomy of Criticism* calls "satire of the high norm," offering "a high degree of the ridiculous" by showing us "society suddenly in a telescope as posturing and dignified pygmies, or in a microscope as hideous and reeking giants. . . ."[12] Wolfe's microscopic view has been much overlooked, however, while his telescopic one has been too much exaggerated. Considering both, future critics may be able to put Thomas Wolfe in proper perspective. Meanwhile, we would do best to heed Wolfe's own words: ". . . Flaubert me no Flauberts, Bovary me no Bovarys, Zola me no Zolas, and exuberance me no exuberances. Leave this stuff for those who huckster in it. . . ."[13]

Notes

1. Sinclair Lewis, quoted in Elizabeth Nowell, *Thomas Wolfe* (New York: Doubleday, 1960), p. 187.

2. Pamela Hansford Johnson, *Hungry Gulliver: An English Critical Appraisal of Thomas Wolfe* (New York: Scribner's, 1948), p. 18.

3. Gerald W. Johnson, "The Horrible South," *Virginia Quarterly Review* (April, 1935), pp. 213–14.

4. Alfred Kazin, *On Native Grounds* (New York: Harcourt, Brace & Co., 1942), p. 484.

5. Stephen Vincent Benét, "A Torrent of Recollection," in *The Enigma of Thomas Wolfe*, ed. Richard Walser (Cambridge, Mass.: Harvard University Press, 1953), p. 155.

6. Bernard De Voto, "Genius is not Enough," in *Enigma*, p. 141.

7. Elizabeth Nowell, ed., *The Letters of Thomas Wolfe* (New York: Scribner's, 1956), p. 447.

8. *Ibid.*, pp. 643–44.

9. Thomas Wolfe, *Look Homeward, Angel* (New York: Scribner's 1929), p. 3.

10. Thomas Wolfe, *Of Time and the River* (New York: Scribner's, 1935), p. 104. The pasage first appeared in a short novel entitled "A Portrait of Bascom Hawke," which appeared in the April, 1932, issue of *Scribner's Magazine*.

11. *Ibid.*, p. 3. Page numbers for the remainder of this discussion will appear in parentheses within the text.

12. Northrop Frye, *Anatomy of Criticism* (Princeton, New Jersey: Princeton University Press, 1957), p. 234.

13. Wolfe, *Letters*, p. 643.

INDEX